Revising Life

Revising Life

Susan R. Van Dyne

Sylvia

Plath's

Ariel

Poems

The

University

of North

Carolina

Press

Chapel Hill

& London

© 1993 The University of North Carolina Press

All rights reserved

Manufactured in the United States of America

The paper in this book meets the guidelines for
permanence and durability of the Committee on
Production Guidelines for Book Longevity of the
Council on Library Resources.

97 96 95 94 93   5 4 3 2 1

Library of Congress Cataloging-in-Publication Data
Van Dyne, Susan R.
  Revising life: Sylvia Plath's Ariel poems /
by Susan R. Van Dyne.
      p. cm. — (Gender & American culture)
  Includes bibliographical references and index.
  ISBN 0-8078-2102-0 (cloth : alk. paper)
    1. Plath, Sylvia—Criticism and interpretation.
I. Title.
II. Series.
PS3566.L27Z947 1993   92-31233
811'.54—dc20   CIP

Contents

Illustrations

All illustrations courtesy of
the Sylvia Plath Collection,
Smith College Library Rare
Book Room.

Acknowledgments

It has often felt like a specially designed punishment to be writing about a poet who complained incessantly about her writing blocks. Yet tempted as I am to attribute the halts and distractions in my own writing process to Plath's influence, I have been more often inspired by her tireless dedication to her craft, the determined business of making and remaking that is visibly evident on every page of her drafts. That this book was partly made and then entirely remade over six years I owe both to Plath's example and to many feminist scholars and friends.

Linda Wagner-Martin has been an important mentor since we met over these manuscripts in the Rare Book Room at Smith; she has unstintingly shared information and sane advice and welcomed my work with characteristic warmth as complementary to her own. She has also kindly offered opportunities for me to share my research with a wider audience in print and in person. Her biography of Plath aided me often, confirming my intuitions through her detailed research and solving several riddles I had puzzled over. Like many feminist critics, I owe much to Sandra Gilbert and Susan Gubar, whose ways of thinking about gender and creativity first informed and inspired my own. Sandra's excitement about my early discoveries encouraged me that there would be an audience for this book. My debts to other feminist critics will be evident in the book itself.

I am more than usually indebted to librarians. I am especially grateful to Ruth Mortimer, curator of the Smith College Rare Book Room and the Sylvia Plath Collection, who very generously allowed my unlimited access to the manuscripts and the collection over nearly a decade; without it, this book simply would not have existed. My own research was considerably hastened by Barbara Blumenthal, who catalogued the Plath Collection at Smith and with whom I shared the exhilaration of our initial detective work. I have appreciated the cheerful efficiency of Sarah Black, who never refused a request to bring just one more draft.

I also want to thank Saundra Taylor, curator of the Lilly Library of Indiana University, and Becky Gibson, assistant curator and cataloguer of the Sylvia Plath Manuscript Collection, for their assistance with my archival research and for their helpful conversations. I need to thank Leonard Scigaj for our conversation at the Lilly Library that led me to the draft for "Tulips" at the Houghton Library at Harvard, and to thank the librarian there who, with considerable disbelief, produced it several years later.

Support for my research, in both time and travel, has been provided by the National Endowment for the Humanities and the Mellon Foundation. Smith College faculty development funds have supported student assistance and travel to manuscript collections.

The confidence of two editors at the University of North Carolina Press in my work kept me writing and made me feel appropriately guilty when I wasn't. I feel wonderfully lucky to have worked with Iris Tillman Hill, my first editor, whose enthusiasm for this project and her freshman memories of Plath brought us together, and Kate Douglas Torrey, my last, whose support, encouragement, and patience sustained me while I reconceived and rewrote the book. Kate especially knew just when to nudge.

I have been fortunate in my readers. Margaret Dickie, Philip Green, Linda Wagner-Martin, and Sandra Zagarell read or heard parts of this project; each of their perspectives has been important in confirming my choices about a different aspect of the book's final structure. Their praise at different stages proved invaluable in bringing it to completion. Betsey Harries's sympathetic attention to matters of argument and phrasing made revising late drafts of most of these chapters much more pleasurable than I expected it to be. I have depended on her friendship and courage in making our department a better place for women to work and to write.

For intellectual companionship and political and personal support, I could have no better allies than my colleagues in the Women's Studies Program at Smith. I profited from the spirited disagreements of the feminist theory reading group whose eclectic tastes helped clarify my own. I owe much of my productivity to the friendship of Martha Ackelsberg, Marilyn Schuster, Ruth Solie, and Vicky Spelman, whose books shared this same gestation period; I learned persistence from them in these and other struggles. I was entertained and encouraged by Nancy Sternbach, who asked, on countless sweaty summer days, "How's Sylvia?" I'm grateful that they always believed I would finish and that, individually, they had the inspired timing to tell me so when I most needed to hear it. Marilyn Schuster did more than even she will admit to make this book possible. She collaborated, as always, on matters large and small; I'm especially glad she remembered life before the book and could imagine one after.

I want to thank my parents for their uncomplicated support of me as teacher and writer and to remember my father whose spirit was with me in writing the final pages of this book.

Abbreviations

CP   Plath, Sylvia. *The Collected Poems.*
Edited by Ted Hughes. New
York: Harper & Row, 1981.

LH   Plath, Sylvia. *Letters Home:*
Correspondence, 1950–1963.
Edited by Aurelia Schober
Plath. New York: Harper &
Row, 1975.

J   Plath, Sylvia. *The Journals of Sylvia*
Plath. Edited by Frances
McCullough and Ted Hughes.
New York: Dial, 1982.

Revising Life

Introduction:
Revising Woman

For Sylvia Plath, revising her life was a recurrent personal and poetic necessity. In her letters and journals as much as in her fiction and poetry, Plath's habits of self-representation suggest she regarded her life as if it were a text that she could invent and rewrite. In her earliest journal entry at seventeen, she already exhibits a sense of her identity as a projected persona: "I think I would like to call myself 'The girl who wanted to be God' " (LH 40). Repeatedly, at moments of crisis, she imagines she can erase the inscription of personal history and be reborn, unmarked as an infant, inviolate as a virgin. In one of the last poems she wrote, Plath regards her life as if it were a completed oeuvre, an already closed book that she has produced in her writing: "The woman is perfected. / Her dead / Body wears the smile of accomplishment" ("Edge").

In the Ariel poems that Plath wrote during the fall and winter of 1962, the rupture in her personal life demanded a refiguration of her identity in and through poetry. In claiming, as I do, that in drafting and revising these poems Plath tried to reconstitute a self, I am not arguing for a "poetics of transparence" in which the woman writer is assumed to be writing directly and authentically from her lived experience.[1] Rather, what I want to examine is the proliferation of masks and performances that Plath produced in her poetry. My reading of Plath assumes that there is no master narrative of her life or her art; neither the pathological understanding of her art as having been determined by her suicidal impulses nor the reading of her actual suicide as a by-product of her textual, metaphoric strategies describes adequately the ways Plath's poems revised her life.[2] Not only is there no single explanatory paradigm; there is no inevitable progression in these poems.

Exploring the nature of the relation between a woman's life and her artistic revision, between her sexuality and textuality, between a psychosexual identity and cultural authority has been the project of feminist literary criticism during the last two decades and is a central concern of this book.

Throughout, this is a book about revision and rereadings. In focusing on the ways Plath revised her life and her art, I am also investigating the ways that we as late twentieth-century readers have revised our understanding of gender and representation. In each chapter I juxtapose three kinds of texts: Plath's private writing in her journals and letters, the interpretive strategies of feminist theory, and Plath's revisions of the Ariel poems. I argue that Plath's dynamic relation to her culture produces an individual negotiation of cultural possibilities, a creative resistance to gender expectations, and a poetic revision of female identity.

In her private writing I locate Plath in the act of reading her culture, especially the competing strains within the dominant discourse from which she formed her expectations of what it meant to be a middle-class wife, mother, and aspiring writer in mid-twentieth-century America. Critics have often construed the gender norms of Plath's historical moment as uniformly oppressive and Plath the woman as their duped victim. Her conformity in life, this argument contends, breeds the rebellious reaction of the poetry. Her journals, however, reveal that the meanings for female experience available in her culture were plural and often contradictory. As much as she assimilated and invested in certain conventional scripts as the paradigms for her own success, her interpretation of her experience was as often a resourceful negotiation of the incompatible possibilities that were embedded in the 1950s ideology of gender.

I assume that the female subject, like any other, does not preexist her awareness of culture but, rather, emerges as a product of historicized experience. Yet her gendered subjectivity is constituted by particular kinds of relations to social reality and its representations. That is, as Teresa de Lauretis argues in extending the insights of Althusser and Foucault, culture makes a "differential solicitation of male and female subjects" who in turn make "conflicting investments" in its "discourses and practices."[3] In understanding Plath's culture as the site of contradictions and her subjectivity as constructed and engendered through her material, social, and psychosexual situations, I emphasize that her subjectivity is fluid rather than fixed and that her dynamic relation to her culture allows for both an individual interpretation and a rearticulation of female identity.[4] Although the issue of personal agency may be among the most vexed matters for critics who posit, as I do, a cultural construction of the subject, Plath's journals demonstrate that she is a "discerning subject," in Paul Smith's phrase, "not simply the *actor* who follows ideological scripts, but . . . also an *agent* who reads them in order to insert him/herself into them—or not."[5] The woman whose life experiences the journals record is engaged in what Judith Butler calls a "daily act of reconstitution"; she apprehends her gender in "an impulsive yet mindful process of interpreting a cultural reality laden with sanctions, taboos, and prescriptions." Her agency is not fully self-determining but is nonetheless present in the interactions through which gender is appropriated, not merely given: "Not wholly conscious, yet available to consciousness, it is the kind of choice we make and only later realize we have made."[6]

Ted Hughes destroyed all but a few entries from Plath's personal journals after 1961, believing they would be too painful for her children to read.[7] Only a few character sketches of her Devon neighbors remain from the period in which Plath wrote the Ariel poems, which constitute almost a third of the poems she wrote in her final decade, including those Hughes selected for his edition of the volume *Ariel* (1965) as well as those composed during the same period and later published in *The Collected Poems* (1980). What Hughes preserved of Plath's journals is part of the Sylvia Plath Collection at Smith College. What he edited and published in 1982 as *The Journals of Sylvia Plath* is a selection from a record that spans her undergraduate career at Smith; her graduate study at Cambridge; her marriage to Hughes; their life together in Northampton, Boston, and London; and the birth of Frieda. Plath's private writing from the last months in London in 1961 (during which she drafted *The Bell Jar*) and the eighteen months in Devon, when Nicholas was born and when she apparently began a second novel about her marriage, called *Double Exposure* (or *Doubletake*), and during which Plath wrote the poems she correctly prophesied would make her name—the journals that accompanied her period of greatest artistic production and personal trial—are missing.

My goal, however, in analyzing her journals, is not to reconstruct the period when Plath composed *Ariel* but to read the larger pattern of conflicts and contradictions that marked her as a woman and as a writer. I have found Plath's private writing from 1957 to 1959, the first years of her marriage and of her life as a professional writer, particularly revealing of the tensions that structured these identities. In these writings Plath significantly revises her narrative of her life and her work. These journal entries provide an especially resonant countertext to the late poems written during a similar period of crisis and revision.

One cluster of concerns in these journals focuses on her relationship to Hughes, specifically her fear of his sexual infidelity, her resentment of his role as tutor and critic of her writing, and her jealous rivalry for poetic recognition. She sought, in these two years, to translate her prize-winning apprenticeship as a writer into a professional identity, first in her year of teaching at Smith and then in her commitment to earning her living exclusively from full-time writing in Boston. Plath's competition with Hughes, disguised in public, is confessed frequently in the journals as an abrasive tension in their marriage that bred a murderous desire for poetic retribution that is fully realized only later in the Ariel poems.

Another group of anxieties and ambitions revolves around the identities of daughter and mother. Even in her rebellion against their expectations, Plath craved the approval of her mothers—that of her intellectual mentor at Smith, Mary Ellen Chase, who had arranged her teaching appointment, no less than that of Aurelia, who welcomed her back to America as a successfully married woman. She also constantly rewrote her literary genealogy, searching for poetic foremothers but simultaneously fearing their precedence, enviously recording her female contemporaries' success and vowing to eclipse it. In her therapy with yet another mother, Dr. Ruth Beuscher, Plath reflected on links between these relationships and her writing. Because she identified her writing as a substitute for herself in her most intimate emotional exchanges, a threat to her ability to write meant the extinction of self; likewise she felt any withholding of love or approval by mother, mentor, therapist, or husband would mean the end of her writing.

As she reconsidered these relationships—literary and personal—and as Plath tried to move from her role as apprentice to professional, from daughter to a mother herself, her goal was to establish an identity that combined sexual authority with poetic generativity. Yet the journals are characterized, as the Ariel poems would be, by fears of insufficiency and an often enraged rivalry. In negotiating these roles, Plath was repeatedly caught up in the contradictory meanings of rage, the female body, and motherhood that become central concerns in her personal life in 1962 and key elements of her poetics in the Ariel poems. Each of these is an engendered situation that is problematic for the woman writer precisely because the cultural representations of their meanings are so densely concentrated. Each of these situations represents a node, a knot, a complication in the narrative Plath conceived her life to be. Each complication required a revision of her poetics; that is, each prompted her to reimagine the relation of gender, sexuality, and poetic authority.

In reading the Ariel poems, I try to account for the reciprocal relation between gender and representation implicit in Plath's texts, to "discover," as Nancy Miller has described feminist critical practice, "the embodiment in writing of a gendered subjectivity; to recover within representation the emblems of its construction."[8] I see Plath's creative choices in the poems as at once symptomatic and strategic, symptomatic in that they suggest her culture's powerful shaping influence on her imagination, yet strategic in that they represent her effort to rewrite her lived experience in a poetics of survival. In her poetry Plath's goal was to rewrite her life; in her practice, I argue, we can understand how she also revised the very notion of "woman."

Plath's rage in her late poems was Vesuvian, to adapt Dickinson's metaphor of the woman poet's dissembling restraint and her potentially destructive expressive power. Plath constructs a highly theatricalized performance of the feminine victim in order to justify the retaliatory script of her consuming homicidal rage. But the feminine victim—mute, confined, tortured, dismembered—

represents Plath's fear of poetic silencing as much as it does her erotic dependency. The extravagantly oppositional stance of these poems, driven by desire and defiance alike, provides the dialectic that defines Plath's sense of self and power.

In the poems in which she confronts the meanings of the female body, Plath resituates the female subject in a refigured body no longer defined by opposition but by appropriation. As she dismantles her earlier poetics in which she was fertile partner to Hughes's inspiring genius, Plath's scenarios move from victimization, through retaliation, and toward dangerous incarnations of female sexuality. She reinvests the male potency and authority that the rage poems protest in a new poetics of singularity. Creative primacy in these poems is asserted as a pleasurable repossession of a body endowed with incandescent energy, unconstrained liberty, and inviolable self-sufficiency.

In Plath's poetry, making babies and making poems are persistent metaphors for each other. As a mother who writes the Ariel poems, Plath explores the dissonance and ambivalence that arise when the conceit becomes a consuming reality. Plath was determined to prove that writing and maternity were both inherent expressive needs of female sexual identity. She depended on both to confirm her generativity and autonomy, yet her journals and her poems alike reveal that she conceived of them as fearful ordeals with uncertain outcomes.

The evolution of feminist theory in the last two decades parallels the critical revaluation of Plath's poetry. My reading of texts from feminist theory serves not only to clarify my own premises but to distinguish them from other possible feminist readings of these engendered situations. In analyzing the critical assumptions and aesthetic criteria of particular works of feminist criticism, I am interested in the logic of certain feminist positions, or reading strategies. I examine the contradictions and revisions within feminist critical practice in order to establish the intellectual framework for my readings and to give a fuller sense of how Plath's poems have been read, and why they may have been misread, in the last two decades. Feminist criticism, like the culture and the literary texts it reads, is dynamic. Janet Todd aptly describes its focus: "Literature and culture are sites at which ideology is produced and reproduced. In imaginative works a moving ideology can be fixed and brought to consciousness and its contradictions made visible."[9] Part of my intention in the theoretical sections is to produce a similar freeze-frame for feminist criticism by isolating the working assumptions of other critics and linking them to the particular analysis of culture from which they emerge.

In thinking and writing about Plath, I remain convinced that, in Nancy Miller's terms, the signature matters.[10] Although Plath as a writing subject is constituted through language and representation, the very fact that representation forces women to adopt multiple and often contradictory subject positions also produces the possibility of resistance and produces a distinctive female signature that marks the texts women produce. In focusing on Plath as a woman revising, I mean to suggest that her journals and poems give us access, in a remarkably densely layered form, to subjectivity in process. The identity she created for herself in these texts is necessarily fictional but, equally important, personally explanatory. Linda Alcoff, following de Lauretis, describes the interaction between available discourses and the female subject as the sort of incessant revision in which I see Plath engaged: "The identity of a woman is the product of her own interpretation and reconstruction of her history, as mediated through the cultural discursive context to which she has access."[11] I locate agency in the female subject not only in the self-conscious performances of these texts but also in Plath's writing of a revisionary history. In her journals we see her as a discerning subject, interpreting her position in her culture. In the poems we see her refiguring the textual representation of that position and in the process rearticulating a changed female subjectivity. Finally, by revision I mean to suggest the ways that Plath repeatedly invested in, dismantled, and reconstructed the personae she performed in her life, in her letters and journals, and in these poems.

The metaphor of Plath revising her life and her poetics has a stunning material reality in the used paper she appropriated to draft the poems in the fall and winter of 1962. In November of 1961, Plath discovered that her poetic scrap could be converted into cash. A London bookseller who had already purchased some of Hughes's manuscripts for Indiana University also bought some of hers.[12] These are, for the most part, typescripts, some with handwritten revisions. Whether because she took her own creative process more seriously once someone else confirmed it was worth preserving, or because she saw these papers as an additional source of revenue, Plath saved and scrupulously dated her drafts and revisions for all of the poems she wrote in the last year of her life. From these poems that I refer to collectively as the Ariel poems, Hughes preserved sixty-seven in successive drafts, which are now part of the Sylvia Plath Collection of Smith College. From this wealth of unexplored textual evidence, I trace the evolution of the major poems in order to formulate a paradigm of Plath's creative process. Unless I mention otherwise, all drafts I discuss are in the Smith collection.

Plath composed her Ariel poems on the reverse of several of Hughes's manuscripts dating from the early spring of 1961 and on the reverse of an edited typescript of *The Bell Jar*, which Plath had completed by August 1961. Underlying both of these earlier manuscripts is the pink bond of Smith College memorandum paper that Plath had systematically pilfered during her year of teaching in 1958.[13] Writing on the pink bond seems a fetishistic appropriation of the authority the Smith English department faculty once represented to her. How important these material reminders of earlier authority and productivity were to Plath is signaled by the request she made to Al Fisher, her former teacher at Smith, to send her a new supply of the memo pads in the spring of 1962 in an effort to break a writing block.[14] If we retrace this history of reusing paper associated with particular periods of her life and with landmarks in her own and Hughes's writing career, we uncover the dynamic of her creative process, especially the interweaving of biography and textuality.

In June 1962, Plath and Hughes had celebrated their sixth anniversary. During her mother's visit later in the summer, Plath had accidentally confirmed Ted's affair with Assia Gutman, which she may have suspected earlier in the spring and summer. In August, Plath decided to seek a legal separation, and in September, Hughes moved back to London for good. In late summer Plath began her new cycle of writing by reinscribing these old manuscripts. "Burning the Letters," the first of several poems that attempt to dismantle and dispose of Hughes's poetry and to articulate her rage, is actually drafted on the reverse of several of his poems, among them one of his most famous statements of his own poetics, "The Thought-Fox." Whether because the primacy of Hughes's poetic example was too strong or her own emotional attachment was still too real, or simply because no time for writing existed without paid child care, Plath wrote no more poems after "Burning the Letters" for more than a month.

In late September, Plath drafted the poems that sought to reclaim a powerful poetic voice for herself on the back of a typed version of The Bell Jar. Beginning with "A Birthday Present" (September 30), and continuing through the five-poem bee sequence she drafted in the first two weeks of October, these poems self-consciously mark a countdown toward Plath's thirtieth birthday at the end of October and a corresponding effort to take stock of her personal and poetic resources. When Plath typed "Wintering," the final poem in the bee sequence, and itself a prediction of her survival as both mother and creative intelligence, she turned to her other major source of used paper for the month, Hughes's manuscript for an unpublished radio play, The Calm.

Hughes's play dates from early 1961 when the couple lived in a cramped London apartment with infant Frieda. Although Hughes borrowed a neighbor's study to write, and earned a steady income that spring from BBC broadcasts of his plays, Plath's own productivity was stalled by depression and the exhaustion of child care. Hughes was at work on The Calm when Plath miscarried their second child. She characterized it as a "dark opposite to Shakespeare's Tempest."[15] In October 1962, the emotional resonance of this manuscript must have included both her earlier hope of financial security and a reminder of her disappointments as mother and poet. Hughes's handwritten draft served as scrap for the next eight poems, among them some of Plath's most devastating reappraisals of Hughes, including "A Secret" (October 10), "The Applicant" (October 11), "Daddy" (October 12), "Eavesdropper" (October 15), "Medusa" (October 16), "The Jailer" (October 17), "Lesbos" (October 18), and "Lyonesse" and "Amnesiac," which were originally a single poem (October 21). *The Calm* ran out, appropriately enough, as Plath drafted "Amnesiac/ Lyonesse," about Hughes's forgetfulness of his family.

Only a few chapters of *The Bell Jar* typescript remained when Plath returned to use it again in the second half of the month. She used the earliest chapters from the novel for seven poems, most of which focus not on Hughes but on Plath's role as mother and on her reconstruction of a poetic identity that was searingly self-sufficient. These include "Stopped Dead" (October 19), "Fever 103°" (October 20), "Lady Lazarus" (begun October 23), and, at the end of this cycle, "Cut," two poems to her son Nicholas, and "The Tour." The last pages were nearly exhausted in the poems she composed on October 24 ("Cut" and the two-part "Nick and the Candlestick"). On October 25, Plath typed "The Tour" on page 1 of chapter 1, and the supply of paper that had prompted and sometimes informed the tremendous rush of creativity—twenty-five poems in less than a month—was gone. No more poems were written until her thirtieth birthday on October 27, when "Poppies in October" and "Ariel" appear, in all their starkness, on the clean bond of the magical Smith memo paper.

Until the middle of November, the next seven poems were written on fresh memo paper.[16] On November 16, Plath reused a draft of "Purdah" from October 29 to begin "The Fearful," and on November 26 she drafted "Winter Trees" on late typescripts of "Stings" (October 16) and "The Arrival of the Bee Box" (October 4). By November, the poems Plath had mailed out in October began to be accepted for publication. The momentum of the last month's creativity and the reassuring number of October poems that were sold apparently made these typescripts and carbons suitably auspicious to reuse as scrap, and the cycle of reinscription began again. It would last until February 5, when Plath composed the last poems before her death over those she had written in the fall, so that the final vision of the "perfected woman" literally overlays the hopeful prophecy of the end of "Wintering."

.ady (azarus (4)

It's easy enough ~~to do~~ it in a cell.
~~It's~~ It's easy enough to do it
It's ~~the~~ theatrical
comeback ~~return~~, in ~~the~~ broad ~~startight~~ day
to the same place, the same ~~face~~,
Amused shout:

'A miracle!'
That really knocks me out.
There is a charge

For fingering my scars; there is a c
For ~~listenostopng~~
~~h~~ my heart —
~~~~. It really goes!

And there is a charge, a very larg
For a ~~~~ word a ~~~~
or a bit of blood

or a piece of my hair or my clo
~~~~ enemy
I ~~burn~~ turn.
~~~~ Her enemy.
You age, & I am new.
I am the baby/on/ your anvil, /I
~~~~
~~~~
You say I am dangerous.

Rage

What a trash
to annihilate

Engendering Rage: The Scene of Betrayal

Plath's Ariel poems of rage react against an act of silencing that is startlingly prefigured in the journals of 1957–59. The period marks her return to America as a married woman; her first experience of work as a professional, first teaching at Smith College, then writing in Boston; and her resumption of psychotherapy. The period ends at the writers' colony at Yaddo, with her first pregnancy and the decision to return with Hughes to make their literary careers in England. Her efforts to define herself as wife and professional poet necessarily included significant revisions of earlier identities. She revisited the scene of her undergraduate success at Smith, hoping to prove herself as a teacher; returned to proximity with her mother, whose approval was always important but apparently never sufficient; and reentered therapy, trying to cure her depression and debilitating writing blocks. The pattern in the journals from these years I want to highlight, however, is the one inscribed in an indelible moment from the spring of 1958. The roles she assigned to Ted in her script for their marriage become superimposed and sedimented in ways that she began to suspect enforced her dependency and threatened to silence her creativity.

> I went alone into the coffee shop which was almost deserted. A few girls. And the back of the head of Bill Van Voris . . . the girl he was sitting with in the booth opposite him could see me. She had very fine black eyes, black hair, and a pale white skin, and was being very serious. . . . He was talking in his way: silly, pretentious, oh yes, fatuous. She stammered prettily. . . . I could see Al Fisher, sitting in the same seat, and me opposite, that official sexual rapport. Al Fisher and his dynasties of students: students made mistresses. Students made wives . . .

> As I came striding out of the cold shadow of the library, my bare arms chilled, I had one of those intuitive visions. I knew what I would see. . . . Ted was coming up the road from Paradise Pond, where girls take their boys to neck on weekends. He was walking with a broad, intense smile, eyes into the uplifted doe-eyes of a strange girl with brownish hair, a large lipsticked grin, and bare thick legs in khaki Bermuda shorts. I

saw this in several sharp flashes, like blows. . . . His stance next to Van Voris clicked into place. (J 231–33, May 19, 1958)

Plath's unspoken rage at male betrayal in this scene, observed on her last day of teaching classes at Smith College and reported in the journals several days later, is equaled only by her disgust at the female gullibility that makes it possible. What Plath learned from the performances she witnessed here provides a key to the poems she would write at the breakup of her marriage four years later. In the layered recognitions of these scenes Plath sees herself uncomfortably inscribed in a repeated scenario of male authority and female collusion. The roles she observed define and depend on each other: the male actor requires a female audience, the teacher a student, the seducer a flirt. Their dynamics also threaten and rehearse the rupture of another pairing Plath considers here, husband and wife.[1]

Initially, Plath poses as satiric, omniscient onlooker at her married colleague's flirtation. Sitting behind him, she appreciatively measures the girl's youthful prettiness against his wife's "dough color" skin and "stretched mouth: grim gripped lips," as if she identified with the male gaze. Yet this male impersonation rapidly dissolves as she sees herself reflected in the mirror of the girl's eagerness to please, her need to have her faltering self-confidence shored up as she, in turn, flatters male pretensions. Leaving the coffee shop to assume the role of teacher herself, Plath's unsettling flashback links her instead to the "dynasties of students" through whom male teachers reproduce their sexual and professional power. She cynically reinterprets her undergraduate identity as prize-winning protegée, once thought special, as serial.[2] Although she rereads her past through this gendered allegory, she believes she is now safely outside the script; its repetition is merely a bad joke on others: "my amusing insight, my ringside seat at Van Voris and Seductive Smith Girl: or William S. is bad agayne" (J 232). But she has not seen all. The final segment of this journal entry anticipates the characteristic inversions that mark Plath's later poems of rage. The flashes of insight that come like blows threaten death: the death of her smug illusions about her perfect marriage and the death of her identity as uniquely beloved wife.

Compared with her ironic detachment from the first performance, her illicit pleasure in her ringside seat, Plath's distance from the second scene of sexual betrayal is a pained, helpless exclusion. Her doubled vision that recognizes how the adoring gaze of the female student and her own serve as enlarging mirrors for the male ego is now triangulated, as the new sight forces her to identify with the deceived wife. The vision has a totalizing effect as images of the three men are superimposed, reducing all three to smiling villains, Plath's persistent trope for Hughes in the Ariel poems. A cruelly depersonalizing metonymy stands in for the girl's sexual availability: a large lipsticked grin, bare thick legs. This time she confronts the male gaze of gratified desire and lacks access to the second female subject in the scene, now substituted for herself: "I could not tell the color of the girl's eyes, but Ted could, and his smile, though open and engaging as the girl's was, took on an ugliness in context" (J 233).

Although a journal entry, this narrative is self-consciously structured to intensify the reader's retrospective awareness of significant patterns and to require our participation in Plath's emotional reversals. The striking conflation of hypermasculinity, fatuous male vanity, and treacherous sexual villainy is reproduced, almost compulsively, in Plath's poetic revenge plots of the summer and fall of 1962. Plath also chooses a similar narrative strategy, a divided or double identification as smug, satiric observer and speechless victim to organize virtually all of the poems in the cycle discussed in this chapter. In Plath's private writings, Ted as teacher and sexual betrayer, fused in the image by the pond, is associated for her with the masculine authority, accomplishment, and approval she doubted she could equal and with the erotic attachment she dreaded might deceive her.

Stoking the Fire: Myths of Masculinity

Plath expected her return to America, with husband triumphantly in hand, to confirm her personal and professional identity: "I told myself, coming over [to England as a graduate student], I must find myself: my man and my career before coming home.... And here I am: Mrs. Hughes. And wife of a published poet" (J 153). But Mrs. Hughes, wife of the poet, confidently proclaimed in England, was an identity more difficult to justify in America than she anticipated. The first major strain in Plath's marriage came during 1958–59, when the couple gave up teaching jobs to become full-time writers, and can be traced in part to how she understood masculinity and work. She may have prized Ted for his un-Americanness, his persona as a rugged, wild man of the Yorkshire moors in touch with nature and the occult, but she consciously measured him against standards for male adulthood that were distinctive of her culture rather than his. The frequency with which Plath itemizes in her journals the things they can do without—"a steady job that earns money, cars, good schools, TV, iceboxes and dishwashers and security First" (J 273)—indicates the tension she felt between social measures of American male success and her investment in a myth of Hughes as romantic genius. Plath had crafted Ted's image in hyperbolic terms from the outset of their affair in 1956. Her very first letters to Aurelia counter the news that he lacks a degree or a job with the representation of Hughes as primal poet: "I met the strongest man in the world, ex-Cambridge, brilliant poet whose work I loved before I met him, a large, hulking, healthy Adam . . . with a voice like the thunder of God—a singer, story-teller, lion and world-wanderer, a vagabond who will never stop" (LH 233).

The American model of masculinity she defended him against is derived from several notions that became the subjects for self-conscious cultural scrutiny and contestation in the 1950s among the middle class: "maturity," the corporation man, and suburban family life. The way each of these served to define masculinity and yet were also attacked as seriously undermining it can help us understand the self-contradictory persona she constructed for Hughes. Plath's journals indicate her conflicting allegiances to humanistic psychologies, which stressed self-actualization and would justify her and Hughes's nonconformity, and to conventional measures of adulthood and achievement.[3] Among the expectations that Plath regarded with mixed disdain and doubt, the criteria for male maturity often involved "settling down," especially to a steady job and raising a family, and "working" at marriage. A man who resisted or delayed becoming sole breadwinner and parent was accused of "evading responsibility."[4] Before he was thirty, an American male needed a steady salary and a family to spend it on to avoid charges of latent homosexuality or infantile attachment to his mother.[5] As Plath worried about postponing children until she and Ted had established themselves as writers and as she hoarded their always unpredictable, sometimes marginal income from selling poems or winning prizes, it is not surprising that she often represented herself and Hughes as late bloomers in the maturity race.[6]

Yet if accusations of sexual deviance were ways of policing the cultural imperatives for men to marry early and earn enough to consume conspicuously, other social critics believed the career path of the organization man was itself the largest threat to masculinity. Plath reported reading David Reisman's bestseller *The Lonely Crowd* and seems to have shared his conviction that the conformity demanded by the middle-class workplace was inherently emasculating.[7] Her disdain for the safe marriage she rejects is tinged with sexual disgust: "Get a nice little, safe little, sweet little loving little imitation man who'll give you babies and bread and a secure roof and a green lawn and money money money every month. Compromise. A smart girl can't have everything she wants" (J 268). The popular culture was also capable of a misogynist logic that made women, in the guise of both parasitic wives and overprotective mothers, responsible for unmanning husbands and sons. The suburbs were responsible for breeding exaggerated gender role separation as the commuting husband left the full-time housewife to raise an increasing number of children largely alone. The centrality of the mother's influence, first sanctioned by baby books and women's magazines, was then decried as a pernicious matriarchy. *Look* magazine ran a special series on American men in 1958, including "The American Male: Why Do Women Dominate Him?"[8] The appearance of *Playboy* magazine in 1953, with Marilyn Monroe as its first centerfold, can be seen not as confirming the dominant paradigm for masculinity but as a self-conscious rebellion against it. In its antagonism to marriage, "conformity, togetherness, anonymity, and slow death," *Playboy* detached virility from social responsibility, bachelorhood from homosexuality, and erected a counterimage of the American male free from the dominance of women who was served instead by interchangeable playmates.[9]

The coexistence in 1950s ideology of these contradictions—the definition of adult masculinity with the steady breadwinner and the counter-identification of escape from marriage with ebullient heterosexuality—also pointed toward corresponding fears of female dependence and female dominance. Plath's particular dilemma in confronting these crosscurrents was to construct a myth of Hughes as manly poet powerful enough to subdue the cultural suspicion of the writer as effeminate and to quiet her own anxiety that as a husband he was improvident. A partial list of what she identifies as "main questions" needing resolution in 1958 reveals several embedded conflicts that pitted Plath against her culture and, perhaps inadvertently, herself against Hughes:

> What to do for money & where to live: practical . . .
> Ideas of maleness: conservation of power (sex & writing) . . .
> Why do I freeze in fear my mind & writing: say, look: no head, what can you expect of a girl with no head? . . .
> Images of Society: the Writer and Poet is excusable only if he is Successful. Makes Money. (J 273)

Undeniably Plath sought to define herself as well as Hughes as a successful writer and money-maker. Still the list makes clear that to endow the unlucrative vocation of poetry with "maleness" would also increase her risk as dependent wife and cast doubt on her own aspirations as a writer of the wrong gender.

What entrapped and enraged Plath was her belated recognition that in attempting to revise the cultural scripts for American success in order to validate her marriage and Ted's vocation, she had assigned to herself a subordinate role as woman and poet. The particular tangle of self-blame for not accomplishing the appropriate feminine developmental tasks in her marriage and her seething yet censored resentment at her role as apprentice poet in the partnership are commonplace in the journals: "Get over instinct to be dowdy lip-biting little girl. Get bathrobe and slippers and nightgown & work on femininity. . . . Must try poems. DO NOT SHOW ANY TO TED. I sometimes feel a paralysis come over me: his opinion is so important to me" (J 295).[10]

"He is a genius. I his wife."

How did Plath, who identified herself at seventeen as a girl who wanted to be God, come to such an impasse? How did she and Ted come to be "strangers in our study, lovers in bed"? Why did the mask of ultrafemininity come to disguise the rage of the thwarted poet? What silenced and estranged Plath in her study was more than the cultural construction of American marriages in the 1950s or her attempted remasculinization of poetry as a profession. If the outward signs of the poet's life did not correspond to criteria for male maturity, the books in Plath's study told another story. The authors she wrote about and later taught at Smith were predominantly, although not exclusively, male; this male dominance of the literary canon was reconfirmed by her graduate study at Cambridge and was affectionately though somewhat ambivalently reproduced in the gift books she received as a serious writer from her mother and then from Hughes. It would be a mistake, however, to imagine that Plath was without female models. As peers and predecessors, women writers provoked Plath's sharpest critical response. What does emerge, however, is an underlying model of literary history that becomes more gendered as Plath matures and in which the male modernists she initially claimed as her masters become increasingly identified with Hughes.

Plath's fondest fiction about her relationship with Hughes was that it was a mutually beneficial collaboration. In their early passion, Hughes evoked poems from her with orgasmic ease: "All gathers in incredible joy. I cannot stop writing poems! They come better and better" (LH 235). This flood of productivity is refined by loving discipline: he "is my best critic as I am his" (LH 243). But even in her initial euphoria, there was a note of competition: "We drink sherry in the garden and read poems; we quote on and on: he says a line of Thomas or Shakespeare and says: 'Finish!' We romp through words" (LH 235). Almost immediately this garden of poetic delights was replaced by a series of cramped apartments in which Ted tutors and tests her: "He literally knows Shakespeare by heart and is shocked that I have read only 13 plays. . . . He is educating me daily, setting me exercises of concentration and observation" (LH 267). While I agree with Margaret Dickie's substantial evidence that in their poetry both were "voracious borrowers" and that Hughes's themes and images show he followed Plath's example as often as he led her in new directions, it is significant that Plath thought herself in Hughes's debt.[11] If she willingly assigned him the role of tutor ("Whatever Ted does I would like to submit myself to it. It would require a long discipleship" [J 283]), she also railed against his demands ("He is didactic, fanatic" [J 246]).[12]

Plath intended to act as Hughes's sponsor in America, introducing him to a market she herself had already broken into. But when his prizes and publication began to outpace her own, she needed to justify his priority as somehow helpful to her: "Strange what vicarious pleasure I get from Ted's acceptances: . . . almost as if he were holding the field open, keeping a foot in the door to the golden world, and thus keeping a place for me" (J 202). The evidence from her private writing shows that Plath consistently imagined the place that Hughes occupied was quite different from her own. The most remarkable pattern is that between the time she met Hughes in 1956 and they separated in the fall of 1962, almost all of Plath's references to male modernists, especially Yeats, were comparisons to Hughes. In fact, in the literary genealogy she constructed, Ted became their direct descendant. An early triumph for Hughes, while he and Plath were still in Cambridge, was being chosen to do a recording of Yeats for the BBC, and during the audition Plath reported, "I made him read one of his own poems stuck between Yeats and Hopkins" (LH 273). Her most frequent terms of praise invoked the male modernists: "Ted is an excellent poet: full of blood & discipline, like Yeats" (J 153) or "It's the most rich, powerful work since Yeats and Dylan Thomas" (LH 287).

Feminist critics propose that a woman writer's relation to the male canon is as metaphoric daughter to patriarchal fathers. At the same time that she seeks through her literary production to please the father, her competition risks his displeasure. While this metaphor explains much of Plath's towering ambition and her self-flagellating fear of writing, in her actual life the male greats frequently played the role of father-in-law. In her particular historical moment the same totem figures could represent distant established greatness—they appeared on the syllabi she studied and taught—and be guests at dinner parties she attended. Their preference for Hughes was not imagined but real: W. H. Auden was a judge for the Harper's competition Hughes won for his first book, Hawk in the Rain; T. S. Eliot was a member of the Faber and Faber editorial board who particularly praised the poems when the volume was accepted for English publication, and he remained a mentor for Hughes's later work.[13] As she watched their mantle unequivocally descend on Ted, Plath could claim a relation to this male literary history only by marriage: "I drank champagne with the appreciation of a housewife on an evening off from the smell of sour milk and diapers. . . . There Ted stood, flanked by T. S. Eliot, W. H. Auden, Louis MacNeice on the one hand and Stephen Spender on the other. . . . 'Three generations of Faber poets there'. . . . Ted looked very at home among the great" (LH 386).

Plath's sense of her own symbolic and real belatedness meant that male literary history was inescapably mediated by Hughes. In her psychic economy he came to stand for the literary tradition she once thought she might enter directly. The intimate rivalry she felt with him in their study was more paralyzing because his approval, or his more frequent criticism, of her work carried the force of an acceptance, or a rejection, by Yeats, Hopkins, Thomas, Auden, and Eliot. Her early fantasy of their collaboration, "a team better than Mr. and Mrs. Yeats" (LH 280) cozily dabbling in the occult, was replaced by the actual humiliation of Hughes disloyally critiquing her work in front of George Starbuck, a dinner guest who gloated over his lover Anne Sexton's success.[14] Outproduced and overcorrected by the husband who had supplanted her, Plath's ire as thwarted poet took the form of wifely nagging, as she recognized in the depths of a writing block in Boston: "Must not nag (anything Ted doesn't like: this is nagging); he, of course, can nag me about light meals, straight-necks, writing exercises, from his superior seat. The famed and fatal jealousy of professionals—luckily he is ahead of me so far I never need fear the old superiority heel-grinding—in weak-neck impulse. . . . Must work and get out of paralysis—write and show him nothing. . . . Smile, write in secret, showing no one. Amass a great deal . . . a woman famous among women" (J 259–60).[15] What is significant in this passage for the forms that rage will take in Plath's later poems is the way wifely submission and poetic concession are the inverse signs of her secret plans. By the end of this intensely ambivalent meditation, she has redirected her ambition away from direct competition with Hughes to becoming a "woman famous among women."

Plath and Hughes spent the fall of 1959 at Yaddo, Ted the invited poet, Plath again his guest. Plath's reading notes in her journals for these months provide a definitive example of the pattern I've emphasized. References to male predecessors dropped out almost entirely, while the frequency of her references to women writers as rivals and sources of inspiration picked up. She foraged among women writers for clues about tone, treatment, character, or reassuring symptoms of weakness like her own. Most likely because she was pregnant at the time, her comments on craft were often linked to speculations about sexuality.[16] The male tradition had become too overpowering or too inaccessible to be confronted directly, as she acknowledged the winter before in Boston: "Why can't I read Yeats, Hopkins, if I love them. Why do I punish myself by not looking at them?" (J 291). When the great male guests arrived at Yaddo, Plath reported, "The famous Board. John Cheever, Robert Penn Warren. I have nothing to say to them" (J 315). I am not proposing that Plath entirely forsakes male models but that her relation to them is focused and filtered by her relationship to Hughes and becomes increasingly embattled and competitive.[17] Some of her most derivative poems, like the sequence "Poem for a Birthday," with its unmistakable echo of Theodore Roethke, date from the Yaddo months. Hughes has claimed that these poems represent her transition from her *Colossus* to her *Ariel* voice. More likely they mark a detour in Plath's development, as Margaret Dickie argues, brought about by another marital competition in imitating Roethke that Hughes set up as writing exercises.[18]

In his editing of the poetry Plath wrote during the Yaddo period, Hughes emphasizes her effort to induce an artistic breakthrough by her tranced impersonation of a male model important to him. What we also need to notice, however, is that, in her fiction from these months, her rage against him, driven underground so often, becomes lethal. The premise for the short story "The Fifty-ninth Bear" is a contest between husband and wife about who can spot more bears in Yellowstone. The dynamic between the couple is a seductive but duplicitous power play in which the wife's apparently pliant will is treacherous: "Her innocence, her trustfulness, endowed him with the nimbus of a protecting god. He fathomed her, enclosed her. He did not see, or did not care to see, how her submissiveness moved and drew him, nor how . . . she led him, and he followed." The husband's macho defense of the campsite from a marauding bear is foiled, at the climax of the story, by the wife's more powerful but unspoken wish that wills the bear to win: "As from a far and rapidly receding planet, he heard a shrill cry—of terror, of triumph, he could not tell. It was the last bear, her bear, the fifty-ninth."[19]

The denouement, though forced, is worth comparing with the end of a short story written in her first year of marriage, "The Wishing Box." In the earlier representation of their rivalry, the wife is repeatedly outdone by her husband's more prolific subconscious (which yields, ready-made, the plots of Hughes's most famous poems, "The Thought-Fox" and "Pike"). When the dream-practice her husband prescribes fails, she attempts to stock her dreams through secret study, but, defeated again, she chooses a suicidal sleep as her way of winning.[20] The first wife's comic earnestness is rewritten in the Yaddo wife's dangerously cunning and violently displaced antagonism. Still, in her journals Plath complained that "The Fifty-ninth Bear" is a "stiff artificial piece" that disgusts her because "little hygienic transparent lids shut out the seethe and deep-grounded swell of my experience" (J 314). When Hughes leaves her almost exactly two years later, Plath plots a similarly displaced murder of her poetic rival in "Burning the Letters" and "Daddy."

Because Plath had so often represented Hughes as the latest heir in the male modernist poetic line, she needed to believe in the myth of their sexual and spiritual fusion in order to claim his patrimony. If she acknowledges their rivalry, the door she once hoped he held open for her slams in her face. But a curious transition occurs in Plath's relation to her most powerful literary father, "my beloved Yeats," once Hughes is gone. In the letters she writes to her mother in the fall and winter of 1962, her pilgrimage to claim and then live "safely in Yeats' house" is clearly an effort to recover her own direct poetic lineage. In London, she is master of Yeats's house, no longer the wifely dependent and secondary genius of Hughes's house. She insists on her mystical election by Yeats, I would argue, as symbolic compensation for Hughes's defection.[21] When Ted unexpectedly abandons her on the vacation she hoped would achieve a reconciliation, Plath rereads the significance of her trip: "I had the uncanny feeling I had got in touch with Yeats' spirit . . . when I went to his tower in Ireland" (LH 480). Lacking one provider, she trusts the recovered father to restore her inheritance: "I opened a book of his plays . . . and read 'Get wine and food to give you strength and courage, and I will get the house ready' " (LH 480). Yeats is the mentor whose tacit approval is unconditional; he is the partner who can never betray her. In rewriting the script of her literary ambition, Plath needs no intermediary; the powerful father-poet himself holds open the door to the house of greatness.

When Vesuvius Speaks: Theorizing Rage

American feminist critics, initially characterized as an angry lot themselves, have elaborated several theories that attempt to explain a woman writer's rage at her position in social and literary history and the expressive forms her anger takes: the silence that explodes when Vesuvius speaks. To see women writers as Vesuvian in their restraint and in their rage assumes that the material, social, and psychosexual constraints that characterize the cultural construction of "woman" will mark not only a particular woman's subjectivity but her writing as well; that is, a woman writer suffers an alienation within herself that is culturally produced and that is textually reproduced in different but discernible forms. In these explanations rage is identified with a narrative need, a desire for a revisionary or oppositional story of female experience that counters the dominant cultural fictions.

In A Room of One's Own and "Professions for Women" Virginia Woolf articulates the logic that links a woman who would write inevitably to anger. These essays, especially *Room*, were among the most frequently cited texts that authorized feminist literary criticism in the 1970s. While later feminists have contested Woolf's conclusions, none have been able to do without her terms: the phenomenon of the split self, the dangerous consequences of this splitting for a woman's psyche and story, and finally, the necessity of compensatory textual strategies for overcoming the anger that the divided self experiences.

Woolf's insights have structured later discussions of rage and the woman writer, although some of her assumptions have become problematic. The very notion of the divided self introduces a series of dichotomies that feminist critics have pondered ever since. In "Professions for Women" Woolf claims murder is the ritual that initiates her into the profession, a necessary self-defense of her right to write: "Killing the Angel in the House was part of the occupation of the woman writer," Woolf asserts; "had I not killed her, she would have killed me. She would have plucked the heart out of my writing."[22] In dramatizing her violent repudiation of ideological constructions of consciousness, Woolf also implies that a separate subjectivity exists, a more authentic self who enacts this rebellion. Many feminists, and virtually all Plath scholars, have posited such a combat between a true and false, socialized self as a central tension in women's writing. Yet the plausibility of such a "true" self, who would exist outside or be somehow immune to ideology, is seriously questioned by postmodernist critics. Woolf herself wondered, later in the same essay, whether such an unrealized, or at least unrepresented, self could be defined: "Now that she had rid herself of falsehood, that young woman had only to be herself. Ah, but what is 'herself'? I mean, what is a woman? I assure you, I do not know."[23] She did know that internalized gender conventions blocked access to the unconscious, balked the imagination which, when it "dashed itself against something hard," censors rather than remembers "something about the body, something about the passions, which it is unfitting for a woman to say."[24] Contemporary feminists might go further to ask whether the unconscious itself is gendered.

From *A Room of One's Own*, feminist critics also borrowed another set of polarities about the divided self. If the parable of Judith

Shakespeare demonstrated that rage, denied its appropriate object, would claim women as its suicidal victims, didn't Woolf also imply that anger could be directed outward? Disaffection might not lead to self-destruction but to a doubled consciousness that is analytically enabling and potentially feminist: "If one is a woman one is often surprised by a sudden splitting off of consciousness, say in walking down Whitehall, when from being the natural inheritor of that civilization, she becomes, on the contrary, outside of it, alien and critical."[25] Later theorists of rage themselves are usually split in their interpretations of female anger: it is either inherently self-wounding or implicitly transformative. While they might disagree about the personal or political consequences, feminist critics have continued to be preoccupied by textual consequences of the split self. Although Woolf judged the enraged text "disfigured and deformed," and argued "it is fatal for any one who writes to think of their sex[,] . . . in any way to speak consciously as a woman," her conviction that gender would leave an indelible mark on the text has proven useful to generations of critics who seek to demonstrate the distinctiveness of the female-authored text. If we are now more interested in reading the signature of gender than in erasing it as Woolf was, her desire for an androgynous consciousness from which to write remains significant, more for the end she imagined than the means. Her goal was to find a narrative strategy that would solve the feminine predicament, repair the split self, and remove the internalized constraints of gender in order to tap creative energy and produce a unified subjectivity; for Woolf, the benefit of the "androgynous mind" is that it "transmits emotion without impediment; that it is naturally creative, incandescent and undivided."[26] Whether and how the text might cure the writer or, through altering discourse, change gender relations have since become fiercely debated questions among contemporary feminist critics.

After Woolf, feminist theorists of rage might be roughly divided into two camps: those for whom explicit anger is valued as a hallmark of creative energy, and another group for whom denials, displacements, and disguises like Woolf's are nearly inescapable expressive strategies and are the chief sources of critical interest and, I argue, aesthetic pleasure in the text. What interests me in tracing these two branches is that they produce remarkably dissimilar critical judgments of rage in a woman's text, both common in readings of Plath's Ariel poems.

Patricia Spacks, Elaine Showalter, and Adrienne Rich are alike in hearing Woolf's voice, played back in the context of the politics of the women's movement of the 1970s, as not nearly angry enough. To the extent that she mutes her rage, they believe, she betrays her art and mutilates herself. The terms of their critique refer repeatedly to failed nerve, avoided self-knowledge, and defensive compromise: she "apologizes for her presumption," "evade[s] confrontation with her own painful femaleness," and wills herself "to be calm, detached, even charming in a roomful of men where things have been said which are attacks on her very integrity."[27] While they ostensibly identify flaws in Woolf's style, these charges also insistently suggest flaws in character.

Adrienne Rich, whose 1971 essay "When We Dead Awaken: Writing as Re-Vision" was invoked nearly as often as Woolf's during that decade, accepts Woolf's split self but articulates an alternative logic of rage that defines this group.[28] For Rich, female rage is constitutively feminist, personally therapeutic, and creatively liberating, releasing the woman writer from defensive narrative strategies and granting access to an authentic and unalienated voice. Rich replaces Woolf's allegory of female suicide with the image of a woman in labor: "Both the victimization and the anger experienced by women are real, and have real sources, everywhere in the environment, built into society. They must go on being tapped and explored by poets. . . . They are our birth-pains, and we are bearing ourselves."[29] Reading Plath, Rich revises Woolf's preferences and praises precisely the qualities Woolf lamented in Charlotte Brontë: "It is finally the woman's sense of herself—embattled, possessed—that gives the poetry its dynamic charge, its rhythms of struggle, need, will, and female energy."[30] The progress Rich charts in her own poetry implies that anger, once spoken, can make way for a psychic and poetic reintegration, a moment when "the woman in the poem and the woman writing the poem become the same person."[31] While the autobiographical identity she asserts between poet and persona is more hypothetical than real, even in her own practice, Rich's premises make possible readings that tend to judge an absence of explicit anger in the text as an artistic deficiency.

For Spacks, Showalter, and Rich, and perhaps even more definitively for Jane Marcus and Paula Bennett in the 1980s, anger does not preclude art but becomes its necessary precondition. They read female anger as demonstrating desirable feminist politics but more significantly, I think, as signs of female psychic health. Marcus cites Freud to justify women's equal right to anger: it is "a result of the ego's first struggle to maintain itself, to find an identity separate from the mother."[32] Bennett praises the poetry written during the 1970s for the "catholicity of its rage" and claims "emotional liberation, the release of rage . . . is psychologically anterior to the integration of the self and makes possible the artist's song."[33] Because these critics maintain that anger is a primary source of creative power, they rank women whose texts appear to lack it, like Elizabeth Bishop and Marianne Moore, as inferior poets. What emerges is a hierarchy of aesthetic value that assumes a text must be a reliable and fairly transparent manifestation of the psychodynamics of its author and that a poet's failure of nerve in confronting her rage necessarily constrains her imagination.

What marks readings of this group is a consistent faith that a wrathful persona in the poem stands for the authentic self in the poet, as in Bennett's equation: "Medusa, the angry or unangelic underside of the self . . . became the passionate symbol for the woman poet's liberated self."[34] Woolf believed that the existence and nature of the self who seeks to cast off her feminine roles is problematic or undefinable; for these critics, it is not. The true and false selves discovered in a text are unambiguously separable; the false self can be "shed," "transcended," or killed off for the sake of an always more powerful subjectivity that is described as "purified," "integrated," "liberated," or "autonomous." In this expressive-purgative logic, the textual enactment of rage effects a cure of the artist's consciousness that is absolute and irreversible. The literary history of women's writing implied by such judgments not only establishes an aesthetic hierarchy of rage but a progressive poetics, as in Marcus's conclusion: "Anger is not anathema in art; it is a primary source of creative energy. . . . Out with it. No more burying our wrath, turning it against ourselves. . . . When the fires of our rage have burnt out, think how clear the air will be for our daughters. They will write in joy and freedom only after we have written in anger."[35] Such a Utopian vision seems to prefer a poetry of affirmation but only at some future date; in their critical practice, these critics uniformly distrust such poetry.

If this first group shares a taste for unequivocal anger, a second group might be said to favor the duplicitous text. The writer's relation to the source of her rage is frequently more complex in these accounts, and its textual signs are more ambiguous. Doubleness itself, however, is prized as a canny narrative strategy, a proliferation of knowing disguises rather than helpless evasions. Instead of willing allegiances to gender conventions that silence part of the female story, the duplicitous text testifies to anxious declarations of nonconformity or sly subversions of hegemonic discourse. Sandra Gilbert and Susan Gubar elaborate a paradigm of the enraged double in *The Madwoman in the Attic* that has been replicated or borrowed by other American feminist critics as often as it has been denounced. Although Gilbert and Gubar propose an identification between the author and her madwoman character that appears, to some, suspect or naive, the relationship they propose is less transparent than the first group's. They stress that the text is the locus for revision, for a refiguration of lived experience; what the writer represses, the text expresses: women writers "project what seems to be the energy of their own despair into passionate, even melodramatic characters," figures who are "bloody, envious, enraged." Because these monstrous madwomen are often suitably punished by their creators or murderously uncontrollable, Gilbert and Gubar argue that "through the double's violence . . . this anxious author articulates for herself the costly destructiveness of anger repressed until it can no longer be contained."[36]

The goal of these narratives, like the narratives of the first group, is to construct through language a subjectivity that revises the prevailing cultural fictions and makes possible self-articulation and psychic wholeness. But Gilbert and Gubar demonstrate in their readings, more than in their theoretical formulations, that these textual doubles are figures with deeply ambiguous significations. Their critical practice, like that of Rachel DuPlessis, Alicia

Ostriker, and Joanne Feit Diehl, yields an aesthetics of anxiety and ambivalence. Together these critics take most interpretive pleasure in palimpsestic texts.[37] Their emphasis on the presence of covert plots and anxious retreats from self-assertion depends in part on how they conceive of women writers' relationship to literary and cultural sources of power. Toril Moi has pinpointed the ways Gilbert and Gubar's central paradigm tends to totalize the operation of ideology as a monolithic, static, and uniformly oppressive patriarchy and to reduce women writers' literary response over two centuries to a single urtext of rebellion.[38] DuPlessis, following Raymond Williams, insists on a more dynamic model of ideology that contains internal contradictions, in which "there is a constant repositioning between dominant and muted, hegemonic and oppositional, central and colonial." While the female subject also experiences herself as divided, her allegiance and resistance are described as an "oscillation," not an unequivocal alienation that can neatly sever all relation to the patriarchy.[39] In fact, what makes Vesuvian rage so often unspeakable, so dangerous to the self once it erupts, is that her ties to her oppressor are often personal, familial, and erotic. In Alicia Ostriker's terms, the woman writer confronts an enemy "at once intimate and historical," "a fatal adversary, by whom she is enthralled."[40] The patriarchal image, according to Joanne Feit Diehl, promises salvation as well as destruction; its power is dangerously irresistible, "a vision of a force at once enticing, provocative, and deeply desired."[41] Instead of arguing that a recoverable, authentic female self survives untainted, somewhere outside of her cultural construction, these critics recognize that a woman writer and her creations are deeply and contradictorily connected to dominant cultural values and to the dominant literary tradition.

If this is so, where does resistance come from, and what are its textual signs? Judith Butler helpfully suggests a conception of gender as performance, a "stylized repetition of acts" that are culturally validated and policed and through which identity is constituted. The style of our gender performance is never fully original or independently volitional, nor is it entirely given or socially determined. Yet if "gender reality is performative," as Butler claims, then "it is real only to the extent that it is performed," and gender identity can be revised by "a different sort of repeating" of its stylized acts.[42] Butler's logic replaces the notion of a preexistent self with an identity that comes into being through performances that are renewed, revised, and consolidated over time in tension with available cultural scripts. Given this understanding, narratives of victimization, rage, and rebellion are not expressions of true or false selves but textual enactments, performances that not only revise but actually constitute identity.

I propose that the textual signs of Vesuvian rage in Plath's poetry are best read not as separable dichotomies but as oscillations or simultaneous performances of contradictory cultural scripts. The text may enact rigid gender conformity or flamboyant transgression. Feelings of powerlessness may be dramatized by adopting the pose of an orphaned child, a sexual victim, or a romantic slave. The retaliatory urge is figured in systematic inversions of these roles, including the punishingly sexual aggressor, the terrible mother, the madwoman, and varieties of male impersonation. In the common sadomasochistic scenarios, the female subject is both the persecuted victim of a cruelly tyrannical and erotically dominating male and at the same time a courageously avenging heroine. Ellen Moers and DuPlessis name this script "female Gothic," a fantasy they suggest is so pervasive among women writers that it may characterize female consciousness.[43] Elaine Showalter proposes these polarized sexual identities are themselves produced by projecting "all the disturbing, dark and powerful aspects of femaleness" onto maleness;[44] or, as Gilbert and Gubar suggest, the oppositional representation of female rage may occur within a single figure, such as the monster, in which the female subject inhabits the misogynist metaphor, now "imbued with interiority," and so changes the meaning of the performance.[45]

In many of these revenge plots, there is a persistent connection between female enclosure, entrapment, and rage and, at the other pole, disclosure, expression, and death. The defining gesture of revenge, whether homicide or suicide, becomes particularly problematic to interpret. Ostriker claims that in women's poems of violence, part of the reader's thrill arises from a "doubleness that demands decoding," a charged presence of the unspoken

and forbidden message, which she identifies as an interchange-
ability between the "desire to die and the desire to kill."[46] Even
when the female subject survives, Feit Diehl notices that her
"murderous poetics" that would reject or destroy the oppressor
have a high cost: being trapped in a repetition compulsion that
does not ease but only intensifies the pain.[47] It seems to me that
we read and reread Plath's poems of rage with something akin to
pleasure not because they produce literary catharsis but because
their interpretive demand is so great. In them we see enacted both
the feminine predicament and the potentially feminist solution.
The poet simultaneously asserts her speaker's agency and, unconsciously, confesses her own cultural formation. In her revenge
plots, Plath imagines triumphant reversals or at least metaphorically refigures her own defeats. Words, the unleashing of verbal
violence, may be either a linguistic cure or the obsessive fingering
of an open wound. The poems tell a double truth that is compelling precisely because of the contradictions it contains rather than
resolves.

Consuming Rage: The Poetics of Victimization

What happens when the two images of Hughes I have traced in
the private writings—the enthralling teacher who betrays and the
helping poet who rewards and confirms—are confounded? What
new fiction would serve Plath when, in the summer of 1962, the
dreadful dreams of her journals all came true? The darker knowledge of the journals—her fear of Hughes's infidelity, her resentment of his role as tutor, her jealous rivalry for poetic recognition—"clicked into place" for Plath in the gallery of male authority
figures by whom she had been seduced and abandoned with the
confirmation of his affair and their subsequent separation. Plath's
myth of her relationship to Hughes as wife and fellow-poet was
constructed, I have argued, in response to her culture's expectations and her own needs, but for the most part quite consciously
by her own hand or, more exactly, pen. The wound to the poet's
identity that Hughes inflicted was not merely a sexual betrayal but
his betrayal of this story that had also defined her. Had she not
insisted so hyperbolically to herself and others that Hughes was

the vital engendering force of her poetic voice, the approving father through whom the blessing of Yeats could be delivered, and the standard of genius by whom her own poetic worth would be measured, her poetic repudiation of this myth and these roles might not have been so extreme.

In the poems of rage written in the summer and fall of 1962, Plath constructs a highly theatricalized performance of the feminine victim in order to justify the retaliatory script of her consuming homicidal rage. Her performance of an enraged woman, capable of murder, depends on separating herself from emotional and sexual bondage to an intimate enemy. Since the fiction of her marriage depended on an ecstatic fusion of self and other, Plath's need for revenge always carried with it the risk of self-destruction. In these poems the poet rigidly polarizes gender identities so that the object of her rage is detestably and more safely other. The oppositional tremor I trace is visible first in the confused narrative line of "Burning the Letters" that moves like a jagged fault line toward the discharge of unexplained violence at the poem's close. The pain of poetic silencing and erotic dependency is figured in a series of poems in which the speaker poses as pornographic victim, starved, raped, and murdered by her partner. The end of this series is "Daddy," in which the chasm that divides wife and husband is constructed as the howling gulf between an orphaned child and the always already absent father. Finally, in the punishingly sexual aggression of "Lady Lazarus," Plath attempts to annihilate both the persona of the female victim and her oppressors.

"Burning the Letters," the only poem she managed to write during that difficult August, is the earliest of several poems that attempt to dismantle and dispose of Hughes's poetry as an obstacle to her own creativity. She appropriated a sheaf of typescripts of Hughes's poems for scrap to compose the first poems in response to the breakup of their marriage; whether the habit of reusing paper was begun in necessity, it is certainly in this instance an emotionally laden gesture with a lengthy prehistory. Plath had served as Ted's typist ever since they met in Cambridge six years earlier. She often used the preparation of his manuscripts as a distraction from her own feelings of stagnation and lethargy. Two months later, in October 1962, a second Hughes manuscript, for an unpublished radio play, *The Calm*, would become another major source of reused paper. Among the six poems she wrote in ten days in October are her most devastating reappraisals of Hughes in "The Applicant," "Daddy," and "The Jailer." The cumulative evidence of these and other drafts for the Ariel poems proves that reinscription was an essential element of Plath's strategies for gestation and revision. Her borrowings from earlier, underlying texts is common enough in the Ariel manuscripts to suggest that Plath read and reread the reverse of these pages while composing, especially to get started or whenever she was stuck. The subversive revenge plots embedded in these poems become fully meaningful only when we read them in the context of his manuscripts that inspired and infuriated her.

How can she confirm her own voice while literally reinscribing the remnants of Hughes's earlier poetic successes? "Burning the Letters" shows more clearly than most what I believe is a richly significant aspect of all of Plath's Ariel poems: how biographical events and earlier texts deeply interpenetrate each other in the composition process. More strikingly than some others where a similar phenomenon occurs, "Burning the Letters" reveals that, during composition, Plath worked on a permeable page. Of the ten manuscript pages that exist for "Burning the Letters," the first six were written on the reverse of six separate Hughes poems from the spring of 1960, among the first poems he had written since his *Lupercal* collection.[48] This poem dramatically arraigns Hughes's old papers as her subject, and then, as if to overcome the threatening dominance of his words, Plath incorporates scraps of his poems into the new fabric of her story. Hauntingly we see the power of his words, especially the manuscripts of his poems on which she composed, as potential sources of inspiration and as oblique objects of her vengeance.

The manuscripts for "Burning the Letters" offer a paradigm of her creative process. To write a poem about burning Ted's papers on actual copies of his poems, among them one of his most famous, "The Thought-Fox," proved riskier than Plath might have anticipated. The whole poem is built upon a central irony: the very fire that the speaker builds to destroy the evidence of betrayal in Hughes's letters unexpectedly betrays her purpose by delivering the name of his lover out of the flames. Plath's ambivalence about whether her gesture was a successful symbolic retaliation or a maddening reenactment of his deception characterizes all of the drafts and marks even the published version of the poem. In the extensive revision of the drafts, however, we witness the poet's deliberate efforts to recast each of the central images of persecution, silencing, and torture to give the speaker the controlling force in the action and the last word in a battle that involves the record of their poetry no less than the history of their marriage.

The plot of the published poem disguises as much as it discloses. The mood of this witch in a housedress is curiously enervated rather than enraged, while Hughes's residual force stored in his writing is animated, hostile, and potentially lethal: "white fists of old / Letters and their death rattle." The discontinuous narrative line marks fissures in the text, places where Plath's revisions fail to resolve fully the tension between the speaker's horrified paralysis and her urge to purge and punish. Significantly, the largest narrative gap occurs at the moment in the poem when the speaker's victimization seems absolute, when the name floats out of the fire to spell her romantic defeat at the end of the third stanza. Plath leaves unspoken the spark of rage that connects this moment to the next, the dismemberment of the fox in the last stanza. To explain these gaps I want to focus on two image patterns that function in the drafts as catalysts for the startling denouement but are suppressed in the published poem: the dog pack that appears only metaphorically in the first stanza and then returns to kill the fox in the final lines, and an image of Joan of Arc seen through the flames of the third stanza that is entirely erased from the finished poem. Each pattern carries the double valence of suffering and aggression in the worksheets.

In the uncertain beginnings for the poem, Plath vacillates between having the dogs serve as mirrors of her own distress and having them function as the "degraded" agents of Ted's antagonism latent in his old papers. In some lines their staring shock mimics her own: "⟨The hounds I saw had the⟩ yellow eyes ⟨of the mad.⟩ / ⟨Peeled open forever on so much lovelessness⟩." In others, the dogs are "holding in their hate" waiting for a signal from their masters, "men in red jackets / With no chins & womenish whinnies." Although Plath's emasculating language hints at a wish to wound, the two impulses coexist uneasily throughout the entire first page of the draft.[49] In her first typed copy of this heavily revised first page (fourteen of twenty-seven lines contain revisions, and fewer than sixteen lines are kept when she prepares clean copy), Plath abandons the dogs and focuses on the fire she has set. The speaker's fire, itself a gesture of both retaliation and self-protection, absorbs the dog imagery and its uneasy ambivalence: "My fire may lick and fawn, but it is merciless. / It is a glass case. / It flickers between me and everything I look at! / *Do not touch.*" The fire also attracts the imagery associated with a bell jar, "a glass case," a frequent shorthand in Plath's drafts for feelings of confinement, paralysis, and muteness. In deploying the fused image of fire/bell jar, Plath cannot decide to whom the fire is merciless, Ted's memory or her own lingering desire: "My fingers would reach through ⟨to you⟩, but are bent back." The confident assertion of the finished poem ("here is an end to the writing, / The spry hooks that bend and cringe, and the smiles, the smiles, the smiles") is compromised throughout the drafts by confessions of lingering attachment that must be consciously erased in revision.

An especially resonant example of Plath's contradictory self-presentation occurs in what would eventually become stanza three of the final poem. The stanza is memorable because Plath summons from the ashes "carbon birds" that "would be coal angels," embryonic forms of the fiery avenging heroines who will later rise untouched out of the destruction of marriage in the brilliant October poems—"Stings," "Fever 103°," "Lady Lazarus," and "Ariel." But in August, in this poem, their consolation for the speaker lies solely in being unable to repeat domestic secrets:

Rising and flying, but blinded, & with no message.
They would flutter off, black & glittering, they would be
    coal angels.
But they have no words to say to anybody.
I have seen to that—
The mouth of this house is shut ⟨up⟩.

They are not yet able to offer the incendiary countertruths that the later resurrected heroines will pronounce. Still, these offspring of the speaker's wrath are typical of this and the later poems because they evolve from the poet's practice of replacing the speaker's feelings of isolation or helplessness with claims of expressive authority. For example, in the first draft the speaker complains, "there was nobody for me to know or go to. / So I burned the letters & the dust puffs & the old hair," which becomes, in the first typewritten draft, "And there was nowhere to go and nothing to do." Finally Plath deletes this passage altogether and substitutes, for the repetitive whine of the trapped and friendless housewife, the oddly defiant smoke signal of the carbon birds: her blinded witnesses and mute messengers whom she controls ("I have seen to that").

The final version of this stanza, however, masks the underlying turmoil in the drafts that surrounds the second message from the flames, the one she cannot control, the name of the lover. The enormous difficulty Plath had in finding words for this revelation marks each of the ten pages of the manuscripts; it will continue to be the most troubled passage in the poem and will be extensively revised even in the last of Plath's six complete drafts. It remains uncertain whose words will win, the taunting reminder of another woman's name preserved in Hughes's handwriting or the poet's refiguring of her torture in a retaliatory script. She poses as a relentless executioner in the first three drafts; the burning letters are expiring saints: "I open the ⟨pages, the⟩ white wads that would save themselves. / ⟨Spirit⟩ Word after ⟨spirit⟩ word ⟨gives itself up⟩ is lit! / They darken like Joan of Arc, the heart is a cinder." The presence of the martyr among the flames has a curious instability once invoked. She appears to stand for the unkillable rival, as in this juxtaposition: "Word after word is lit / Then darkens, a little Joan of Arc, / And the name of the girl flies out." Or she is associated with the speaker's interminable suffering and speechless persecution, "⟨red & dark & dumb as an old heart⟩." Through several drafts Plath fails to resolve whether the burning words in her "little crematorium" are more dead than alive or whether she murders or is herself ghoulishly tormented by "letters ⟨crawling⟩ spidering ⟨like hands⟩ ⟨by hooks and hands⟩ on a skin of white."

In five separate drafts Plath worries over the fatal vision that concludes this section, the name that cannot be suppressed; she sees a "death card" or a "funeral announcement, black-edged and that fatal." Logically such an image should announce the lover's death, but emotionally it is clearly the speaker's funeral. The unburnable word, the unkillable rival, the unredeemable situation—these are the elements that disturb the coherence of the poem throughout its long gestation. Frequently Plath settles for naming her rival through a private metonymy; her gray eyes and Germanic name are evoked in the first draft by "⟨an infatuation of pale eyes and gutturals⟩." Similarly displaced recognitions are diffused over the vegetables, in the second draft, turning "red cabbage" to "German cabbage." Apparently for Plath the most resonant totem for Ted and Assia's adultery was an orchid.[50] The image may have been inspired by the visual appearance of wood ash ("a white wood flower, an orchis"), or Plath may have intended an etymological pun, since *testicle* is the Greek root of orchid. By the sixth draft, the orchid acquires suggestively sexual epithets: "⟨Now⟩ a name ⟨is alighting⟩ with black edges / Wilts at my foot ⟨it is in your writing⟩ / ⟨A notorious⟩ Sinuous orchis / In its nest of root hairs and boredom." In the published version of the poem, Plath replaces the tangled snares of the drafts with a wordless gap; the climactic event occurs in the stanza break between the third and the final stanza: "And a name with black edges / Wilts at my foot."

Curiously, in the drama of "Burning the Letters," the event that precipitates Plath's powerful final assertion of immortality, the killing of the fox, seems at first unrelated to the funeral pyre the speaker has arranged for her marriage. Yet the violence finally unleashed on the fox and the full resonance of the fox's unstoppable cry provide the most dramatic proof of the remarkable permeability of Plath's page. Hughes's "Thought-Fox" is not merely invoked here but literally underlies the draft of Plath's poem. "The Thought-Fox," written in 1957, contrasts significantly with the other poems Plath now reused as scrap.[51] Compared with the slighter, new poems from the spring of 1960, which were published in magazines later that year but were never collected into one of Hughes's major volumes, "The Thought-Fox" was already a talisman of Ted's talent and success for the couple. Published first in *The New Yorker* (the coveted pinnacle of success for Plath), then included in the prize-winning *Hawk in the Rain* volume, the poem

It never snows in this country. That is the trouble. 2

~~There is never a gutter of white on the dustip~~

The rain ~~drags~~ its rags. The ~~~~ lukewarm droplets

~~~~ ~~split~~ ~~their skins on varnish,~~

Grease my

The rain smells like ~~~~ wool.

And here is your handwriting, ~~paper~~ ~~the paper~~, the spry hooks, the lies.

I got tired of looking.

And there was nobody for me to know a goto.

So I burned the letters & the dust puffs & the old hair.

At least it will be clean in the attic.

~~At least it will smell ~~~~ ~~~~~~

At least I won't hang underneath it, dumb as a fish,

My tin eye waiting for glints & a signal,

~~My fins holding up the wake of those~~

Riding the cold, pure arctic

That was the space between your speaking, your thinking time.

So I poke at the carbon birds in my housedress.

They are more beautiful than the cry of an owl, they console me.

~~Rising & flying, but blinded, + with no message.~~

They would flutter off, black & glittering, they would be coal angels.

But they have no words to say to anybody.

I have seen to that—

The mouth of this house is shut ~~up~~. With ~~the cut~~ of a rake

I open the ~~page white~~ wads, that would save themselves.

~~Scald~~ of the ~~wood~~ ~~~~ ~~~~ is lit!

My ~~pe~~ darken like Oran of arc, the heart is tender →

~~A ~~~~~~ rain greases my hair, but ~~it ~~~~~~ extinguishes nothing.

My veins glow like trees love

The dogs are tearing a fox. my this is what it is like—

"Burning the Letters," draft 1, page 2, composed August 12–13, 1962 was one of Ted's favorites and often was a touchstone in his poetry readings. In a BBC broadcast in 1961 he had boasted, "Long after I am gone, as long as a copy of the poem exists, every time anyone reads it the fox will get up somewhere out in the darkness and come walking towards them. . . . It will live for ever, it will never suffer from hunger or hounds. I have it with me wherever I go. And I made it. And all through imagining it clearly enough and finding the living words."[52]

Hughes's poem is set in a snowy midnight when the speaker-poet confronts a writing block; the fox is evoked as an unconscious agency that comes "about its own business" but suddenly accomplishes the poet's task as "it enters the dark hole of the head" and "the page is printed." Composing her own poem in mid-August, Plath ends the first page of her draft focused on the bonfire of burning letters but addresses the absent Hughes: "O love, it is giving me a suntan. I am sweating." The complaint that begins a new stanza on the second page is such an unexpected contrast that it strongly suggests Plath, stalled in her own composition, got her fresh start by rereading "The Thought-Fox": "It never snows in this country. That is the trouble. / There is never a gallon of white on the doorstep." Still, Plath's dialogue with Hughes's poems is always competitive and her strategy revisionary.[53] Hughes's poem surfaces even more dramatically at the end of the second page of Plath's draft. Here Plath first imagines the burning papers "darkening like Joan of Arc, the heart is a cinder" and then, in a non sequitur that indirectly confesses as much anger as it censors, observes with icy detachment, "The dogs are tearing a fox, my love, this is what it is like." The stanza that begins the third page of the draft superimposes the image of the mutilated fox on that of the smoldering martyr: "The ⟨red flash⟩ burst heart & the cry / That splits from its ripped bag & does not stop." If, in the implied logic of the metaphor she creates by layering her poem on Hughes's, the fox is Hughes's poetic agency, he is set upon and devoured by his own deception (the degraded hounds seen in his old letters in the first stanza) while the speaker stands by un-bloodied yet unequivocally avenged. But the burst heart might as plausibly be hers, proving she is no Joan of Arc (whose allegedly intact heart established her saintliness) but a mortal woman whose only immortality is her anguished death cry and, of course, this poem. Like the endings of the later "Stings" and "Lady Lazarus," "Burning the Letters" produces an alter ego who both perishes and survives the forces that threaten her.

"Burning the Letters" demonstrates that all of Plath's revenge plots from the fall of 1962 have twin objects for her rage: Hughes's sexual betrayal and his poetic primacy. The fox's dying cry repays and overrides the death-card announcement of the lover's name: it lingers, "telling the particles of the clouds, the leaves, the water / What immortality is. That it is immortal." In quarreling with Hughes's telling of the fox's story, Plath contests his prior claims to immortality, vindictively diminishing the thought-fox to "the dead eye / And the stuffed expression." Her counterclaim defies Hughes's visionary equation of his own poetic genius with the mysterious powers of nature; it also defines the engendering source for the next cycle of Ariel poems: the voice of suffering and murderous desire.

In three poems written in October—"The Detective," "The Courage of Shutting-Up," and "The Jailer"—Plath recasts marriage as a criminal act, an intimate violation that robbed her of her poetic voice. In these scripts the roles of the partners are unvarying; the abjectness of the victimization her speakers perform is the necessary counterpart to the depravity of the oppression she would assign to the male enemy. In each, the poetic silencing the speaker suffers but claims she cannot speak of is figured as domestic confinement and physical dismemberment. Reflecting the threat to her self-consciously crafted identity that the end of the marriage posed for Plath, the wife in "The Detective" has disappeared entirely. The textual symptoms of inadequate selfhood, Ostriker observes, include invisibility, muteness, and a representation of self as dissolving or deformed.[54] In Plath's narrative, the poet investigates her own absence from the scene in an act of ventriloquism, speaking the poem through the disembodied voice of Sherlock Holmes. In re-creating the murder that was marriage, the detective reports, "The fingers were tamping a woman into a wall / A body into a pipe, and the smoke rising." The image evokes the grisly methods of a serial killer, unsuspected by the neighbors, disposing of the corpse. It also suggests the translation of poet into housewife is a literal and imprisoning transmutation of woman into house. But it speaks more duplicitously of rage, of the confined woman as loaded gun, ominously undischarged.

In the progressive fragmentation of the once articulate self all three poems report, the poet's tongue is always the first casualty:

> The mouth first, its absence reported
> In the second year. It had been insatiable
> And in punishment was hung out like brown fruit
> To wrinkle and dry.

The insatiable mouth recalls the conflation, frequent in the Boston journals, of emotional hungers and her appetite for artistic success, and Plath's habit of looking to Hughes to feed both: "The old god of love I hunted by winning prizes in childhood has grown more mammoth and unsatiable still" (J 322). She recognized even then that their exclusive intimacy that demanded all inspiration and admiration be derived from each other could be destructive: "Do we vampirelike, feed on each other?" (J 260). In the first draft for "The Detective" the competing appetites of the couple are even more explicit. Plath's subordinate role as wife and her poetic defeat are rendered as a literary allegory in which the poet's shriveled mouth is devoured by the scavenging crow: "Then there was no mouth at all / To polish the crow's wing." Hughes's poetic persona as crow, already emerging in the early 1960s, was a violently anarchic trickster with an abusively vulgar voice.[55] The duel for poetic survival ends more ominously than in the published poem. In a landscape littered with the dismembered tongue and breasts of the wife, Plath positions their literary totems: "There is only the moon, embalmed in phosphorus ⟨the barren queen⟩ ⟨her light like a⟩ the bright scalpel. / There is only a crow in a tree. Make notes."

In "The Courage of Shutting-Up" (originally titled "The Courage of Quietness") the speaker claims her silence is elected rather than enforced, yet her unarticulated anger is no less disabling. Like the broken record that serves as the organizing metaphor of the first half of the poem, the speaker gets stuck repeating a litany of

"Bastardies, usages, desertions and doubleness" that "revolve" in the brain "like the muzzles of cannon." This repetition of injury without relief, reparation, or expressive release produces a poet of diminished capacity:

> The needle journeying in its groove
> Silver beast between two dark canyons,
> A great surgeon, now a tattooist,
>
> Tattooing over and over the same blue grievances,
> The snakes, the babies, the tits
> On mermaids and two-legged dreamgirls.

The poet turned tattooist must retrace male fantasies of desire, mapped on the body as tawdry sexual symbols. The aggressive phallic sexuality of this whole passage suggests the poet's imagination has been taken over by this dominating male inscription. Plath revised these lines in her first draft, substituting "snakes" for the more innocuous "tiger heads, American flags" to insist on the sexual nature of the injury and the dulling redundancy of the images that now obliterate all others.

The speaker owns that her tongue is a weapon; "indefatigable, purple," swollen with rage, it is a whip with "nine tails" that "flays" when it speaks. Only by cutting it out can she perform the self-censorship the poem promises. Still the tongue has taken its trophies; if she must be silenced, the lethal wish of the speaker is that her severed tongue be "hung up in the library" alongside Hughes's decapitated poems, "the fox heads, the otter heads, the heads of dead rabbits." The poet's vital organs of expression and perception perish in the claustrophobic confinement of her anger; her eyes, like her brain and tongue, reflect and repeat the death of the self who loved and the murder of the beloved:

> But how about the eyes, the eyes, the eyes?
> Mirrors can kill and talk, they are terrible rooms
> In which a torture goes on one can only watch.
> The face that lived in this mirror is the face of a dead man.

The torture the poet undergoes in these poems and the punishment she would inflict are in fact murderous mirrors of each other.

The sadomasochistic necessity of torturer to victim is nowhere more evident than in the sexual script of "The Jailer." The blamelessness of the speaker who has been "drugged and raped" is confirmed by the depravity of her oppressor who has been "burning me with cigarettes, / Pretending I am a negress with pink paws." Plath's adoption of the role of woman as colonized, dehumanized subject is a strategic choice with several consequences, some of them contradictory. Because of historical associations of woman with body, Ostriker contends that psychic hurt is often figured by women poets in somatic terms.[56] Jane Marcus proposes that the representation of rape in a woman's text has symbolic resonance as a "speaking text" that figures the destruction of a woman's sexual and creative power. For Marcus, the literary representation of a woman with her tongue and hands cut off stands for the silencing of the woman writer through the cultural forms of male dominance that prevent and punish her speech. In writing the scene of rape, the woman writer as victim possesses only a "wrested alphabet" and produces deformed and constricted texts whose only subject appears to be the naming of her oppressors.[57] Certainly the extreme victimization that Plath's speaker performs in "Jailer" testifies to an identity reduced in scope and size, mute, even comatose, in her incarceration. Plath's images of exploitation in this poem are heavily freighted with associations of other experiences of powerlessness, entrapment, and the extinction of articulate selfhood. Her drugged sleep is a small death that not only recalls the suicidal caul of The Bell Jar, and of "Daddy" (written the week before), but that also resembles the engulfing darkness of "Wintering":

Seven hours knocked out of my right mind
Into a black sack
Where I relax, a foetus or a cat,
Lever of his wet dreams.

In one of her most desperate October letters to her mother, the poet who had been left behind in Devon rants, "Stuck down here as into a sack, I fight for air and freedom and the culture and libraries of a city" (LH 465). A few days after this poem, the image will reappear in "By Candlelight" to stand for the forces that constrict her imagination and threaten the survival of mother and child: "The sack of black! . . . everywhere, tight, tight!"

How seductive Plath found these images of victimization for absolving her of responsibility and for vilifying Hughes is more evident in the draft of "Jailer" in which the wife is not just an unconscious partner but a surrogate for the absent Assia, whom, as in "Burning the Letters," Plath's deforming anger can name only by a string of verbal approximations: "I have been raped, dark funnel / For your dreams of burly queens, international oysters. / Swedes who love you in another language." In "Burning the Letters" the speaker projects her suffering onto the landscape; here, everything in her environment participates in her persecution: "Carapace smashed, / I spread to the beaks of birds." In the first draft the birds are merely irritants who pierce the cocoon of the wife's drugged sleep. Plath's revisions progressively sexualize and brutalize their attack until the birds' violation imitates that of the rapist-jailer and again evokes the consuming appetite of the barbarous crow. Re-seeing marriage as rape also revises another very early fiction of Plath's. During the spring and summer of 1957 she worked on a novel that was apparently never finished, focused on her "irrefutable meeting" with Hughes in Cambridge. In her journal she notes, "Novel: *Falcon Yard*: central image: *love, a falcon*, striking once and for all: blood sacrifice" (J 162).[58]

In the poem Plath systematically inverts earlier roles she had self-consciously played; the supportive wife and nurturant husband she had constructed in her private writing she now rereads as her self-starvation and his devouring male egotism, "in whose shadow I have eaten my ghost ration."[59] Each of her revisions intensifies the gender antagonism that drives the poem. The initially intimate dialogue of "I" and "you" between husband and wife in the first draft is replaced by consistently renaming the jailer "he," thus further stylizing the jailer's otherness while granting the victim an interiority. Although the portrait of her oppressor is obviously conceived in anger, writing the scene of her poetic silencing as rape limits her imagination to these one-dimensional projections. Several early drafts contain a penultimate stanza in which the speaker tries to imagine her release: "That being free. / I look through the holes of eyes. / I look through the hole of a heart. / The sky is a boot-sole. Will it crush me?" The model of Hughes as treacherous tyrant erected in the poem completely controls the speaker's vision of what might lie beyond.

Finally, in "Jailer," Plath cannot detach her need to punish the sadist from her desperate need for attention as suffering victim. The ending confesses a continuing dependency that is self-wounding even as it is self-validating. "I am necessary," the speaker contends, just before the final stanza in the first draft. The poem closes not with the violent reprisals that are present in "Burning the Letters," "Detective," and "Courage," even if only covertly enacted, but with the anxious wish that her torturer's perverse needs must be satisfied only by her willingness to serve as sacrificial object: "What would the dark / Do without ⟨my⟩ fevers to eat? / What would the ⟨day⟩ light / Do, without eyes to knife, ⟨open⟩ what would he / ⟨Be⟩ Do, do, do without me? ⟨without me?⟩." The danger of these polarized performances is that they are mutually constitutive of identity; both partners cease to "be" if either stops "doing" them, as the last line reveals.

"Jailer" dramatizes the risks of Vesuvian rage when its subject is the very relationship that has constituted identity for the woman writer. Yet I disagree with those critics who argue that Plath cannot imagine a performance that will discharge her anger at the intimate enemy without simultaneously wounding herself. The more subtle critics of Plath recognize that Plath's speakers operate in a figurative system that has its own logic and consequences independent of her biography. Their readings tend to assume, however, that her speakers' performances are either determined by cultural constraints or are self-deluded, assumptions that my own readings intend to counter. Jane Marcus believes the speakers' revenge plots always mask an erotic dependency that goes unquestioned and certainly unbroken. Steven Axelrod reads Plath's victim roles as flawed politics, a submission to illegitimate and destructive authority. These readings both assume that the sexual scripts Plath uses are imposed by the cultural construction of gender and inhabited with little or no critical self-awareness.[60] Margaret Dickie, Margaret Homans, and Joanne Feit Diehl propose more emphatically, as I do, that Plath's performances are strategic narrative choices intended to refigure and verbally control gender relations. Still, they would insist that her representational strategies are entrapping and inherently self-defeating.[61] I would argue that Plath's performances are always self-conscious and frequently parodic. The evidence in the manuscripts demonstrates that Plath intentionally dichotomized gender roles in her poetry of rage in order to demystify, if not dismantle, the erotic dependency that underlies these poems. We also need to resist a critical habit of collapsing all of the poems powered by anger into a single script with a uniform logic. The poems I have discussed so far represent the experience of being silenced as their primary subject. The retaliation they perform is more often oblique than overt; revenge is taken on scapegoats, like the ripped fox, or accomplished through characterization, like the jailer's. In "Daddy" and "Lady Lazarus" murder moves to center stage.

Performing Rage: "Daddy" and "Lady Lazarus"

In "Daddy" balked rage erupts into speech. The confused elliptical narratives that characterize the poems about silencing are replaced, in Plath's description of "Daddy," by an "awful little allegory." Although Plath invents a plot that is starkly clear, the language of its naked aggression is far from lucid. Few critics have liked the tone of "Daddy." Commenting nearly a decade apart, Irving Howe calls it "monstrous" and "utterly disproportionate," and Helen Vendler finds it adolescent and unforgiving. Even a sympathetic ear like Margaret Dickie's hears it as "hysterical."[62] It may well be that Plath's audacity in appropriating images from the holocaust as analogies for the damage of her family history deserves Howe's rebuke; other critics have been embarrassed, as Vendler is, that a woman of thirty reverts to baby-talk in her fury at parental injuries. The critical disapproval of Plath's tone, it seems to me, indicates doubts both that the speaker's excesses are altogether appropriate to the occasion and that Plath is entirely in control of her tone. Readers who hear the tone of "Daddy" as extreme, childish, and regressive are responding to textual cues, yet Brenda Silver suggests that how readers describe the tone they have heard in an angry text depends, in part, on a construction of whom they imagine the author to be. In other words, in unconsciously conflating the voice in the text with the voice of the author, readers may be judging whether the writer's anger is morally justified rather than whether the text is aesthetically effective.[63]

I grant the tone that critics have heard in "Daddy" is indeed present, but I believe its excesses are part of Plath's conscious strategy of adopting the voice of a child, of creating a persona who is out of control. To speak as a woman in the guise of a child may be one of the most duplicitous narrative strategies of the woman writer. Feminist critics of Emily Dickinson, who, like Plath, adopts the persona of the child to articulate her relationship to male authority, have identified some of the motives and consequences of this voice. The child persona dramatizes a woman writer's powerlessness; it mirrors the cultural allegation that woman is child, and it gives form to her experience of being treated like one. To pose as a child also authorizes a naughty deviance, a mad playfulness in which blasphemy might be uttered but go unpunished. Because words are instrumental in a child's effort to gain approval and independence, choosing to become a child as an aesthetic strategy may give access to the rage, pain, and deprivation that are a necessary motivation to make words. The child's oppositional stance, driven as it is by desire and defiance, may provide the dialectic that defines the speaker's sense of self and power.[64]

The voice of "Daddy" contains and exploits all these tensions. The female self performed is helplessly infantile, defensively repetitive, unrelenting in her complaints of abuse. The speaker's accusations that the dead father has played Hitler to her Jew and has imprisoned her tongue "in a barb wire snare" are more scathing because voiced by a needy dependent, yet their very recklessness points toward the child's confidence about escaping punishment. But is it the frenzy of excited word-making or frustration that makes the speaker stutter so often, that makes her accuse others of the clotted speech ("your gobbledygoo") she most dreads in herself? The repetitiveness of Plath's language has struck more than one critic as symptomatic of a disordered psyche and poetic incontinence. While the evidence of the manuscripts shows that Plath regularly deleted repeated words from key passages, the finished poem certainly retains more of this verbal tic than any other she wrote. Plath's use of regressive, repetitive language for "Daddy" is probably overdetermined. Ostriker claims that infantile language testifies to sexual trauma, the power of sexual pain to infantilize the woman writer.[65] Clearly the aggressive back talk of the poem is aimed not merely at the patriarch of the title but at the cultural construction of masculinity that is first enacted by the father and later reproduced in the vampire husband who also tortures and abandons the daughter. We might read the uncensored excess of "Daddy" as stemming from its double source; the repetition compulsion the poet now recognizes in her life, she risks reproducing in her language.

In her crisis of October 1962, superimposing husband on father is an efficient way for the poet to reinterpret both past relationships. The father's death and abandonment now prefigure the husband's defection; Hughes's unavailability for retribution echoes her father's speechless remoteness in death. What we can infer from the poem is not an accurate portrait of either Otto Plath or Hughes but Plath's sense of her role as orphaned daughter and as woman infantilized by sexual pain, and of the roles she makes these male arch-villains play in her struggle to claim poetic authority.[66] In her psychic economy either male had the power to confirm her poetic identity or her monstrosity. Casting Hughes as a resurrected father figure was Plath's favorite trope for his engendering force: "my own father, the buried male muse and god-creator risen to be my mate in Ted" (J 223). On the other hand, the absent father could also prove the murderousness of his daughter: "If I really think I killed and castrated my father may all my dreams of deformed and tortured people be my guilty visions of him or fears of punishment for me? And how to lay them? To stop them operating through the rest of my life" (J 301). This journal entry anticipates Plath's gloss on "Daddy" as a cathartic ritual ("a girl with an Electra complex . . . has to act out the awful little allegory once over before she is free of it"), yet it reveals a darker logic that may also operate in the poem. The guilty daughter has now gotten the punishment she deserves as the unlovable wife. The daughter who can never prove herself innocent of desiring her father's death now performs it extravagantly in the poem; since she has been punished already by the loss of the husband, she has nothing left to lose.

I want to focus on the conflicts that arise when the speaker of "Daddy" dares to do the murder Plath fears she could never be forgiven for. I also want to uncover in the drafts, and in the densely cross-referenced intertextuality of the poem, the poet's duplicitous substitution or conflation of father and husband at key moments. Plath constructs the willed recklessness, the verbal ferocity of her child-woman by disguising and deflecting our attention from the poem's second murder, that of her poetic rival. The drafts for "Daddy" are again layered on texts of Hughes's successful work, a handwritten draft of his radio play The Calm, which also underlies "The Jailer," composed a few days later. The play, like the poems Plath reinscribed in drafting "Burning the Letters" in August, also dates from the spring of 1960, when Hughes wrote and recorded a number of radio plays for the BBC. For the young couple these represented their hope for substantial fees and a steady income from rebroadcasts of the plays over a period of years.[67]

The monolithic "man in black" who dominates our attention in the completed poem is actually a composite portrait drawn from her earlier poems as much as from life. In a 1959 poem titled "Man in Black," Hughes appears as an apocalyptic silhouette who anchors the entire landscape. A month after she wrote it, Plath calls it "the only 'love' poem in my book [Colossus]" and speculates about its genesis: "The 'dead black' in my poem may be a transference from the visit to my father's grave" (J 301–2). In late January 1963 in London, when Plath drew up a table of contents for her projected second volume of poems, "Daddy" was one of several alternative titles for the book. The collection, which is unlike Hughes's final selection and arrangement of Ariel, contains only nine poems written before July 1962, when she discovered his affair; the majority are from October, and none were composed after "Death and Co." on November 14.[68] All four of the poems discussed earlier in this chapter were included, although Hughes chose later to delete them.[69] For Plath, the central subject of the volume was her reevaluation of her marriage; "Daddy" was a key document in this revisionary history. Of course the poet's dismantling of patriarchal authority in "Daddy," as emblem of the new book, would also recall the towering father figure the daughter and apprentice poet labors to rebuild in the title poem of her first collection, The Colossus.

The speaker marks a series of anniversaries in the poem: her father's death when she was ten, her attempted suicide at twenty, her marriage of seven years, and her own thirtieth birthday. The pattern of dispossession and restitution further confounds husband and father in an uneven exchange over which the speaker now realizes she has no control but the verbal magic she intends to work. The male power that the speaker seeks to repudiate is extreme in both its cruelty and its desirability to the abased female victim: "Every woman adores a Fascist, / The boot in the face, the brute / Brute heart of a brute like you." The drafts reveal the tension between the desired and renounced male antagonists even more emphatically. In the deletions from the last third of the first draft of "Daddy" we can recover evidence that, for the poet, the father and husband were, for the moment, interchangeable. In the eleventh stanza, "black man" and "black daddy" are alternate choices for the man "who / Bit my pretty red heart in two." In the thirteenth stanza, after failing to recover the father through suicide, the speaker makes "a model of you," a "man in black" who recalls Plath's 1959 poem to Hughes. He has, in her first inspiration, a "sexy look," then a "Nazi" look, and finally a "Meinkampf" look; in the brief evolution of these revisions the intimate enemy of the family romance is translated into historical villain. We also see an extreme form of a verbal tic, which appears frequently in the drafts in passages of intense conflict. In the twelfth stanza (obscured by multiple cross-outs), she tries "back" no fewer than six times: "At twenty I tried to die / And get ⟨back, back, back⟩ back ⟨through the black⟩ back, back to you." In revising, Plath always questions whether the verbal jags of her drafts can be suppressed or contained; typically she deletes most, though in "Daddy" she retains the compulsive repetition to mark the moments in the poem of greatest longing and rebellion.

What we remember most vividly about "Daddy" is the vehemence of its denunciations, as if the child speaker had increased both the nastiness and the decibels of her performance to be sure her intended male audience is paying attention. These verbal gestures are attempts to wound the men who have victimized her, deforming and disfiguring the myth of masculinity with each abusive epithet: "panzer-man," "swastika," "Fascist," "devil," "vampire," "bastard." With her furious hexes and charms the speaker seeks to ward off, since she can no longer attract, the powerful male forces. She severs communication and performs a symbolic castration: "So daddy, I'm finally through. / The black telephone's off at the root." This phallic displacement is another duplicitous gesture that only partially hides her desire to wound Hughes sexually. In both the July poem about discovering his affair, "Words heard, by accident, over the phone," and the drafts for "Jailer," the telephone is a "muck funnel" that represents for Plath both illicit intercourse and the power of words to wound.

Still, the ferocity of the tone should not deafen us to the residual ambivalence that also informs the poem. What is most remarkable about the drafts is how long it took Plath to accomplish the ritual murder that concludes the poem. In the original ending of the first draft of the poem, the speaker's confession ("If I've killed one man, I've killed two") unexpectedly frees a loving benediction in the final line: "Daddy, daddy, lie easy now." This draft reminds us that if the poem is an act of verbal vengeance—vilifying the father for setting up the model of manliness she admired and later married and which has now disappointed her—the poem also struggles to be an elegy. "Daddy" might have turned out, if Plath had kept her initial draft, more like Anne Sexton's "All My Pretty Ones" or Robert Lowell's *Life Studies* (both of which she knew and admired) in which unsatisfactory fathers are exposed in all their faults by the unfilial poet and then finally forgiven in the last stanza by the equally flawed children. In subsequent drafts, changing the nature of the ending demanded most of Plath's attention.

Simply saying she is through with this erotic dependency that drains her blood is not enough. To exorcise the demon and her desire for him, the speaker must stage an even more dramatic re-performance of polarized gender roles. To widen the gap between male threat and female powerlessness, Plath projects onto

Daddy (3)

You stand at the blackboard, daddy,
In the picture I have of you
A cleft in your chin instead of your foot
But no less a devil for that, no not
Any less the black ~~man~~ who

Bit ~~my~~ pretty red heart in two—
I was ten when they buried you.
At twenty I tried to die
And get ~~back back back~~ to you.
I thought even ~~the back back~~ bones would do.

But ~~they~~ they ~~stuck~~ pulled me out of the sack,
And they ~~stuck~~ me together with glue.
And then I knew what to do.

I made a model of you,
A man in black, with a ~~Meinkampf~~ look

And a love of the rack & the screw.
And I said I do, I do.
So daddy, Im finally through.
The black telephone's off at the root,
The voices just can't worm through.

If ~~I've~~ killed one man, I've killed two—
The vampire who said he was you
And drank my blood for a year,
Seven years if you want to know.
Daddy, daddy, lie easy now.

"Daddy," draft 1, page 3, composed October 12, 1962

the male specter an urge for sexual domination she had once acknowledged as her own: "The vampire is there, too. That old, primal hate. The desire to go round castrating the arrogant ones who become such children at the moment of passion" (J 100). In the second draft, the poet invokes a chorus of dancers ("villagers [who] never liked you") who stamp out the father-husband's image; they represent an inversion of the image of the original oppression (the adored boot in the face) that opened the poem: "They are dancing ⟨shoe, boot, shoe⟩ and stamping on you." Equally important, the stylized ritual reconfigures Plath's courtship dance with Hughes, rapturously reported in the journals in 1956. Hughes storms a party and bellows a conversation with Plath, "colossal, in a voice that should have come from a Pole," that ends with a bloody, biting kiss: "I was stamping and he was stamping on the floor, and then he kissed me bang smash on the mouth. . . . And when he kissed my neck I bit him long and hard on the cheek, and when we came out of the room, blood was running down his face" (J 111–12). Such violent eroticism, Butler would remind us, is itself a stylized gender performance of heterosexuality.

Although the poet supplies, in the community killing of the vampire, the magical gestures that should assure that the composite ghost cannot rise again, the speaker stops short of claiming the homicide is her own. In a surprising retreat from agency the speaker observes, "there's a stake in your heart," but Plath will not (or cannot) say who put it there. The final revision of the third draft demonstrates how hard it was for Plath to keep this powerful male image subdued:

> Daddy, you can lie back now.
>   fat black
> There's a stake in your heart.
> And the villagers never liked you.
> They are dancing and stamping on you.
> They always knew it was you.
> Daddy, daddy, you bastard, I'm through.

The new final stanza almost totally obscures the kindly elegiac ending of the initial draft ("daddy, daddy, lie easy now") and adds, as the latest revision, the gratuitous "fat black" heart as if to insist one last time his monstrosity, not hers, sealed his fate.

The enraged speakers I have discussed so far are distinguished by their constraint: they are subdued, dismembered, silenced, confined. Even the speaker of "Daddy" is small compared with the power she objects to and rebels against. Unlike these, the persona of "Lady Lazarus" is searingly self-confident—a taunting, bitchy phoenix who appears to loathe her earlier incarnations (so much "trash / to annihilate each decade") almost as much as she does her present audience, the "peanut-crunching crowd." In the worksheets, the ire of this poem is directed not at the monolithic brute of "Daddy" but at multiple forms of male authority; many more are named in the drafts than in the finished poem: enemy, professor, executioner, priest, torturer, doctor, God, Lucifer. What Lady Lazarus suffers is not male brutality but the gendered asymmetry of her relationship to power in which her role is always defined as dependent and defective: to male professor she is student; to executioner, criminal; to priest, sinner; to doctor, patient.

Yet the audience who matters most in the drafts, for whom these other names may be only aliases, is an other she calls "love." What the speaker wishes to accomplish by sheer force of will is precisely the inversion of what she fears. Rather than be consumed by the fires of sexual jealousy and helpless rage that appear repeatedly in the imagery of the drafts, the speaker wants to separate herself from her fused identity with Hughes, to eliminate the threat of his superior power as sexual partner and literary competitor, and, finally, to appropriate his male powers to herself in a consuming gesture of her own fierce self-sufficiency. The poet's revenge is to turn the tables on the husband and fellow-poet who, she now recognizes, objectified her as product of his creative performance, his "opus," his "valuable," his "pure gold baby." She contests not merely the fact that he possessed her but her own myth that he produced her.

In "Lady Lazarus" Plath borrows the miracle of Lazarus, the horror of the holocaust, the hype of the circus, and the legend of the phoenix to construct for herself a blazing triumph over her feeling of tawdriness and victimization. The speaker's agility in performing these roles is what will make good her opening bravado that she is in control, that what we witness is an act and that she will "manage it." The stunt she is famous for is impersonating a suicide:

Dying
Is an art, like everything else.
I do it exceptionally well.

I do it so it feels like hell.
I do it so it feels real.
I guess you could say I've a call.

To leave no doubt that Lazarus produces a performance with an illusion of reality, not reality itself, Plath replaces a line in the first draft, "I guess I'm a natural," with a clearer acknowledgment that she's an actress, "I guess you could say I've a call." She claims not only to manage this daredevil feat but to manipulate her audience's response. Her suicides are so compelling that her self-produced resurrection, "the theatrical comeback in broad day," is applauded as a "miracle." A perverse eroticism binds actress to audience: the brazen, cynical persona flaunts her objectification, knowingly poses as spectacle to the voyeuristic male gaze. Nonetheless, her exhibitionism, "the big strip tease" of her deathly intimacy, is staged to intimidate, not to please.

Plath tried out a variety of voices during these months to unmask the essential antagonism underlying gender relations, from the wheedling, seductive entreaties of "Birthday Present" to the sarcastically hostile interrogation of "The Applicant." The caustic humor with which Lady Lazarus assaults her audience is a tone Ostriker names the "exoskeletal style" in poetry by women since 1960. Ostriker hears the brittle aggressiveness of this voice as a mask for vulnerability: "The equivocal treatment of the reader as lover-antagonist [is] a formal invention elegantly designed to illuminate the dilemma of inadequate selfhood."[70] Pretense or not, Lazarus's voice arrogates power that the careening vituperation of "Daddy" lacks. Her belittling disdain for the peanut-crunching crowd is a defense against the risk of uncontrolled explosion that erupting anger can produce, destroying the self along with the enemy. Vesuvian rage is the voice of the weak, the small railing against the all-powerful; disdain is the prerogative of the strong.[71] Yet if Lazarus feels contempt for the prurient observers, she seems to exhibit no less for herself. Plath tests Gilbert and Gubar's contention that the woman writer can inhabit the misogynist metaphor without being imprisoned by it. Lazarus's grotesque theatricalization must be read as intentional self-parody; her analogies are knowingly presumptuous, and her caricature of cultural horrors ("my skin / Bright as a Nazi lampshade / . . . / My face, a featureless, fine / Jew linen") is an affront to taste. Yet such self-parody has at least two meanings. Her burlesque of suffering both confesses the damage of gender and uses it as a weapon. Lazarus as walking corpse enacts the male metaphor of woman as monster, yet it is a mask she would gladly wear in order to terrify. The persistent double consciousness of "Lady Lazarus" is not the split self of alienation that marks Plath's other poems of rage but a strategy for control. Lazarus is simultaneously the performer who suffers and the director who calculates suffering's effect. The victory may be only a stage effect, an attribute of voice, but as Gilbert and Gubar claim for Dickinson, "the creative subject impersonating the fictionalized object[,] . . . the eiron, who both impersonates and stands apart from her impersonation, always triumphs over her naive interlocutors."[72]

"Lady Lazarus," like "Daddy," is a poem whose symbolic anniversaries are part of Plath's anxious countdown to her own thirtieth birthday at the end of October. During that month she wrote nearly a poem a day, and during the week preceding her birthday she composed eight poems, starting with "Fever 103°" on October 20 and ending with "Ariel" and "Poppies in October," both written on her birthday, October 27. The monumental "Lady Lazarus" was alone in being revised over a period of six days. In only a few poems from these weeks in October, such as the pivotal poem "Stings" in the bee sequence, did Plath make substantive revisions of a stanza or more after the initial draft or two. I think Plath's hesitation about being done with these poems marks her conviction that they were major works. Even more, I believe her prolonged attention to them and the nature of her revisions indicate the materials and areas of feelings she longed to order and control. Although the published version of the poem brags that the voracious, terrifying self is unencumbered by her past, the manuscripts reveal the strain of reconstructing a self that could define itself in opposition to the dependent, derivative definitions linked to the strong male figures in her life.

Evident throughout the drafts is her fixation on a male figure as her primary audience; even more obviously than in the published version, the speaker's performance depends on him to validate it. In the snarl of what was initially the third stanza of the first draft, the speaker regards a male figure whom she must name, within the same breath, her greatest love and her greatest enemy, and who she demands must know her:

> Peel off the napkin
> ⟨My⟩ ⟨Great⟩ Love, ⟨my⟩ ⟨great⟩ enemy.
> ⟨It is certainly I!⟩ Do I terrify?
>
> Yes ⟨yes⟩ Yes Herr Professor
> ⟨It is I⟩ I is I
> Can ⟨You⟩ you ⟨cannot⟩ deny
> The nose, the eye pits, the full set of teeth?

She insists on her unmistakable identity—she is the walking corpse he cannot walk out on—but her anxious assertions seem to expect only denial. Suppressing this direct interrogation of "my love" by replacing it with "Herr Professor" is the final revision Plath would make in the poem six days after she began.

The fourth page from the first draft reveals the sexual nexus of the poem's antagonism and the smoldering fusion of the tortured speaker with her partner. In return for her miraculous "comeback," the speaker warns, "there is a charge." "Charge" comes to stand for the high-premium, high-voltage exchange between Lady Lazarus and her audience; it is the reciprocal thrill produced by the speaker's grotesquely public disclosure of her wounds and the crowd's greedy consumption of her performance. In this draft, the parody of venerated sainthood is clearly derived from other intimate acts that are experienced as progressively more violating:

> There is a charge
>
> For fingering my scars, there is a charge
> For ⟨hearing⟩ ⟨stethoscoping⟩ my heart
> . . . .
> And there is a charge, a very large charge
> For a ⟨night in my bed⟩ word, or a touch
> Or a bit of blood.

In another heavily reworked passage, later almost entirely deleted, the speaker revolves in a fire that tortures ("I burn and turn" reappears three times) but fails to punish the oppressor or purge the victim.

> ⟨So love, so enemy⟩
> So, Herr enemy.
> ⟨I burn & turn.⟩
> You age, & I am new.
> I am the baby/ on/ your anvil,/ I eat fire.

The enflaming, repetitive suffering echoes the fevers of the earlier poem "The Jailer," in which these lines also figured in the drafts. The speaker struggles to recast the sexual slang of the husband's "pure gold baby" into an image of herself as born again, but though the rage simmers in this passage, it cannot free her. Because Lady Lazarus is consistently the abrasive carnival barker and suicidal stuntwoman in the finished poem, passages of unguarded vulnerability in the drafts are particularly surprising. Plath originally cast the third suicide as a pleasurable martyrdom:

> I am supple, I breathe gently
> And shall sit ⟨here⟩ a ⟨while⟩ little, ⟨uncommon⟩ ⟨on this
>   green common⟩
> Loving the death that killed me like a lover.
> Now it is over
> ⟨And⟩ I am involved & still, a wax madonna.

The wax madonna's suffering is passive, even erotically willing; her tone is elegiac rather than acerbic. In her self-involvement she looks toward the grave rather than toward the crowd.

The evidence of these passages suggests that even to name the male antagonist as "love" proved an obstacle for Plath in constructing the Lazarus persona. By consistently excising these images of agonizing or erotic fusion with the intimate enemy in the drafts, Plath redirects her anger at public, gendered performances of power: "Herr Doctor," "Herr God," "Herr Lucifer." In the process of negative definition that organizes the poem, these roles function as a composite projection of the speaker's fear and desire. As Plath works to tighten the defense of her speaker's macabre self-irony in revising, a consistent pattern emerges. Initially, the persona's love is fused with death; ultimately, Lady Lazarus's new life is fueled with hate. The violent fantasy of the poem is informed by the wish to incorporate the forces that threaten to destroy her.

A few poems were vexed from start to finish, like "Burning the Letters" and "Medusa" or the incoherent, splenetic outbursts of "Lesbos" and "Eavesdropper." Plath rarely doubted the beginning impulse for most poems, however, and revised the first stanzas relatively little. Her dramatic first lines often emerge at once and remain untouched as they do here. By contrast, she almost always reworked a large section of the final movement of a poem in three or four successive revisions even within the initial draft. Nearly three entire pages of the six-page handwritten draft for "Lazarus" focus on recasting the ending. What would release her heroine from the grip of male definitions, the bloody desire for revenge or a staged disdain? Plath's first effort to bring Lazarus back from the dead contains both contradictory impulses: "Each time I rise, I rise a ⟨bloody⟩ ⟨blooming⟩ ⟨sweet white⟩ virgin." In other poems from this period, Plath is equally drawn to a conception of the reconstructed heroine as emphatically carnal ("Stings" and "Ariel") or imperviously virginal ("Fever 103°").

In whatever guise the reborn self appears, her performance always commands the attention of a male observer. In imagining the punishing scenario of the conclusion, Plath refigures the scene of "Burning the Letters." In the August poem, the speaker's ritual fire fails to purge the past because Hughes's words rise out of the flames to assault her anew. The language of the first draft of "Lazarus" is remarkably similar, but now it is the male figure who lady Lazarus (4)

It's easy enough to do it in a cell.
~~It's~~ It's easy enough to do it & stay put.
It's the theatrical
~~comeback~~, in ~~the~~ broad ~~sunlight~~ day
to the same place, the same face, the same brute
Amused shout:

'A miracle!'
That really knocks me out.
There is a ✓ charge
For ~~fingering~~ my scars; there is a charge
For ~~the listening~~ to my heart —
~~It~~ It really goes!

And there is a charge, a very large charge
For a ~~~~ word a a touch
Or a bit of blood

Or a piece of my hair or my clothes!
So, ~~Herr Doktor~~ ~~So~~ ~~I am~~ ~~enemy~~
I ~~burn & turn~~.
So, Herr enemy.
You age, & I am new.
I am the baby, on your anvil, I eat fire.
~~~~
I ~~~~
You say I am dangerous.
I ~~burn & turn & have no need of you~~.

"Lady Lazarus," draft 1, page 4, composed October 23–29 and revised after
October 30, 1962, perhaps as late as January 1963

fails to incinerate the protean female force and who must witness her fiery ascension:

> Out of that ash
> You poked
> till it lay in a hush
> Without cough or stir
> I rise with my red hair ⟨terrible, feathery hair⟩.

Here the adjective "terrible" echoes the speaker's rhetorical question, "Do I terrify?" in stanza three. For Plath, "terrible" was the secret sign of Vesuvius. It signaled both rebellion, her Medusa-wish to terrify, and constraint, the recognition such a desire was monstrous. Her speakers have hinted at the capacity before. In "Birthday Present," the speaker warns that her withheld gift has latent, explosive potential: "You are terrified / The world will go up in a shriek, and your head with it." If in "Lazarus" it is the "pure gold baby / That melts to a shriek," an alchemy has turned the cry of suffering to the voice of anger. In both poems the shriek is the sound of an old order that perishes in the frisson that passes between performer and voyeur. Even more memorably in "Stings" it is the inscription of poetic authority as the queen rises, "More terrible than she ever was, red / Scar in the sky, red comet."

In her last revisions, Plath grants Lady Lazarus an appetite equal to the predation she fears. Her devouring orality steadily becomes more threatening to her male opponents, from the baby's initial boast, "I eat fire," to the first version of the phoenix, "I rise, ⟨I eat the air⟩," to the final oracular warning:

> Beware
> Beware
>
> Out of the ash
> I rise with my red hair
> And I eat men like air.

Unlike the starving, deprived speakers of the earlier October poems, Lazarus now fattens on men. In her retaliatory logic, Lazarus reacts against each of the relationships from which she might have grown through love, care, and nurturance and turns instead to anger to enlarge herself. Writing about Dickinson, Barbara Mossberg identifies the link between eating and hating that Lazarus enacts: "Anger is put forth as a form of hunger for some primal satisfaction which food symbolizes: the less she is fed, the larger her anger grows."[73] Lady Lazarus invokes as her last witnesses "Herr God" and "Herr Lucifer"; she magnifies her adversaries to make her victory more significant, yet in her final gesture she trivializes them to make it more secure.

In "Lazarus," for the victim to become fiery avenger, she must demonstrate her ability not only to suffer but also to "manage it." From the psychic deaths caused by her father's death, her attempted suicide, and her husband's departure, Plath creates a performance of the poetics of rage. The subjectivity structured and articulated through these relationships must die in words so convincingly that "it feels real" and yet must survive in the awareness that this performance, though constitutive of identity, is not coextensive with it. Through parody Plath is able to create a distance between her creative agency and the roles of daughter, lover, and suicide. The risks of poetic rage are high, as Joanne Feit Diehl observes in Dickinson's similar struggle: "The war with the Father is more than a war with the world because it is an internal struggle between an introjected patriarchal force and that aspect of consciousness Dickinson experiences as self. This is why the terms of her language are so extreme, why the violence of murder meshes with the desire for suicide."[74] It is true that both the male and the female roles of Plath's poems are her own psychic constructs, yet I do not believe, as Ostriker claims, that gender polarity has unalterable meanings, that whether a woman poet plays God or victim she cannot rewrite the sadomasochistic script.[75] We have mistaken the arena of combat in imagining that what a poem would change is either the social and material conditions of gender relations or the intrapsychic structures of the poet's mind. What Plath has won is a verbal contest of representation. Only in "Lady Lazarus," among the poems of rage polarized by the dialectic between power and deprivation, phallic mastery and erotic dependence, and speech and silence, does the speaker claim her performance is self-conscious. In this lies her claim to power.

The Body

O bright beast I

Ariel

Stasis in darkness,
Then the substanceless blue
Pour of tor & distances.

God's lioness!
How one we grow!
Pivot of heels & knees! the furrow

Splits & passes.
Sister to the brown arc
Of the neck I cannot catch,

Nigger-eye
Berries cast dark
Hooks, ~~but do not scribe black~~

~~black~~ sweet blood mouthfuls!
Shadows!
Something else

Hauls me through air—
Thighs, hair;
Flakes from my heels.   white
                                                     Godiva
                                                     dead

And now I
Foaming to wheat, a glitter of seas.
The child's cry

Melts in the wall.
O bright beast, I
Am the arrow, the dew that flies

Suicidal, at one with the drive
Into the red
Eye, the cauldron of morning.

Reading the Body: The Awful Stink of Women

The little white house on the corner with a family full of women. So many women, the house stank of them. The grandfather lived and worked at the country club, but the grandmother stayed home and cooked like a grandmother should. The father dead and rotten in the grave he barely paid for, and the mother working for bread like no woman should have to and being a good mother on top of it. . . . A stink of women: Lysol, cologne, rose water and glycerine, cocoa butter on the nipples so they won't crack, lipstick red on all three mouths. (J 267, December 12, 1958)

What is sickening in this journal entry is Plath's inclusion of herself in the revolting stink of women. In her angry recitation of her family's efforts to enact a middle-class suburban script, she demonstrates not only her disaffection from the litany of "shoulds" governing women's behavior but also her revulsion against the lessons of femininity inscribed on the female body itself. She takes her place in this lineup of three generations of female bodies, carefully prepared and ironically preserved for the absent male. What is shocking in this portrait is the sexual disgust that informs it; the antipathy of Plath's presentation of woman's body as sexualized spectacle suggests a knowing distance from the scene, but her own participation in this ritual is part of what she sees. The Ariel poems considered in this chapter give evidence of Plath's attempts to exorcise or reimagine the burden of the sexual body and the ways she had been taught to read it.

Plath claimed that in the therapy she undertook in 1958 she gained a "sanction to hate one's mother" that freed her from the "smarmy matriarchy of togetherness" that was the approved reading of this houseful of women. In finding words for the pain and rage she felt, Plath also articulated the embattled terrain of the female body shared by mother and daughter yet always surveyed and judged by an implied male gaze. In two dreams she reports from this period, Plath reads her sexual body as a carnal fact that is dangerous to display but impossible to hide; it is a source of violence and betrayal in the family romance she constructs. In sardonically retelling a dream of Aurelia's about her in her own journal, Plath exposes her mother's interpretation of her sexuality as shameful, excessive, and deadly: "Her daughter was all gaudy-dressed about to go out and be a chorus-girl, a prostitute too, probably. . . . The poor Mother runs along the sand beach, her feet sinking in the sand of life, her money bag open and the money and coins falling into the sand, turning into sand. The father had driven, in a fury, to spite her, off the road bridge and was floating dead, face down and bloated, in the slosh of ocean water" (J 268). The daughter's unspoiled sexuality appears in the dream as her mother's only coin, a hoarded resource now prodigally wasted by the ungrateful daughter who is both her fortune and her ruin. The daughter is also guilty of robbing the mother of her own sexual happiness. The mother can forestall neither her daughter's fall nor the father's fury but helplessly flees one and vainly tries to prevent the other. Perhaps the dream also confesses, in its final image of the bloated male figure in a "slosh of ocean water," Aurelia's own punishing dread of the father's potentially incestuous desire.

In a dream of her own during the early months of her first pregnancy, Plath imagines that she learns the body's shame in a family ritual that resembles a religious ceremony. First Plath drinks milk from a golden chalice, then her mother appears "furious at my pregnancy, mockingly bringing out a huge wraparound skirt to illustrate my grossness . . . Shaving my legs under the table: father, Jewish, at the head: you will please not bring your scimitar to the table" (J 319). Although the chalice of milk promises a consecration of motherhood, the mother's scorn betrays the daughter whose body now imitates her maternal model. The mother colludes with the patriarchal judgment of the female body as unsightly, in either the natural fact of procreation or the feminine arts of beautification. In this dream, unlike Aurelia's, Plath is censured not for her deviance but for conformity. She situates her pregnancy within the sacralized communal myth of female fulfillment, yet her efforts to present her body in a form pleasing to either the mother's or the father's gaze fail; the body is inherently obscene, its practices barbaric. In these dreams Plath records the profound ambivalence toward female sexuality that underlay the 1950s valorization of the virginal wife and the prolific mother. She also locates her mother at the root of her own bodily uneasiness;

Aurelia is the victim ruined by the daughter's sexuality and at the same time the treacherous ally of the patriarch who contributes to her humiliation.

Reading Female Desire: The Monstrous Modern Woman

If Plath inevitably internalized her decade's distrust of the body, other journal entries and her later poems demonstrate her struggle to negotiate these cultural interpretations. This transformation was problematic for Plath because to reject her mother's advice and example about the meaning of her body implied, in the terms current in the 1950s, she wanted to become a man rather than a woman. After the social dislocation and disruption of traditional gender roles during World War II, American postwar psychologists and sociologists increasingly reified a functional Freudianism that based gender distinctions on a sexual dimorphism so extreme that men and women might have been separate species. Ferdinand Lundberg and Marynia Farnham's Modern Woman: The Lost Sex, published in 1947 and recirculated as the popular wisdom of magazines, sex handbooks, and films throughout the 1950s, presented the sexually normal woman as naturally passive in disposition and exclusively procreative in ambition. The unmarried career woman was not merely pitiably unfulfilled but dangerous, a menacing man-imitator who must be barred from contact with children, especially as teachers. The vehemence of Lundberg and Farnham's denunciation of feminism as warped "masculinism" marks it as an extreme, and probably minority, conservative viewpoint. Yet its totalizing premise, which held that gender relations were troubled and that women were sexually unfulfilled because they had "lost" their feminine ability to please and be pleased by men, reflected the genuine cultural malaise and proposed a single coherent explanation that faulted individual women rather than family structure or economic opportunities.[1] The emphasis on a woman's natural satisfaction in homemaking and mothering did not exclude her as a sexual body but merely stringently limited the expression of that sexuality. Marriage manuals directed at men and child-care manuals aimed at women promoted a consistent image of feminine sexuality; men should work hard to please their wives, and women should labor to remain sexually attractive in order to save the children from the damage of a domineering mother. Good sex, defined as heterosexual, vaginal, and often assisted by hyperfeminine costuming, was not an end in itself but an antidote to bad mothering.² Equally important cultural landmarks, the two Kinsey reports on the sexual behavior of largely middle-class men and women in 1948 and 1953 only confirmed the worst fears of The Lost Sex; modern women's interest, appetite, and experience of sex suggested a competition between men and women for orgasmic outlets both inside and outside of marriage. Kinsey's statistics exposed a vast hidden world, an extensive subterranean knowledge of the body's pleasures that contradicted the publicly espoused norms.³

For Plath the dichotomous rubric that distinguished good girls from bad, her mother from herself, and women from men was the contrast between virginity and promiscuity. Her worries about promiscuity reveal an embittered sexual competitiveness alongside a conviction that she is naturally monogamous: "Promiscuity: my ingenious, evasive self-deceiving explanation: I had to give out affection in small doses so it would be accepted, not all to one person, who couldn't take it. . . . So I was trying to be like a man: able to take or leave sex, with this one and that. I got even. But wasn't really meant for it. What about exhibitionism? The whore, a male-type woman?" (J 291). If she appears to blame herself for betraying her gender identity, she also associates her transgressions with self-defense, a desire to get even for masculine autonomy or indifference. In a journal entry in which she brainstorms the plot of what would become The Bell Jar, she recognizes her theme will be to expose the cultural hoax of virginity: "Virgin girl brought up in idealism expects virginity from boy her family raves about as pure." Duped by male hypocrisy, her heroine would demand not an apology but parity: "Kiss the earth and beg pardon. No, that wouldn't be enough. The modern woman: demands as much experience as the modern man" (J 284). Although she warns herself in the Cambridge journals to "be chaste" and not to make "indiscriminate love," her more frequent complaint is of insatiable and violent sexual desire: "Oh hungry hungry. I am so hungry for a big smashing creative burgeoning burdened love. . . . I am dressed in black, white and red: violent, fierce colors" (J 131).[4] I am not arguing that Plath's resistance to the sexual mores of the decade was particularly profound or entirely consistent. The pattern of her journals suggests to me that Plath felt she inhabited two bodies: one she believed she had inherited from her mother and read as a source of disgust and embarrassment; the other she interpreted as male in its ambition, sexual appetite, fierce pride, and potential violence.

Hollywood Projections: "With love, from Betty Grable"

Maternal prohibition and adolescent rebellion were not the only ways, of course, Plath learned to read her body. Despite the disclaimers of Esther Greenwood in The Bell Jar, Plath's journals and letters indicate a lifelong intense interest in fashion. Lois Banner characterizes the 1950s taste for steadily enlarging breasts, shrinking waists, and hobbling skirts as a combination of Victorian repression and sexual exploitation.[5] When Plath was a guest editor for Mademoiselle in 1953, a photo spread was shot at Smith College, featuring Smith and Amherst couples. The photos feature "the blond boom" (a style Plath imitated in her "platinum summer" of 1954 after her breakdown and during her senior year) and another six-page layout titled "When There's a Man Wear Red." As in the summer after her suicide attempt, Plath's interest in bodily perfection often masked her emotional or intellectual insecurity. In the spring of her first year at Cambridge, worried about end-of-the-year exams, Plath was accepted onto the mostly male staff of the weekly, Varsity. An early assignment, and the first she sent home to Aurelia, shows her modeling cocktail dresses and ball gowns. On the clipping of a full-length shot of her in a swimsuit, she's added, "with love, from Betty Grable" (LH 235–37). Whether ironic or not, Plath's inscription suggests that she and her mother were expected to be allies in producing and enjoying her success as sexual spectacle.

In Hollywood cinema of the decade, the female body was pushed in extreme directions, toward voluptuous but vulnerable sensuality and toward an impish asexuality. Underlying both inscriptions is an association of the female body with the child. Feminist film theorists have shown that, even in movies directed primarily at women, what the female viewer reads is not herself but projections of male fantasies. In the antitypes of Debbie Reynolds and Marilyn Monroe, the exaggeration of physical differences becomes synonymous with moral values; body becomes character, and each body has its unvarying script. In the Debbie Reynolds plot, the sunny, ingenuous, freckled heroine is corny but cute, comically inept but always a good sport; she is thoroughly competent, however, in her main project, which is to become a wife, often by tricking her unsuspecting mate into marriage for his own good. Marilyn Monroe, and her dark twin, Liz Taylor, offer erotic gratification without commitment. Sultry, languorous, sexually experienced, and usually undereducated, they can be maternally understanding and yet are rarely rewarded with wifely success. Film critic Molly Haskell suggests that the polarized excess of each category promotes an awareness of its falseness. The woman viewer is likely to see in Monroe a cartoon of sexuality, the unsettling performance of a woman "in drag." Likewise the guileless sweetness of Reynolds masks a "professional virgin" whose calculating innocence is deployed for material gain.[6]

Plath saw herself in both figures. As a young wife she viewed all women as her rivals, and in observing Reynolds's defeat she mirrors her own insecurities: "Liz Taylor is getting Eddie Fisher away from Debbie Reynolds, who appears cherubic, round-faced, wronged, in pin curls and house robe. . . . How odd these events affect one so" (J 259). In Monroe's marriage, Plath reads her own more ambitious script: "Marilyn Monroe appeared to me last night in a dream as a kind of fairy godmother. . . . I spoke, almost in tears, of how much she and Arthur Miller meant to us." Whether Miller and Monroe meant the same thing (or the same thing to Plath and Hughes) is unclear, yet their union seems satisfying proof that the sexual body can be linked to the intellectual artist, at least by marriage. To Plath, Reynolds is the monitory image, the cautionary tale of sexually inept virgins who are unable to hold onto husbands. Monroe is not punished but rewarded for her extravagant sexual appeal and, in Plath's dream, will gratify Plath's similar aspirations by sharing her beauty secrets: "She gave me an expert manicure. . . . She invited me to visit her during the Christmas holidays, promising a new, flowering life" (J 319).

In thinking about her body Plath displays an unremitting self-consciousness; her self-perception always includes an awareness of herself as spectacle, and her self-representation contains an element of performance. If her mother tried to teach her that her body was her greatest resource and her most dangerous liability, Plath learned for herself that performance of its sanctioned roles did not guarantee success. Although she inevitably read her body's meanings through the cultural grids available to her, in her journals she frequently noted their slippage, that the match between cultural interpretations and her bodily experience was imperfect. Whether she found her body punishable, as in her dreams, or praised, as in her Betty Grable posturings or her adoptive identification with Marilyn Monroe, Plath seemed inclined to identify herself with bodily excess. The body and its gendered meanings became increasingly problematic for Plath in the Ariel poems as bodily autonomy came to stand for poetic authority. In "Medusa" and a group of related poems Plath tries to recover her body from symbiosis with her mother; in the bee sequence, "Fever 103°," and "Ariel" she reclaims it from the erotic thralldom and sexual humiliation of her relationship with Hughes. Rather than renouncing the flesh, however, as some critics contend, Plath chooses to exploit the sexualized body for its disruptive powers.

The Carnal Subject: Theorizing the Body

Dualism. Imaginative women thinking about the body inevitably confront it: the habit of binary thinking that, in linking man to thought and woman to body, would suggest the project itself, women theorizing the body, is a contradiction in terms.

Although the body seems a stubbornly insistent fact, feminist theorists soon discovered that we have almost no direct access to it. Between a woman and the body she would think about lies a potential minefield of polarized stereotypes. Her physicality is represented as feeding, breeding, bleeding, and decaying; her sexuality is animalistic and excessive, engulfing, castrating, and contaminating. Or woman is represented as disembodied, desexed, and, in her Victorian incarnation which continues to circulate in the twentieth century, angelic and altruistic. Feminists have amply demonstrated how these stereotypes function to mask male vulnerability and to maintain masculine privilege. These images serve as powerful instruments to organize gender relations and to embody cultural hierarchies, underscoring the superiority of mind to matter, masculine to feminine. Because women and their bodies enter the social world through this network of received interpretations in which they read the meaning of their bodily experience, feminist literary critics have asked whether the cultural mapping of the female body as polluted and demonic has deformed or constrained the female imagination. Will these images inevitably structure a woman writer's self-representation? Can a woman express her body as subject in ways that contradict or correct the images meant to confine and objectify her?

In following a few feminist critics in search of the body, I am most interested in focusing on these twin issues: the apprehension of the female body and its gendered meanings by women, and the qualities inherent in these stereotypes that might make them, in the hands of women writers, susceptible to revision. Throughout this discussion certain images reappear like magnetic poles, attracting cultural meanings and theoretical interest: the primal mother and the virgin, the fresh young girl and the aging hag, the sexual monster and the angelic corpse. These figures circulate not only in the culture at large but also in various mutations throughout the Ariel poems.

In 1949 Simone de Beauvoir in *The Second Sex* identified the paradox of the female subject that feminist critics have continued to debate for three decades: "One is not born, but rather becomes, a woman."[7] In demonstrating that gender and the gendered body's meanings are not natural but socially constructed through the myriad practices of everyday life, Beauvoir laid bare the female body as an object mapped by male desire and dread: "For him she is sex—absolute sex, no less. She is defined and differentiated with reference to man and not he with reference to her. . . . He is the Subject, he is the Absolute—she is the Other." But even as we see our Otherness, our confinement to the realm of sexual body, reflected in the gaze of men and incorporated in our sense of self, women, Beauvoir proposes, must also know themselves as subjects capable of resisting or contesting this construction through individual acts of will: "The drama of woman lies in this conflict between the fundamental aspirations of every subject (ego)— who always regards the self as the essential—and the compulsions of a situation in which she is the inessential."[8] We have since discovered that Beauvoir's survey of female history is flawed and that she is blinded by bourgeois individualism when she persistently blames women for colluding in their oppression.[9] But she does make available for later feminist critics the terms of our struggle. She makes clear that the battle over the female body pits male representation—historical, nonnatural, and yet seemingly inescapable—against the female need for revision—urgent, but apparently impossible.

What do we need to revise? For Beauvoir, women needed to recognize that not only their bodies but their imaginations had been colonized; the oppression of women is justified by and expressed through the degradation of the body by women and men alike. Further, the root of our cultural somatophobia can be traced to the awful power of the primal mother: "What man cherishes and detests first of all in woman—loved one or mother—is the fixed image of his animal destiny. . . . From the day of his birth man begins to die: this is the truth incarnated in the Mother."[10] The dreadful mystery of the maternal body is that it threatens death with the same gesture that it promises life. Onto woman's body man projects the "horror of his carnal contingence" and feels for her corruptible flesh the disgust he seeks to flee in himself.[11] If the primal mother threatens to engulf man's hope for immortality, man seeks to reconfirm his identity as informing spirit of female matter, Beauvoir argues, in his possession of the virginal body: "Grotto, temple, sanctuary, secret garden—man, like the child, is fascinated by enclosed and shadowy places not yet animated by any consciousness, which wait to be given a soul: what he alone is to take and to penetrate seems to be in truth created by him."[12] The woman's body serves man's imagination as a blank slate, a dark, material absence of meaning on which to inscribe his presence. What remains unknown by man is inchoate, inexpressible; men feel a "sexual repugnance in the presence of maidenhood too prolonged. . . . The curse is in their flesh itself, that flesh which is object to no subject. . . . It becomes an oddity, as disturbing as the incommunicable thought of a madman."[13]

The Body | 75

How can women, who apprehend their bodies through these imprisoning images, resist the reductive cultural equation of woman and engulfing, mortal, morbid body? Beauvoir suggests that, despite the power of patriarchal representation to construct and control the meanings of "woman," women escape or exceed the symbols meant to contain them: "[Men] did invent her. But she exists also apart from their inventiveness. And hence she is not only the incarnation of their dream, but also its frustration. There is no figurative image of woman which does not call up at once its opposite."[14] While Beauvoir recognizes the instability of the categories, she offers little hope that female excess or deviance can outpace the hegemonic desire to police and punish it by inventing new and equally oppressing images.

Still, Judith Butler argues that Beauvoir provides, albeit in embryonic form, a conceptualization of the body that makes revision of these stereotypes possible. Beauvoir proposes, according to Butler, that "we understand the body as a cultural situation"; thinking about one's body as situation enables a woman to imagine the intersection of body and gender as a dynamic position, according to Butler, a site of interpretation in which she plays some role. Women are not passive, entirely constructed objects but resourceful interpreters of cultural possibilities: "Becoming a gender is an impulsive yet mindful process of interpreting a cultural reality laden with sanctions, taboos and prescriptions." For Butler, the very recognition that gender is culturally constructed through everyday practices opens the possibility for reconstruction, for a "modality of inventiveness" in the ways we appropriate what we are given, for "the possibility of autonomy within corporeal life" as one "becomes" a woman.[15] Beauvoir unequivocally demonstrates that women are never in simple possession of their bodies but have, consciously or not, internalized culturally specific interpretations of female flesh and sexuality. Since then, feminists who theorize the body have sought to explore, as Butler does, the possibility of female resistance, the ways in which the carnal female subject may express an I that is not merely Other.

Adrienne Rich's project in *Of Woman Born* is to revise the meanings of childbirth and motherhood by trying to articulate the gap between her experience as bodily subject and the culturally sanc-

tioned representations of mothering. For Rich the lie that is per-
petuated in the institution of motherhood depends on the same
mind/body dualism Beauvoir observes. Rather than accept dualism as a phenomenon as "primordial as consciousness," Rich attempts to repair the split. Like Beauvoir, she grants the cultural construction of her self-perception: "As my father's daughter, I suffered
the obscure bodily self-hatred peculiar to women who see themselves through the eyes of men." Yet her formulation suggests that
the position of being a "father's daughter" may be forestalled or at
least retroactively reimagined. For Rich the solution to somatophobia is not to emulate our father's transcendence, as Beauvoir
would advise, but to revise our damaged relation as daughters to
our mother's body. In terms that are remarkably similar to Beauvoir's central insight, Rich defines matriphobia as "the fear not of
one's mother or of motherhood but of *becoming one's mother.*" What
we dread in our mother's example is the very process of becoming
a gender that Beauvoir identifies, the transformation from the subject we imagine ourselves to be into the devalued, objectified other
our mothers have become. Daughters see in their mothers, according to Rich, not only the source of their bodily inadequacy and
sexual defilement but a social betrayal of their own possibilities: "A
mother's victimization does not merely humiliate her, it mutilates
the daughter who watches her for clues as to what it means to be a
woman."[16]

To break from the mother can be a rejection of her victimization. Other feminist literary critics have recognized that for the
woman writer such a rupture has sometimes seemed an imaginative necessity, that to be a poet or novelist requires not being the
woman her mother has become. Barbara Mossberg describes the
"daughter construct" of Emily Dickinson as a psychological and
literary rebellion against the conventions embodied in the
"mother matrix"; the daughter perceives in the mother matrix the
mother's wish to enforce her own degradation on her and to deny
the daughter who would be exceptional.[17] The humiliation and
feared mutilation of being entrapped in such a network of maternal and cultural expectations produce Plath's violent repudiation
of feminine conventions in her poems about her mother, particularly "In Plaster" and "Medusa." Marianne Hirsch also claims

that in the nineteenth century the writing daughter's quest for a "singular" heroine produces plots in which the heroine disidentifies with the fate of other women, particularly mothers.[18] Plath's contradictory identifications with both the exceptional queen bee and the drudging female laborers in the hive in the narratives of the bee poems mark a similar search for status and an altered destiny. Rich's understanding of the operation of matriphobia not only explains the strategies of particular women writers, including Plath, but also the focus of many feminist critics in the 1970s. Because a refusal of the mother's example seems a potentially feminist revision of the meanings of female gender, feminist critics often praised monstrous self-assertion and imaginative autonomy in women writers.

Rich's own position in *Of Woman Born*, however, is not to endorse matriphobia as a necessary stage in female individuation. Instead she advocates a loving reconnection with the mother's body. Only by rejoining imagination to flesh could the carnal subject find full expression: "We must touch the unity and resonance of our physicality, our bond with the natural order, the corporeal ground of our intelligence." Rich goes beyond Beauvoir's understanding of the body as a culturally marked situation susceptible to revisionary rereadings and nonhegemonic enactments. She proposes that repossessing the body may transform consciousness itself: "I am really asking whether women cannot begin, at last, *to think through the body*, to connect what has been so cruelly disorganized— . . . its fertility, its desire, its so-called frigidity, its bloody speech, its silences, its changes and mutilations, its rapes and ripenings."[19] In her effort to refigure the form of the singular female poet, Plath also redeems the shameful, sexual female body as the ground of her creative intelligence. The revalorizing of the female body as a source of gender-specific wisdom recommended by Rich became an important project for other feminist critics in the 1980s. Interest in redeeming the mother's body, not surprisingly, has increased as feminist critics who began their careers as rebellious or seduced daughters become biological mothers themselves. For feminist critics, theorizing the body has always involved, in a particularly self-conscious way, both the critique and the extension of available discourses and a self-interested reflection on the critic's own bodily identity.[20]

The example of these critics reveals that the body's meanings are products of particular historical moments and that theories informed by new historical understanding may enable us to read a body in ways the subject inhabiting it could not read or represent herself. Rather than rehearse the complex history of feminist theorizing about the body born of Beauvoir and Rich, I focus on those literary critics who analyze the nineteenth-century legacy that structured the consciousness of Plath's literary forebears, as well as on feminist critics who write out of a historical moment, and perhaps a consciousness, near her own. In different ways, each critic identifies within flesh-loathing images a source of dark potency. Each also brings to the surface the strains that threaten to disrupt the apparent rigidity of the polarized images that separate a woman from her body.

Mary Ellmann in *Thinking about Women* itemizes, with considerable wit and an unapologetic lack of system, patterns she finds among male misrepresentations of women. Her literary sample includes the male modernists Plath revered along with novelists and reviewers who were contemporaries of Plath. She, like Beauvoir and every feminist since, notices that women exist in the male imagination only as extremes: a "consistent quality of feminine stereotypes is the repeated effort to move women in two directions away from a premised, though indefinable, human center." Yet the dichotomizing of women's nature is guaranteed to backfire: "Each stereotype has a limit; swelled to it, the stereotype explodes."[21] Nina Auerbach reveals a similar explosive tendency in the diametrically opposed conceptions of women in the Victorian imagination. In *Woman and the Demon* Auerbach argues that the absent center identified by Ellmann is a woman's true cultural location; she exists not at either pole but at the "junction between the social and the spiritual, the humanly perishable and the transcendently potent."[22] Auerbach claims Victorians were fascinated, as the twentieth century would continue to be and Plath certainly was, by the conjunction of women and corpses. In examining the paradigm of the female life-in-death figures who are subject to "fits of vampirism, somnambulism, mesmerism, or hysterical paralysis," who appear prone victims in the power of devouring male masters, Auerbach uncovers a barely suppressed and "boundless capacity for mutability."[23] These swooning maidens are drugged, hypnotized, and eroticized in their passivity, she claims, in figurative gestures of cultural self-defense, lest they awake to their devastating powers. Likewise the comic or pathetic figure of the old maid domesticates, in the form of a household dependent, the earlier incarnation of the single woman as witch. Although the old maid figured the embarrassment of the "redundant" woman in Victorian society, she also appeared in novels as the harbinger of a new race of women for whom marriage and men were inessential and who defined themselves by public careers. Disparaged, dismissed, and pitied as unfulfilled in their feminine nature, "the impassioned and protracted virginity" of these manly women endows them as well, in Auerbach's reading, with "heroic immortality."[24] What men feared and unconsciously confessed in the visual and verbal representations of high art and the stereotypes of popular culture is the protean nature of the female body: its instability, especially its rapid deterioration from purity to corruption, but also its seductive and disruptive powers.

Ellen Moers reminds us how much mothers seem to be the fathers' allies in coercing daughters to hate the female body. In *Literary Women* Moers suggests the twentieth-century version of the "female Gothic" gives "*visual* form to the fear of self." We learn to regard ourselves as spectacle first in the mirror of our mother's glance and read there our cultural degradation. The woman writer's anxious fantasy dramatizes the alienation of a female subject becoming her gender and finding the transformation freakish. The female psyche creates "haunting monsters of ambivalence" who shadow her own sense of dreadful deformity. In her list of "freaks" who populate the "horrid sideshow" of the Gothic scenario, Moers identifies "masqueraders" and "aberrant creatures with hideous deformities or double sex: hermaphrodites."[25] Although Moers does not comment on it, these terms may hint, in their ambiguous gender and masks, at the woman writer's resistance to gender conformity as much as to her internalization of herself as monstrous. In a psychoanalytic rereading of Moers,

Claire Kahane further interiorizes the Gothic horror: "The heroine is imprisoned not in a house but in the female body, which is itself the maternal legacy. The problematics of femininity is thus reduced to the problematics of the female body." Yet where Moers finds only the poison of incorporated self-hatred, Kahane sees in the mixed-gender grotesques of the daughter's fantasies a transgressive wish to join the power of the phallus to the vulnerability of feminine identity.[26]

If the post-Freudian feminist reader can expose what the male unconscious tries to repress, other feminist critics remind us that these images do, nonetheless, have a coercive force over the female writer's imagination. The monstrous woman in male texts serves as a powerful monitory mirror to curb female ambition. Gilbert and Gubar persuasively link the images of women's "filthy materiality" not just to male sexual nausea and ambivalence about carnality but to a contempt for women's intellectual and literary aspirations. By reducing woman to her disgusting bodily functions, they suggest, these loathsome monsters warn women against presuming any higher function, especially forms of creativity reserved to men.[27] But the burden of Gilbert and Gubar's argument is that women will write, and the carnal subject will have its say and will shape its own narrative by testing the explosive potential of these imprisoning images. The enduring problem for the woman writer, however, is that at either pole of the angel/monster dichotomy lies the death of the body. To imagine herself as either the virginal corpse preserved in the "glass coffins of patriarchy" or the self-assertive queen destroyed by her passionate but "suicidal tarantella" means sacrificing the body. Confronted with these options, Plath registers the same ambivalence Gilbert and Gubar identify in nineteenth-century writers. No matter how often the female body is confined to death-in-life traps, however, Plath also suggests that the sexualized body has an uncanny capacity for horrifying resurrections.

For Patricia Yaeger the female body is the site of pleasure rather than horror, while the transgressions she identifies among women writers are linguistic rather than sexual. *Honey-Mad Women* explores the metaphor of female appetite, a consuming orality that excessively feeds on language. In a shift characteristic of post-structuralist critics, Yaeger relocates the female body in a set of discursive practices that she identifies as "emancipatory." The metaphor of the title defines female writers as pleasurably demented "women who consume to an excess the language designed to consume them." Although she argues that reckless, hyperbolic wordplay can preempt and usurp the culture's power to contain or control the female imagination, she cannot obliterate, it seems to me, the regressive dimension of orality that reduces woman to body and to nature.[28] Yaeger's reading of the body as a rhetorical instrument responds to an understanding of subjectivity as discursively constituted, yet feminist post-structuralist critics often still betray, as she does, a sense that the female body remains unspoken. We can witness the textual signs of its disruptive presence, but the carnal subject itself can be only indirectly expressed in terms of what it is not.

All these critics posit, nonetheless, that the opposite poles of the cultural interpretations inscribed on the female body which appear rigidly fixed are destabilized by a fluid exchange between them; that any stereotype displays an explosive, disruptive power when it is exploited to its extreme; and that a woman writer may exist at the mutable junction between these opposites, scarred by ambivalence yet teeming with only temporarily suppressed powers of transformation.

Of course what a woman writer inherits as her literary and cultural legacy are not merely discrete images but entire scripts. In questioning the roles assigned to monstrously embodied women in patriarchal narratives, women writers engage in what feminist critics have called revisionary myth making or writing beyond the ending. Alicia Ostriker, Teresa de Lauretis, and Rachel DuPlessis would include in the category of myth a broad range of received stories from scripture, history, folktales, and popular and canonized literature. In echoing these sources in her own poetry, Plath, like other modernist and contemporary poets, also ironically critiques their earlier meanings. Revising mythic material is particularly appealing to women writers, according to Ostriker, because its existence in the public domain confers an authority, a participation in cultural dialogue that the confessional mode lacks. Yet myth continues to permit self-exploration because it is "intimate material, the stuff of dream life, forbidden desire, inexplicable motivation—everything in the psyche that to rational consciousness is unreal, crazed, or abominable."[29]

Teresa de Lauretis proposes that enigmatic figures like Medusa or the Sphinx represent unanswered, because unasked, questions about gender. They possess no story of their own but function as "markers of positions—places and topoi—through which the hero and his story move to their destination and accomplish meaning."[30] These monsters are liminal figures who, in their animal-woman incarnations, metaphorize boundaries; they stand as tests or limits, luring the male gaze, yet these horrifying spectacles cannot be fully seen and survived. But what do we know of their own ends, motivations, and desires, de Lauretis asks, not as spectacle but as subjects? Women artists can remake the story, she claims, can open up "a space of contradiction in which to demonstrate the non-coincidence of woman and women" through several revisionary strategies: "The only way to position oneself outside of that discourse is to displace oneself within it—to refuse the question as formulated, or to answer deviously (though in its words), even to quote (but against the grain)."[31]

Rachel DuPlessis emphasizes that the ideological power of myths depends on their apparent forgetfulness of history and politics. In imaginatively appropriating these narratives, the woman writer stands "at the impact point of a strong system of interpretation masked as representation." Yet the politics of narrative authority can be contested through a "committed identification with Otherness," by adopting the muted object as subject in a gesture like de Lauretis's "displacement." The woman writer can also destabilize and potentially transform meanings through "delegitimation," which creates a critical and unexpected story, questioning the inevitability of roles or endings.[32] All three critics would agree that these revisions do not erase or replace familiar interpretations but "release meanings that were latent but imprisoned all along in stories we thought we knew."[33] The woman writer remains drawn to the inevitable, the seductive power of the culturally sanctioned story, and yet partial to the inarticulate, the liminal body whose story has not been told.

Transgressions and Transformations: Embodying the Poet

"Ocean 1212-W": A Myth of Origin

In January 1963, at the same time she drew up her plan for the *Ariel* volume and made final revisions in the poems she chose to include, Plath wrote a memoir about her early childhood, "Ocean 1212-W."[34] In it she tells two stories: the first is her traumatic severing from fusion with the maternal body; the second is the originating moment of self-consciousness as a poet, a state she represents as singular, autonomous, marvelously given, and in which her gender is insistently suppressed. In her self-portrait as an infant, she is intrepid, recklessly greedy for experience: "When I was learning to creep, my mother set me down on the beach to see what I thought of it. I crawled straight for the coming wave and was just through the wall of green when she caught at my heels" (21). Throughout the narrative, Plath situates herself as poet at the liminal shore, poised for a transformation into the mermaid she expects to greet her in the foam. Meanwhile the boundary between herself as daughter and the cautious controlling mother of this initial image becomes increasingly distinct and finally uncrossable.

In her story of the birth of the poet, the bartering of symbolic equivalents is knowing and calculated. Plath scripts this moment according to a paradigm Freud and Lacan have taught us to read: her fall into self-consciousness ("this awful birthday of otherness") spells the end of her "beautiful fusion with the things of this world," marks her as an individual ("I felt the wall of my skin. I am I"), yet also indelibly inscribes her loss. The burden of the piece is to illustrate how the loss of the mother's breast prompts her entry into language, whose pleasures give her "a new way of being happy." To compensate for an identity structured by lack, loss, and rejection, Plath substitutes her election as a poet. Even without Aurelia's scrupulous corrections to the facts of these events, Plath's cues throughout the narrative announce that this autobiography is a carefully reconstructed, even mythicized fiction.[35] Aurelia offers her account of Plath's introduction to the alphabet in her own memoir that opens *Letters Home*. To distract Sylvia from her rivalry with Warren when he was being nursed, Aurelia set her the task of picking out letters in a newspaper at her feet (LH 16). In both Plath's mythic account and Aurelia's literal one, the scene of maternal nurture gives access to the medium of language at the same time that the breast is denied, while the rupture of this exclusive dyad, through sibling rivalry, reinforces the daughter's need of the word's compensatory pleasures.[36]

Plath includes in her narrative what is noticeably absent from the psychoanalytic paradigm, the problematic awareness of her gendered body in this symbolic transaction. To become a poet, for Plath, means to resist becoming her gender. In her solitary walk along the beach the poet as daughter mourns her replacement at her mother's breast by her baby brother, a male rival whom the mother, in her "desertion" of the daughter, seems to prefer. In the fate of a "stiff pink starfish" she reads her own: "It lay at the heart of my palm, a joke dummy of my own hand." While she once "nursed" starfish until they grew back "lost arms," she now recoils from its reproduction of the female body as wounded and deficient. She violently repudiates the equivalence she once nurtured, flinging the starfish against a stone: "Let it perish. It had no wit" (23). The starfish is the signature of gender she will not own, a counterfeit of her own identity, a wordless body without wit. In rejecting the starfish she also mimics the maternal body's rejection of its copy in her. To counter the image of the starfish, Plath evokes at several places in the narrative the figure of the mermaid. The mermaid is the deeply desired but always elusive embodiment of female gender with protean possibilities.

Listening to her mother read Arnold's "Forsaken Merman" ignites Plath's poetic sensibility. In Arnold's poem, the spontaneous, magical forces of the artist are associated with the merman, deserted by the faithless mortal woman who was mother to his children. In recalling this moment as her birth into poetry, Plath transposes the gender of Arnold's boundary-crossing figure; it is the undersea world of woman posing as mermaid that stirs her longing. For Plath, mermaids are the mirror image of the self she would become, yet which is frustratingly inaccessible. In her childhood cosmology they are linked to unseen omnipotence: "I often wonder what would have happened if I had managed to pierce that looking-glass. Would my infant gills have taken over, the salt in my blood? For a time I believed not in God nor Santa Claus, but in mermaids" (21). Later when she looks to the sea for a sign of her "election and specialness," the tokens she desires are "a mermaid, a Spanish infanta," emblems of fantasy and power. What the sea yields instead is a wooden monkey.

In the series of metaphoric substitutions in which the daughter is figured in her vulnerability by the starfish and in her desired omnipotence by the mermaid, the monkey appears anomalous. Yet onto the monkey Plath projects everything the starfish is not. Rather than the familiar, witless, perishable dummy of her own body, the monkey is a "simian Thinker," "remote and holy, long-muzzled and oddly foreign." In a maternal gesture of adoptive kinship that seems oddly reminiscent of Emily Dickinson's spider poems, and the antithesis of disowning the starfish, the poet claims her special gift: "Out of a pulp of kelp, still shining, with a wet fresh smell, reached a small brown hand" (24). Unlike Dickinson's spider, however, who as the sign of her creative genius is identified as male, Plath's monkey is conspicuously ungendered. In declaring her allegiance to the "Sacred Baboon," Plath appropriates a body that, in its strangeness and its artificiality, is available for her imaginative reinscription. The monkey serves as charm against or compensation for the newly arrived presence of the male rival in the house; more significantly it also functions as muse and, I would argue, as the unnatural, slightly monstrous figure of the female body shorn of gender and endowed with thought.

If Plath's situation as woman poet required refiguring the female body, it also demanded a mythic genealogy. Throughout the narrative Plath claims her true descent from the sea, which is insistently portrayed as sexual and violent as well as maternal. While the biological mother is unavailable, rejecting, or overcautious, the oceanic mother is seductive, mysterious, and generous. Rather than producing a rival, the sea gives birth to a totemic confirmation of Plath's poetic election. In the biological mother, the daughter is reminded of her infantile dependence. In the sea, Plath imagines her own capacity for vengeance: "Like a deep woman, it hid a good deal; it had many faces, many terrible, delicate veils. . . . If it could court, it could also kill" (21). In this description we recognize the veiled antagonism of "The Birthday Present" and "Purdah," while in the "dozens of tea-sets" the sea has swallowed we see those the speaker of "Tulips" lets sink in her anesthetized forgetfulness. The sea's final gesture is to throw up a dead shark in a storm that disfigures the domestic landscape. Plath ends her narrative as if it were the foreclosed dream of childhood possibility: "Those first nine years of my life sealed themselves off like a ship in a bottle—beautiful, inaccessible, obsolete, a fine, white flying myth" (26). Yet the timing of its composition demonstrates that such a myth was an adult necessity. A mother herself, and a daughter who still feared her mother's disapproval for her failed marriage, Plath knew the liabilities of her sexuality and the fragility of her identity as poet.[37] To counteract these anxieties, she constructs a myth of origins that proves, instead, that her identity as poet was preordained and was continuous from earliest childhood. In this mythic autobiography she self-consciously reads the cultural inscriptions of gender but refuses to be bound by them, claiming instead a bodily singularity that is born of the imagination through language.

Corporal Punishments: The Burden of the Body

A pair of poems from 1961, "Mirror" and "Face Lift,"[38] confront what Beauvoir calls the "carnal contingence" of the human subject. While both men and women find in their bondage to perishable flesh a dreadful premonition of their mortality, women see their aging bodies refracted through masculine aversion as well as their own anxiety. In "Mirror" the body's death sentence appears ominous and inescapable; in "Face Lift" it seems optimistically, if gruesomely, malleable.

Originally titled "Mirror Talk," the first poem was written just before Plath's twenty-ninth birthday, otherwise an auspicious moment that marked the English publication of The Colossus. The tale the mirror tells, however, is of hidden violence. Locating the center of consciousness in the mirror marginalizes the woman;

her presence in the mirror's vision is intermittent, and then only as a reflected object. The source of the mirror's image, the observing woman, does not exist as a subject at all. In the first stanza of this neatly bipartite riddle, the mirror speaks with the implacable voice of justice: "I am silver and exact. I have no preconceptions." Its omniscient gaze is "the eye of a little god." Its discretion is assured: "Whatever I see I swallow immediately." Yet the woman's desperate need to know herself through this reflection and the mirror's jealous wish to control her self-perception are revealed in the second stanza: "A woman bends over me, / Searching my reaches for what she really is. / Then she turns to those liars, the candles or the moon." With cold rationality, the mirror insists that it is the only valid source of enlightenment because it can see the woman as she cannot see herself: "I see her back and reflect it faithfully. / She rewards me with tears and an agitation of hands."

As the poem progresses, the mirror's exactness comes to seem a cruel tyranny; the woman's dependence, a helpless compulsion. In revising her draft, Plath removes the single hint in the entire poem that the woman's subjectivity may exist apart from the mirror's knowledge of her. "Her thoughts are deeper than mine" is replaced by the smug assertion, "I am important to her." Bound to the mirror that claims to contain her entirely, the woman cannot retreat from the threat of the final lines: "In me she has drowned a young girl, and in me an old woman / Rises toward her day after day like a terrible fish." The terror of this vision is its reduction of woman to inexorably aging flesh. But in the dichotomizing of that body between the drowned but desirable young girl and the hideous specter of death in the terrible fish we detect the bias of the male gaze, the flaw in the mirror that would represent itself as god.

"Face Lift" was composed on February 15, 1961, midway between Plath's miscarriage and her appendectomy, both occasions of bodily vulnerability. Although the poem incorporates imagery from her appendectomy and memories of her childhood tonsillectomy that appear in her letters, its immediate occasion is Dido Merwin's face lift, which Plath regarded as a pathetic effort to remain sexually attractive to her husband, the act itself a concession of defeat.[39] In the poet's ambivalent treatment of this occasion we can see signs of the dialectic that Butler proposes exists between a woman's acceptance of gender as a matrix of preexisting meanings and her local resistance to or reinterpretation of these cultural possibilities. The speaker voices the homicidal antipathy toward her aging flesh we saw reflected in "Mirror," but she also boasts that the agency for the mysterious transformation of this bodily situation is her own. Her tone oscillates between two moods: a quiescent detachment from the body that will reappear in "Tulips," a passive life-in-death in which her body is relinquished to "Jovian surgeons"; and a parodic self-awareness of the resurrected body as grotesque. Like the later "Lady Lazarus," the speaker of "Face Lift" disassociates herself from her body in order to control it. She suffers the small anesthetized death with tranquility because it promises to erase history: "For five days I lie in secret, / Tapped like a cask, the years draining into my pillow." But the new creature she gives birth to, like Frankenstein's monster, comes from the grave. The emergent self as walking corpse, flinging off her "mummy-cloths," shares Lazarus's exhibitionistic bravado about her disfigurement: "Skin doesn't have roots, it peels away easy as paper. / When I grin, the stitches tauten." In managing her comeback the speaker pretends to reverse the mirror's sentence, but only by doing violence to an objectified, repulsive shadow self: "Now she's done for, the dewlapped lady / I watched settle, line by line, in my mirror— / Old sock-face, sagged on a darning egg." The close of "Face Lift" implies that the repeated death trance of feminine passivity is a temporary mask, as Auerbach argues, for the protean self, secretly incubated: "Mother to myself, I wake swaddled in gauze, / Pink and smooth as a baby." This self-engendering gesture also previews Plath's Ariel poems of reincarnation. What makes the body intolerable in the later poems is its history of sexual suffering or maternal exhaustion. Rather than leave the body behind in a search for spiritual transcendence, Plath insists she can remake it; she can deliver by her own violent agency an unmarked body innocent of, and sometimes immune to, conventional sexual inscription.[40]

To repossess the body in order to rewrite the meanings of gender meant, for Plath, to do battle with the figure of the mother. Two poems written on the same day, March 18, 1961, contest the cultural situation of mother from opposite perspectives. The daughter's strategy in "In Plaster" is a planned insurrection; the mother's ploy in "Tulips" is an attempted evasion. Together they demonstrate that either subject position was vexed.[41] Plath's efforts in both poems to cast off any link between the maternal body and her own may indirectly suggest the guilt and resentment she felt because, in her miscarriage the month before, she felt she had failed Aurelia.[42] "In Plaster" is a neat allegory that exposes the dualistic mechanism of gender formation. The mother, and the conventional definitions of femininity she models, is a plaster cast that both sustains and constrains the "ugly and hairy" daughter within. To break free of that construction means destroying the mother or denying the self; for the speaker there are no compromises, "I see it must be one or the other of us." Rich describes such oppositional self-definition as a symptom of matriphobia: "a womanly splitting of the self, in the desire to become purged once and for all of our mothers' bondage, to become individuated and free. The mother stands for the victim in ourselves, the unfree woman, the martyr."[43] Although Plath's metaphor promises that the daughter's bondage to the mother is temporary and pragmatic, the speaker's defensiveness, her sense of herself as monstrous, proves that gender is not so easily shed.

"In Plaster" also exhibits the signs that Moers and Kahane have associated with the modern female Gothic. The trapped voice, rebellious and persecuted by turns, speaks from within the prison of the maternal body that Kahane suggests represents the "problematics of femininity" and is "perceived as antagonistic to the sense of self, as therefore freakish."[44] The mother is a ghastly twin: "She lay in bed with me like a dead body / And I was scared, because she was shaped just the way I was / Only much whiter and unbreakable and with no complaints."[45] Her tolerant silences, her unflinching self-sacrifice are, to the speaker, a frighteningly unnatural inversion of her own jealous, manipulative self-interest: "You could tell almost at once she had a slave mentality." Kahane argues that in the Gothic narrative the woman writer reproduces the infant's experience of the primal mother. The speaker's reviling of the mother and her anxious dread of abandonment certainly recall infantile fantasies. In the first half of the poem the violence of the speaker's aggression against the mother is afford-able because the daughter assumes her devotion is absolute and interminable: "Without me, she wouldn't exist, so of course she was grateful." In the second half of the poem the speaker's reluc-tant dependence breeds paranoid projections: "Secretly she be-gan to hope I'd die." Although abraded by the relationship, the child that the adult daughter continues to be finds any suspicion of the mother's self-interest intolerable. She imagines a sexual rivalry as if it were a morbid impersonation, the mother desiring to "wear my painted face the way a mummy-case / Wears the face of a pharaoh." Compared with the swaggering irony of the first four stanzas, the tone of the last four is self-pitying, apologetic, covertly plotting: "I wasn't in any position to get rid of her. / . . . / So I was careful not to upset her in any way / Or brag ahead of time how I'd avenge myself." The only remaining draft of this poem is a typescript with very few significant revisions; yet "revenge" in this line is emended to "avenge" as if to underscore the speaker's portrait of unjustified victimization. The poem ends with a fantasy of escape that is threatened but postponed: "one day I shall man-age without her, / And she'll perish with emptiness then, and begin to miss me." In the typescript the speaker is more cautious about her self-sufficiency but more candid about her hatred of her dependence: "I shall ⟨learn to⟩ manage without her, / And she'll perish with emptiness when they cut her throat." The daughter boasts that she will eventually be separate and free of the mother's body, but her imagined revenge reveals the hold she would still have on it, the response she still desperately desires from it. Her vindication would be to punish the mother for daring to do without her.

To perish with emptiness seems a desirable fate for the speaker of "Tulips." The antagonism that structures this poem arrays her "learned peacefulness" against the intrusion of the "too excitable" tulips; the speaker longs to sever her blood connection to the body and its sexual consequences, both of which she has imag-inatively displaced onto the tulips.[46] Demanding as an "awful baby," the tulips' behavior seems to accuse her of failed maternity: "Nobody watched me before, now I am watched. / The tulips turn to me." In their needy and blaming eyes, her separate subjectivity is reduced to the spectacle of an unnurturing mother: "I see myself, flat, ridiculous, a cut-paper shadow." Throughout the poem the speaker attempts to defend herself against the guilty ambivalence the tulips excite by adopting a tranced passivity. Her effort to evacuate the body of maternal significance and to recover a nunlike purity results in a willing imitation of death: "I only wanted / To lie with my hands turned up and be utterly empty. / How free it is." Complete effacement proves impossible, however; in its extremity, the speaker's emptiness becomes untenable and is destabilized by its polar opposite, the "explosions" of the tulips.

In the drafts for the poem the speaker's confrontation with the tulips happens much earlier than in the published version, and the speaker appears a more vulnerable, permeable subject. In the second stanza the eye that is propped open is "helpless"; a "Stupid pupil, it has to take everything in: ⟨the tulips.⟩." The tulips are also more explicitly linked to the speaker's fears of carnal and contaminating flesh:

I have no face, I have wanted to efface myself
⟨The tulips are frightening⟩
The vivid tulips ⟨bleed & are⟩ eat⟨ing up⟩ my oxygen.

In the final poem the speaker's progressive erasure of the body's social inscriptions is, for the most part, pleasurably unimpeded: her name, day-clothes, personal history, family photo, tea sets, linen, books all fall away as so much unnecessary baggage in her journey toward a "peacefulness . . . so big it dazes you." In the first draft, however, Plath oscillates between representing this as an unwilling loss ("They didn't let me take a thing with me") or as a more hostile repudiation of family ties ("Now I have lost myself I am sick⟨ened by bondage⟩ of baggage").

In revising, Plath sharpens the dichotomies in the poem. The speaker's drift toward anonymity and irresponsibility is uninterrupted and unregretted. She postpones any attention to the tulips for five full stanzas while the speaker describes her self-forgetful serenity. When the tulips finally do appear in the poem their disruptive, wounding presence seems more threatening because so long delayed. They are significantly more corporeal than the speaker: they compete for breath, space, and attention. The speaker recognizes that "their redness talks to my wound, it corresponds," but this likeness is dreadful. To her the tulips are signs of the procreative body perceived as a deadly liability; in her anxious projections the tulips become a "sunken rust-red engine" or "a dozen red lead sinkers round my neck." The tulips' designs on the speaker are a terrifying magnification of Plath's image of infant appetite from "Morning Song," written a month earlier. In her poem to Frieda, the mother wryly observes, "your mouth opens clean as a cat"; here the speaker shrinks from them, "opening like the mouth of some great African cat."

This poem closes with a return to the body that is as reluctant and incomplete as the daughter's boasted escape from the maternal prison was in "In Plaster." The speaker transposes the tulips' imagined aggression into an image of her body's astonishing affection:

> And I am aware of my heart: it opens and closes
> Its bowl of red blooms out of sheer love of me.
> The water I taste is salt, like the sea,
> And comes from a country far away as health.

She apparently weeps in relief at her body's resistance to her attempted defection. Yet the split between the female subject and her body remains. Although the metaphoric exchange between speaker and tulips promises a reincorporation of their vital, instinctive force, the final lines confess her enduring disease with the flesh.

"Medusa": The Body that Swallows Speech

In her original title for her most extreme poem of matricidal rage, "Mum: Medusa," Plath identifies an unspeakable equation: her intimate familiar, the mother who nourished life, becomes a ghastly vision of death. The title suggests both an interdiction, what a daughter is not permitted to say about the mother, and the instrument for enforcing that silence, the threat of speechless paralysis. Composed in mid-October of 1962, "Medusa" is a companion poem to "Daddy," written four days earlier. In her struggle to exorcise the figure of the parent in each, Plath wars against an emotional dependency that she felt thwarted her ability to write. Since childhood, Plath had considered her mother's praise and love as returns for the gift of her writing: "Writing, then, was a substitute for myself: if you don't love me, love my writing and love me for my writing" (J 281). If she could not write, she would not be loved. Yet she also feared that her mother's self-sacrifice for her children had been so profound that no return from her daughter could ever balance the debt. In her 1958 journals Plath tries to disrupt this logic:

> MY WRITING IS MY WRITING IS MY WRITING. Whatever elements there were in it of getting her approval I must no longer use it for that. I must not expect her love for it. . . . I must change, not she. Why is telling her of a success so unsatisfying; because one success is never enough: when you love, you have an indefinite lease of it. When you approve, you only approve single acts. Thus approval has a short dateline. The question is: so much for that, good, but now, what is the next thing? (J 281–82)

In therapy Plath began to believe that her writing blocks were rebellion against the indebtedness to her mother and that her debilitating blocks were an unconscious attempt to punish her mother and, inevitably, also to punish herself for her selfish ingratitude. The poet's first full-time commitment to writing during that year was a risky decision Plath felt her mother disapproved; she feared the independence of her decision was compromised by the six-month writing block that followed. In journal entries from early July 1958, at the beginning of this period, Plath reveals that the punishing mother and the unwritten text were interchangeable metaphors. Plath felt "unable to speak human speech, lost as I am in my inner wordless Sargasso. . . . I must cure this very destructive paralysis and ruinous brooding and daydreaming. If I want to write, this is hardly the way to behave—in horror of it, frozen by it. The ghost of the unborn novel is a Medusa-head" (J 246). Later her worst blocks came after the births of her children, when the drain of mothering left her without the concentration or stamina for writing but when her urge to better her mother's example went unabated. The image of Medusa came to represent a death threat to her identity as a writer and, shadowing this, a guilty dread of losing maternal love.

How deeply conflicted and apparently unbreakable Plath's habit was of bartering poetry for love and then blaming Aurelia for blocking one and withholding the other is revealed in a letter she wrote on the same day as "Medusa." The letter contains some of her most grandiose claims of literary accomplishment: "I am a genius of a writer; I have it in me. I am writing the best poems of my life; they will make my name. I could finish the novel in six *weeks* of day-long work. I have a gift of an inspiration for another."[47] The manic moments in this letter strive to maintain the established script of Plath's relation to Aurelia even as the poem works to rupture it. The poem breaks silence about a number of taboo subjects; one of these is her seething resentment at the fictions "Sivvy" and "Mummy" created of and for each other. Plath self-consciously wrote the poem, and her mother later read it, against the countertext of their letters.[48] The persona of the letters models her femininity on Aurelia's example and even claims to exceed it; the persona of the poem, in denouncing Aurelia, risks hating the very aspect of herself she has constructed in order to be loved.[49]

In the earlier poems Plath wrote to scrutinize her fear of becoming her mother, the figures she chose to represent her antagonism enabled her to imagine that gender could be separated from self. That is, in order to resist or revise the cultural interpretation of femininity or maternity, she needed a script or a metaphor that differentiated, and often dichotomized, woman and her mirror, rebellious flesh and plaster cast, self-effacing patient and devouring tulips. In "Medusa" Plath fails to create a metaphoric narrative that safely exteriorizes the threat that her mother's gender embodied. Several narrative lines are generated by the psychodrama of the mother's parasitic solicitude that consumes what it nurtures, but none are dramatically coherent or entirely intelligible. The drafts contain more traces of a sea battle in which the speaker is pursued by an armada of jellyfish, who are "sister stooges" to the maternal medusa. At the end of a transatlantic chase, the besieged speaker warns, "Off, off, eely tentacle! / I shall break my oar on you." Yet this seascape is also the boiling, inchoate topography of the mother's body from which the speaker is incompletely delivered. The miasmic scene is imagined with the sexual disgust Beauvoir and Kahane associate with the primal mother. The predatory jellyfish seem a cancerous proliferation of "wild cells"; pulsing "like hearts" with "red stigmata at the very center," the sign of their sickness is the brand of the martyr. The speaker is caught in the treacherous "rip tide" of the mother's womb, dragged back by her "old barnacled umbilicus," engulfed by a fat, red "placenta / Paralyzing the kicking lovers." The steaming sea, the "hiss" of the mother's censure, the tears of "Blubbery Mary," and the amniotic fluid in which she stews are indistinguishable: "I am sick of hot salt. / I am sick to death of ⟨maternity, you, Mary, Mary!⟩."

The speaker's revulsion at her maternal prison is overwhelming in the poem, yet some images suggest it is also seductive. The transatlantic phone calls that keep the idealized mother-daughter myths "in a state of miraculous repair" are recalled in the drafts in terms that suggest the daughter's neediness and urge to control as well as the mother's almost sexual responsiveness:

> you are always there,
> Tremulous breath at the end of my line,
> Curve of ⟨Bright⟩ water upleaping
> To my water⟨-finder⟩ rod, dazzling & grateful
> Touching & sucking! ⟨O silver tentacle!⟩.

Rich would explain the emotional crosscurrents that warp Plath's narrative as the unconscious motive for mother loathing: "Where a mother is hated to the point of matriphobia there may also be a deep underlying pull toward her, a dread that if one relaxes one's guard one will identify with her completely."[50] Ostriker claims that poems by daughters about identification with mothers, whether they express a nostalgic longing for pre-oedipal fusion or furious attempts at individuation, also testify to a "fear that femaleness means formlessness" or that "motherly attachment . . . means infantilism and shapelessness for both mother and daughter."[51] In "Medusa" the rigid oppositions of "In Plaster" are replaced by a series of hideous conflations. The lifeline of the old barnacled umbilicus becomes a murderous weapon, an eely tentacle; the mother regresses to a needy infant, touching and sucking, or more horrifically in the drafts, a host of leeches, "A million little suckers loving me." Throughout the poem the primal mother displays the freakish sexual ambiguity that makes her a Gothic horror according to Kahane. Her hermaphroditic omnipotence is revealed in the confusion of the gorgon's phallic snakes and the devouring, womblike mouth of the jellyfish "dragging their Jesus hair." Yet if the "unnerving" "God-ball" of the poem evokes infantile dependencies, for Plath it also represented her disgust at the heroic martyrdom of Aurelia's superhuman mothering during her adolescence: "She had to work. Work, and be a mother, too, a man and a woman in one sweet ulcerous ball" (J 267).[52]

The bodily transgressions in the poem are symptomatic of both the maternal appropriation and her own dependency that Plath feared. The most dangerous aspect of Aurelia's maternity was her self-sacrifice; her material and sexual self-denial had to be repaid by Plath's literary productivity and marital happiness, a debt in which Plath was always in arrears. Because Plath as a child had demanded Aurelia not remarry, she developed a guilty logic that her adult sexual life had been paid for by Aurelia's abstinence.[53] Paradoxically, in Plath's emotional economy, Aurelia's selflessness made her into a suspected rival: "Jealousy over men: why jealous of Ted? Mother can't take him. Other women can. I must not be selfless: develop a sense of self" (J 279). The extravagant blame of her mother's saintly altruism in "Medusa" seems motivated, in part, by Plath's sexual guilt; now that Aurelia's suffering on behalf of her daughter's fulfillment seems wasted, Plath's debt is correspondingly magnified. In the drafts, the culturally sanctioned images of motherhood are represented as a grotesque cannibalism in Plath's Gothic translation:

> Wh⟨at⟩o do you think you are?
> A Communion wafer? Blubbery Mary?
> I am no pieta.
> I refuse to be.
> Pulse by, pulse by!
>
> I shall take no bite of your body.

She denies the offer of the mother's body not only because she refuses to incorporate the values her mother represents, but also because she dreads that such nurture, feeding the daughter with the mother's flesh, masks a similar appetite: "And your kisses are the worst of all— / They eat me away! / I shall not let you swallow me!"

The central tensions in "Medusa" are organized around two monstrous figures: the jellyfish who is all mouth and the gorgon who is all eyes. Just as the stigmata of Aurelia's ulcerous body reminds Plath of her emotional and sexual debt, so her mother's look contains her sexual shame. Plath most succinctly reports her encounter with the gorgon in a letter written the week before this poem: "The horror of what you saw and what I saw you see last summer is between us and I cannot face you again until I have a new life" (LH 465).[54] Her description reveals that the mirror of the mother-daughter gaze produces an infinite regression. Plath both suffers the humiliating spectacle her mother sees and must see herself reflected as horrifying object in her mother's eyes. Frozen between them is the death of the persona perfected for the mother's approval. Such a mirror is intolerable for Plath; she vows in the letter what she has already begun in the other October poems, to give birth to a new self. In the drafts, the mother's stare is not only lethal but gloating. In its "cobra light" the daughter "could draw no breath, / Dead and moneyless, / ⟨I watched that loony white martyr's smile.⟩." The sight of the mother's face provokes a tirade of name calling: "That martyr's smile! / That loony pivot! / That stellar jelly-head!" For the most part, however, Plath's primary strategy for retaliation in the poem is to rob the mother of any face and to reduce her instead to the repulsively entrapping anatomy of the female body. Despite her claim at the close of the poem that "There is nothing between us," the speaker's struggle to break her bond with the maternal body and to erase the horror of the maternal mirror fails.

Feminine Singular: A New Poetics

Recovering the Queen: Reinflecting the Body

In the bee poems Plath began to articulate a new poetics. During October she oscillated between dismantling a poetics in which she was fertile partner to Hughes's genius and articulating a new

Medusa (2)

    I didn't call you.
    I didn't call you at all. // Never the less, never the less
~~Nevertheless, ~~ ~~please~~ ~~with~~ ~~tentacle~~ ~~a~~ ~~dhan~~ ~~dhan~~
~~From~~ ~~you~~ ~~the~~ ~~moon~~ ~~can~~ ~~took~~ ~~blow~~ ~~rose~~ ~~the sea~~ ~~fat~~ ~~red~~ ~~midnight~~
    Fat & red, ~~a~~ ~~place in it~~ ~~to me~~ ~~midnight~~
    Paralyzing the kicking lovers.
    Cobra light
    Squeezing the breath from ~~the~~ the blood bells
    Of the fuchsia! I could draw no breath, ~~dead & more~~
    Dead & moneyless, ~~for~~
    I ~~watched~~ ~~that~~ ~~the~~ ~~mystified~~ ~~state~~
~~As~~ Overexposed, ~~like~~ ~~in the~~ ~~glory~~ ~~arena,~~ ~~& pale~~ ~~Eyes~~ like ~~an x ray~~
~~Rocking~~ ~~with~~ ~~as mine~~ ~~X ray~~ ~~of~~ ~~an~~ ~~insomniac!~~ ~~insomnia~~
    That martyr's smile!
    That ~~is~~ my pivot!
    That stellar jelly-head!
And A million little ~~fishes~~ suckers loving me!

    What do you think you are?
    A Communion wafer? Blubbery Mary?
    I am no pietà.
    I refuse to be.
    Pulse by, pulse by!

    I shall take no bite of your body.
    There is simply nothing I want to be in touch with. In re
    No mercy, no mercy.
    I am sick of hot salt.
I am sick to death ~~of~~ ~~the kisses~~ ~~of the~~ ~~faithful.~~ ~~your~~ ~~Mary~~ ~~Mary!~~

"Medusa," draft 1, page 2, composed October 16, 1962

vision of the female poet as singular. In the obsessive figures of erotic thralldom and sexual defilement that characterize her poems of Vesuvian rage, she repudiated both the partnership and the poetic silencing it entailed. Reconstructing an alternative poetics meant Plath had to rethink the relation of gender, sexuality, and poetic authority; it also meant she had to reimagine the female body. In the poems discussed so far we have seen that Plath represented the intersection of poet and body as a site of rebellion. To define herself as poet she must contest the gendered inscription of her body as feminine by shattering the plaster cast, by effacing the maternal body in "Tulips," or by demonizing it in "Medusa." Yet these oppositional strategies by their very nature ensnare the speaker in a dependent attachment to the gender identity she reacts against. They also produce a subject who is either monster or corpse, that is, a subject who continues to reproduce, despite her rebellion, the flesh loathing of her culture.

In the sequence of October poems that includes the bee poems as well as "Fever 103°," "Lady Lazarus," and "Ariel," Plath resituates the female subject in a refigured body no longer defined by opposition but by appropriation. Rather than trying to erase the polarizing markers of gender, she would exploit and recombine them. I read these poems not as a struggle to free herself from the burden of a sexualized body but as her effort to find in it an adequate figure to embody a poetics of singularity.[55] Compared with the stalled, repetitive suffering of the poet as enraged wife or the anxious Gothic imprisonments of the poet as rebellious daughter, the figures for the poet in these poems exhibit incandescent energy. These fiery heroines emerge from feigned sleep, chilled stupor, sullen fevers, or static darkness to articulate themselves in searing, uniformly rising trajectories. They claim an inviolable self-sufficiency in contrast to the battered, dismembered speakers of the rage poems or the ambivalently enmeshed speakers in the daughter group. Yet in their combustible energy these personae are also extremely mutable; each new incarnation seems unstable in its excess and unpredictable in its final form. Although Plath's emphasis on the protean nature of the poet might seem to leave the female body behind, the figures she chooses are transgressive rather than transcendent. Female sexuality is extravagantly intensified to outlaw status in the hermaphroditic queen of "Stings," the autoerotic "acetelyne virgin" of "Fever," and the daring exhibitionist of "Lady Lazarus" and "Ariel." Self-engendered and self-delighting, these heroines appropriate male potency as their own. They frequently trespass on male prerogatives; they are violent in their self-assertion and unrestricted in their liberty. By contrast the male figures who appear in these poems are mute, shrunken, disfigured, immobilized, or dead.

In less than a week in early October, Plath completed a sequence of five poems about keeping bees at her cottage in Devon. At the end of January, she gathered and ordered the poems for her second collection of poetry and set these poems last.[56] When Plath chose to conclude *Ariel* with this group of poems (an order Hughes did not honor in his ordering of the volume), she recognized that the series pointed, at least figuratively, toward survival. She remarked that her selection "began with the word 'Love' and ended with the word 'Spring.' "[57] Nevertheless, the bee poems look backward to the unfinished emotional business of childhood and her relationship to her father as much as they respond to immediate betrayals or optimistically claim a certain future. In the earliest versions, Plath's notations indicate that she conceived of the group as an ordered sequence. The five separate poems are numbered consecutively in both her handwritten drafts and her typescripts, beginning with the draft of "The Bee Meeting" and concluding with "Wintering" five days later. The first typed draft of "The Bee Meeting" is dated October 3, 1962. "The Arrival of the Bee Box" came the next day. "Stings," "The Swarm," and "Wintering" arrived at one-day intervals on October 6, 7, and 8. All but "Stings" evolve from the first draft to a clean typescript of what would become the final published version mostly within a single day. During the week of composition, Plath tried several working titles for the group. "The Beekeeper" was her initial choice, self-consciously echoing a change in her role since the poem "The Beekeeper's Daughter" in *The Colossus*. By the time of "The Arrival of the Bee Box" on the following day, Plath had substituted "The Beekeeper's Daybook," and when she was typing "Stings" midway in the cycle, she settled simply for the running title "Bees." She mailed the completed sequence to *The New Yorker* on October 10; by January 25 she had successfully placed all but "The Swarm."[58]

The unerring drive with which Plath composed the sequence is further substantiated by her habit of drafting her first handwritten copies and earliest typescripts of each poem on the back of a typed draft of *The Bell Jar*, itself composed on the reverse of Smith College memo paper. Whether dictated by frugality, a rage for order, or a desire for sympathetic magic, Plath's earliest drafts are recorded on the reverse of *The Bell Jar* papers with hardly a page skipped or used out of its numbered sequence. Almost without interruption, Plath worked her way through a stack of the novel's pages from back to front. Her worksheets begin with the conclusion of chapter 6; by the time she typed "Wintering," she had worked down to within five pages of the beginning of chapter 4. About half the total of what Plath and subsequently Hughes preserved, some twenty-six of fifty-seven pages of the manuscripts for the sequence, including each of her handwritten drafts and her first heavily revised typescripts, appears on *The Bell Jar*. For later typescripts she used clean bond. The novel had been safely in the hands of her publisher since November 1961; it would be published in England in January 1963. Meanwhile she had collected a quarterly stipend from the Saxton grant during 1962 for this already completed work.[59] Nothing gave Plath such a sense of security and conviction of her own generativity as the tangible evidence of past success. The impressive stack of novel manuscript was at once satisfying proof of her productivity and a familiar stimulus to feelings of creativity. The determination with which Plath apparently used each page in sequence may indicate too that she felt a challenge to match her earlier prose output with her current poetic activity. Her choice was more likely emotionally overdetermined than accidental. It seems too neat to be coincidence that Plath began composing these poems that respond so immediately to the breakup of her marriage at the point in the novel that marks Esther Greenwood's discovery of Buddy Willard's sexual infidelity. Chapter 6 contains Esther's devastating comment that Buddy's proud display of male flesh reminded her of a "turkey neck and turkey gizzards." In drafting "The Bee Meeting" on the reverse of chapter 6, Plath's indelible image reappears parodically in the speaker's vulnerable overexposure: "I am nude as a chicken neck, does nobody love me?" Although the three *Bell Jar* chapters make up the bulk of material Plath reused during this week, she drafts smaller sections on equally significant scraps borrowed from other sources. Four versions of an earlier aborted attempt at "Stings" begun in August each appear on the reverse of several versions of a poem Hughes wrote in May 1960 marking Frieda's birth.[60] At the very end of this cycle of composition, on October 9, Plath types the final poem on another Hughes manuscript, this time a handwritten scene from his play *The Calm*, significantly a deadly quarrel in which a wife accuses her husband of fraudulent artistic ambitions.

Plath's choice of the queen to represent the woman poet as carnal subject is riven with contradictions. The queen's singular status is uncontested inside and outside the hive. Without her, the hive dies, production ceases. Yet because her distinguishing characteristic is her excessive generativity, her queenly estate is, in fact, perpetual confinement; and the end of the queen's story is her biological exhaustion and inevitable replacement by young virgins. What is more attractive to the poet about the queen is her murderous instinct toward her mate, a characteristic Plath initially emphasizes in drafting the central image of the queen in "Bee Meeting": "The fine upflight of a murderess in a swarm of wooers." What is most significant about Plath's choice, however, is that she joins the queen when that bride flight is behind her. The queen's situation is the pivotal moment in her history when the virgins dream of killing her. In her imaginative alliance with the aging queen, Plath situates herself within the spectacle she had previously loathed. In "Mirror" and "Face Lift" the apparition of the old hag meant self-murder; here Plath invests old flesh with secret intelligence that guarantees survival. In borrowing the queen's story to tell her own, Plath accomplishes the kind of narrative displacement within dominant discourse that de Lauretis and DuPlessis describe. She invests the position of Other in the culturally sanctioned script with subjectivity, and she grants the queen a will and purpose that resist her dead-end role. The plot the queen harbors is incubated in secret; repeatedly in the sequence she is thought to be hiding, sleeping, or dead. She governs the action but, except for "Stings," never appears. Plath's queen represents the explosive potential that Moers and Auerbach contend exists at the extremes of patriarchal dichotomies; she contains in her sequestered deathlike repose the possibilities of more dangerous transformations.

Still, throughout the sequence there is a constant undertow in the other direction that is also directly contingent on Plath's choice of the hive as the site of her new poetics. In both "The Arrival of the Bee Box" and "Wintering" the powers of creation represented by the bees threaten to become agents of destruction. If the regendered female body could become the corporeal ground of her poetic intelligence, in Rich's terms, the maternal body continued to threaten the poet's extinction. I read the entire bee sequence as Plath's struggle to bring forth an articulate, intelligible self from the potential death box of the hive. One of the most terrifying words in these poems is "dumb." To be dumb means to have been duped into silent complicity in her own imprisonment, like the willing bees in "The Swarm" who are "dumb banded bodies / Walking the plank . . . / Into a new mausoleum." More forebodingly, it also calls up the torpid woman, "her body a bulb in the cold and too dumb to think," in "Wintering" who is inarticulate without being insensate.

To take up beekeeping, and even more to write about it, was deeply resonant for Plath. The bee poems participate in an extended autobiographical narrative that had mythic status for Plath, involving as it did her initiation into starkly polarized gender identities, forbidden desires, and transgressive appropriations of power. They rework the earlier psychodrama she had already reconstructed several times in the 1959 poem "Electra on Azalea Path," in "The Beekeeper's Daughter" from Colossus, as well as in a prize-winning undergraduate poem called "Lament," and in her short story from the same period, "Among the Bumblebees." In setting up her own hive in Devon, Plath was self-consciously imitating her father's authority, a mastery she both desires and disdains in "The Beekeeper's Daughter." Keeping bees also served to validate and extend her sense of her own reproductive health. Plath enjoyed the neat parallel that the same woman, Winifred Davies, who taught her beekeeping served as midwife at the birth of Nicholas. Davies also provided significant material help to Plath by securing nannies who would free a few hours a day for her poetry again in October. Written out of the matrix of this layered experience, the bee poems represent not only a revisionary history of her role as daughter, wife, and mother but a simultaneous search for an adequate shape in which to reconstitute herself as both a generative and an authoritative poet.

In "The Bee Meeting" (originally titled simply, and more ominously, "The Meeting") the speaker belatedly reads the setting up of the hive as her own initiation into the received meanings of female gender. She participates simultaneously as a willing accomplice and unsuspecting victim in a village ritual that seems to require female sacrifice or at least sedation. She fears equally being without the protection shared by the rector, the midwife, and the sexton and assuming the disguise they offer her: "Now they are giving me a fashionable white straw Italian hat / And a black veil that molds to my face, they are making me one of them." Not only the villagers and the social order they represent but the natural order appears to collude against her: in signs of fertility she reads only injury ("Is it blood clots the tendrils are dragging up that string?"); in its female scents, her own stupefaction ("Is it the hawthorn that smells so sick? / . . . etherizing its children"). Significantly, the pattern of Plath's revisions enhances the speaker's feelings of vulnerability and co-optation. What were originally assertions about the identities and purpose of the villagers in the first draft are consistently recast into apprehensive questions. In the draft the speaker robes herself, while in the finished poem another woman is "buttoning the cuffs at my wrists and the slit from my neck to my knees." She also intensifies the ambiguity of the speaker's identification with the villagers, especially whether it is chosen or enforced, by revising the key phrase "I am one of them" to read "they are making me one of them."

The speaker's fearful passivity in accepting her gendered role as given by her community seems to guarantee her conformity. Yet in imagining the contest within the hive, she reveals her disloyalty to the normative script. As an initiate, her sympathies might be expected to lie with the "new virgins" who "dream of a duel they will win inevitably." But she prefers the duplicitous queen's self-interested plotting to their sleeping biological certainty: "She is very clever. / She is old, old, old, she must live another year, and she knows it." In positing the queen's "ungrateful" resistance to the villagers' intentions, Plath opens a space for her own contradiction to this inevitable story, in de Lauretis's terms. In telling the story of the hive, Plath focuses on the generational antagonism between females but from a devious perspective; for both the aging queen and the dreaming virgins, the apex of female identity is the singular "bride flight," the violently self-defining "upflight of the murderess into a heaven that loves her." Oddly, this flight is only remembered and anticipated within the narrative; although this escape is deeply desired by the speaker, she has not yet witnessed it. Instead the poem ends with the speaker's premature burial in the queen's long box (explicitly identified in the draft as "that coffin, so white & silent"), an even more frightening and permanent incarceration than "In Plaster." The communal "operation" of conventional gender formation would seem a success: "The villagers are untying their disguises, they are shaking hands." But the speaker's chilled torpor may only be feigned. She resembles another of Auerbach's swooning maidens who knows more tricks than she lets on: "I am the magician's girl who does not flinch." Still this is an identity in hiding; she, like the old queen, has not shown herself.

What powers are incubated in the guise of this corpselike pose? In "The Arrival of the Bee Box" the speaker experiences frightening, uneasy intuitions of a poetic pregnancy. The unknown interior harbors dreadful possibilities: "I would say it was the coffin of a midget / Or a square baby / Were there not such a din in it." Like the shrouded and ominous "awful baby" of "Tulips," the dark, locked box of the body contains archaic mysteries, primitive appetites, and anarchic potential. The beekeeper's doubts about her ability to control what threatens to feed on her mimics a woman's experience of pregnancy which, Kahane suggests, is an inherently Gothic scenario, provoking apprehensions about her bodily integrity as it becomes host to parasitic, alien inhabitants.[61] The grasping, teeming life within would overthrow the conventional, hierarchical authority the speaker has allegedly acquired:

How can I let them out!
It is the noise that ⟨terrifies⟩ ⟨appals⟩ ⟨alarms⟩ ⟨dismays⟩
    appals me most of all,
The unintelligible syllables.
It is like a Roman mob.
Small, taken one by one, But my god! together!

I ⟨put⟩ lay my ear to furious Latin.
I am not a Caesar, I am not a Caesar.

Much as she is worried about mothering in this poem, Plath is also wittily experimenting with fathering. She reenacts, with a subversive difference, the role her father played in "The Beekeeper's Daughter." In the earlier poem, the mounting, pulsing sexuality of the female bees threatens to overwhelm the father's capacity to regulate it. The "maestro" in a "frock coat" is an inadequate bridegroom for the queen bee, but still he dominates. In "The Arrival of the Bee Box" the female owner anxiously asserts and retreats from her mastery. When she chooses to claim control, her tone is comically imperious: "They can be sent back. / They can die, I need feed them nothing, I am the owner." Her gestures are self-consciously unmaternal; she can starve or reject these dependent beings rather than teach them speech. This elaborate little dance around the bee box suggests at once Plath's ambivalence about following in her father's footsteps and her antipathy toward defining herself exclusively in terms of her biology. Both these issues are involved in her hesitation about authoring the queen who would be born in "Stings." When she finally decides to play "sweet God" and set the bees free, her act speaks less of feminine Christlike mercy than what she associated with the unconstrained exercise of male power.

The manuscript of "Stings," the third poem and the stunning centerpiece of the sequence, shows the most dramatic signs of revision. In August Plath began and abandoned an early fragment, also titled "Stings," about an incident that occurred when she and Hughes purchased the hive in June. Writing her mother on June 15, Sylvia describes the bees getting into Ted's hair because he neglected to wear a hat while they were moving a queen (LH 457).

Most of the events recounted in June are later transmuted into the first poem in the sequence, "The Bee Meeting." The August fragment focuses entirely on Hughes and is the initial portrait of the scapegoat figure from "Stings" who provokes the bees' "suicidal" attack; it contains early versions of several lines that survive into the October version of "Stings," most notably, "They think death is worth it." Most of the speaker's sympathy in the fragment is given to the "ignominious" defeat of the bees: "Gelded and wingless. Not heroes. Not heroes." When Plath returned to the poem in October, she used the incident to tell another story; the wounding of the male figure by the bees takes second place to the speaker's recovery of the queen. As in each poem in the series, the speaker of "Stings" broods about her ability to control or order generation, the bees' as well as her own.

In "Stings" the question of ownership, and of access to power, especially through the enigmatic sexuality of the queen, is initially posed with deceptive tranquility. The poem opens with a delicate and dangerous image of barter and sexual exchange as the barehanded speaker and an unnamed male transfer the honeycombs: "He and I / have a thousand clean cells between us." The male and female figures appear innocently exposed ("Our cheesecloth gauntlets neat and sweet, / The throats of our wrists brave lilies"); the man smiles at the transaction. Yet the pretty domesticity of setting up the hive and the honeyed sweetness of these images barely hint at the antagonism that is acknowledged in the drafts. The earlier versions show the speaker engaged in a definition of herself that is primarily vengeful. She is the wronged wife and deserted mother whose verbal assault disfigures, emasculates, and finally destroys a male opponent. During the process of revision, Plath redirects her energy toward resuscitating the queen.

The cameo appearance of a "great scapegoat," who mysteriously watches in the eighth stanza and vanishes punished by the avenging bees in the tenth, is curiously unmotivated in the narrative. In the first handwritten draft, he looms larger and much uglier. He also enters the poem a stanza earlier. A distrusted voyeur, he is neither partner nor midwife to the speaker's dangerous labor:

It is almost over
I am in control, I am in control.
⟨Who is this third, this extra
Who watches & helps not at all?⟩.

His monitoring gaze threatens the self-possession the speaker attempts, rather unconvincingly, to assert in her nervous, repetitive phrases. He intrudes again six lines later:

There is a third one, watching.
He has nothing to do with me or the bee-seller
Now he is gone

In eight great bounds, a great scapegoat.

The amount of space and the intensity of affective response devoted to the scapegoat in the drafts reveal the inhibiting power this figure held for Plath. "The sweat of his efforts a rain / Tugging the world to fruit" recalls father Otto Plath, the "maestro of the bees," as much as Hughes, who fathered her children and, not incidentally, often fathered her poems by suggesting subjects; both are condensed in this jealous spy on her creative process:

Now he peers through a warped silver rain drop;
Seven lumps on his head
And a ⟨great⟩ big boss on his forehead,

Black as the devil, & vengeful.

The name-calling and the grotesque caricature in these lines make explicit the emotional projection throughout the poem. Plath's uncertainty about her self-engendering poetics underlies her representation of the male figure as a deformed troll who might hex her labor or appropriate its fruits. Significantly, this passage remains in the finished poem until a final revision ten days later on October 16.[62] By then Plath had completed "Daddy," a poem wholly devoted, as we have seen, to subduing this doubled male force. Extended treatment of the male antagonist played an important cathartic role in the drafts, I argue, but was later intentionally suppressed in favor of a primary focus on the transfiguration of the queen.

In the first handwritten draft, Plath recognized the authority of her claim "I / Have a self to recover, a queen." She began this section over four separate times in her handwritten drafts; she rewrote the concluding vision, beginning "more terrible than she ever was," another four times in the first typed draft. Her first attempts remain largely reactive. The power Hughes has literally exercised, Plath would figuratively restore in the poem to the queen. She is imagined "Rising this time, on wings of clear glass, / Over the deserted nurseries," or again, "⟨Leaving the stiff wax, / The dead men at the lintel⟩ / Clear as glass ⟨& merciless⟩ / A lens of the sun." She enacts the mother's unspeakable wish to desert the nursery and the jealous wife's preemptive desire to abandon "the stingless dead men." With each successive revision, the men are literally done to death: they are "stingless," then "rejected," then "old dead men," then simply, flatly, "dead men." In the same line, "deserted nurseries" remains constant and appears as part of the closure in every draft until the last. In these early versions, poetic authority is equated with the liberty to deny relational bonds. In revising "Stings" Plath consciously checks her urge for retaliation; what she requires, instead, is uninhibited self-expression. Her process of recasting the ending demonstrates vividly that the re-covered self longs to leave her mark elsewhere than in the faces of her children. The queen's "more terrible" need is to reinscribe her identity on the heavens.

To give primacy to the singular woman poet, Plath reworked cultural myths as well as autobiographical narratives. Another submerged narrative demonstrates how Plath moved from a reaction to the situation of gender toward a revision of its possibilities. She depended less on oppositional strategies and more on an appropriation of male potency and a reinvestment of these qualities in a transformed female body. In a shadowy but insistent way, the manuscript for "Stings" reads like a subverted Cinderella story. The speaker is inwardly convinced of her specialness although she is bound in servitude with her unlovely sisters:

⟨I think I am being cheated⟩
I stand in a column

3. Stings (2)

The sweat of his efforts a rain
Tugging the world to fruit.
Now he peers through a warped silver raindrop,
Seven lumps on his head
And a big boss on his forehead,

Black as the devil, and vengeful.
The bees found him out,
Molding onto his lips like lies,
Complicating his features.
They thought death was worth it, but I

Have a self to recover, a queen.
Is she dead, is she sleeping?
Where has she been,
With her lion-red body, her wings of glass?
Now she is flying

More terrible than she ever was,
~~Over~~ glass. A red scar in the sky ~~A~~ A red scar a comet
Over the engine that killed her, the white stiff wax,
The deserted nurseries, the stingless dead men.

More terrible than she ever was, shimmering
A red scar, a comet in the sky, a comet
Over the engine that killed her,
The white, stiff wax,
The deserted nurseries, and stingless dead men.
rejected
mausoleum

More terrible than she ever was, a red
A red Scar in the sky, a comet
Over the engine that killed her,
The mausoleum of wax,
The deserted nurseries and rejected dead men.
and old

More terrible than she ever was, red
Scar in the sky, a comet
Over the engine that killed her,
The wax mausoleum,
The deserted nurseries and old dead men.
The desertion of   The desertion of

"Stings," draft 2, page 2, composed October 6 and revised perhaps as late as October 16, 1962

Of winged, unmiraculous women,
Honey-drudgers. ⟨I am no drudge⟩
I am no drudge
Though for ⟨seven⟩ six years I have eaten dust
And dried plates with my dense hair.

And seen my strangeness evaporate.

In this version from the handwritten draft, the speaker's worry over whether she has bought "wormy mahogany" rather than a queen is linked more explicitly with her own feelings of unrecognized worth. As in this passage, the worksheets frequently specify significant numbers reminiscent of fairy tales: there are eight combs of honey; the monstrous male figure has seven wens and vanishes in "eight great bounds"; the speaker's dense hair has been wasted in domestic drudgery for six years (the actual length of her marriage, although the more magical number seven also exists as an alternate choice in the same draft). After this archetypal period of servitude, the heroine is ripe for a magical transformation from scullery maid to royalty, from honey-drudger to spectacular glass-winged queen.

Yet in superimposing her narrative on the fairy tale motif, Plath also critiques its gendered logic. Her greatest necessity in borrowing either the queen bee's story or Cinderella's was to rewrite the ending since, in both, queenly authority is inevitably linked with producing biological heirs. Throughout the worksheets, Plath reinflects the gender of the major figures. The mysterious male departs in haste, leaving his slippers and a "square of white ⟨handkerchief⟩ linen" but without leaving his name. The hidden queen meanwhile is becoming distinctly unfeminine: "her long body / Rubbed of its plush—, / Poor & bare, ⟨poor & bare⟩ unqueenly & even shameful." A specifically female identification of the queen who "dreams of a second bride-flight" is discarded in the handwritten draft and replaced with a male association, her "lion-red body." Through these systematic refigurations, Plath's poetic avatar gains her power not by marrying the prince but by appropriating his phallic possibility. The lion-red queen who scars the sky like a "red comet" in her flight is clearly a blood relative of the virgin who burns like a blowtorch in "Fever," the red-haired Lady Lazarus whose prodigious appetite incorporates male authority as her own, and the lioness in "Ariel" who flies like an arrow into the "red / Eye, the cauldron of morning." Plath was preoccupied throughout October with producing a psychic and sexual metamorphosis in herself as woman and poet as she approached her thirtieth birthday. "Fever" and "Lady Lazarus" were both begun in the week before it, less than two weeks after she completed the bee sequence; "Ariel" was composed on her birthday, October 27. In the endings of each of these poems, she predicts not only the luminous energy of the sexualized body but its resilient mutability.

Plath intended "Wintering," the last poem in the bee sequence, to close her second collection of poems. In "Wintering" Plath takes the greatest risk in the sequence in associating the female body with nature; in the drafts for the poem she also shows the greatest resolve that the comatose body can be willed back to life. Like "The Arrival of the Bee Box," this poem confronts the intractable otherness of physicality. "Wintering" lacks, however, the manic metaphor-making wit used by the earlier speaker to discipline her fear of the dangerous contents of the bee box. Here, the speaker dares herself to descend to the interior, to know herself engulfed by "Black asininity. Decay. / Possession." This time, rather than encountering ungovernable appetite clamoring for release, she confronts a deathlike stupor. That this poem was typed on the reverse of one of Hughes's plays (their shared earlier hopes for wealth) gives poignance to the speaker's hoarded reserves:

> I have whirled the midwife's extractor, I have my honey,
> ⟨Half a dozen⟩ Six jars of it,
> Six ⟨gold, clear⟩ corn nubs, six gold teeth,
> Six cat's eyes in ⟨my⟩ the wine cellar.

Images of accumulation struggle against premonitions of attrition in these metaphors; the midwife's extractions resemble the leavings of corpses. What did she have to show for this summer, these six years of marriage, this, her thirtieth year? Anticipating her mother's visit the summer before, Plath associated the cellar with country husbandry and her mother's traditional domesticity: "Have you any canning advice? Maybe you will supervise some of my canning this summer. We have a fine, dark 'wine cellar' which asks to be crammed with bright glass jars full of good things" (LH 455). In the draft for "Wintering" her stores are counted and recounted as a charm against "the black bunched in there like a bat." On the eighth of October, when she began the poem, they seemed uncertain protection against a winter alone. The authority she claimed in the earlier poems as owner of the hive, or as its ascending queen, is reduced to the defensive claim that the female body is nature's basic resource:

> They have got rid of the men,

> The men have only their sex & they eat too much honey
> ⟨They will make men again⟩
> ⟨Anyway⟩ Winter is for women—
> ⟨It is for⟩ The woman still at her knitting,
> At the cradle of Spanish walnut,
> Her body a bulb in the cold & too dumb to think.

In her body's imitation of the bees' minimal survival, the poet is nearly immobilized, her consciousness on the verge of extinction. What the poet's corporeal interior promised or threatened changes throughout the sequence. The bee box delivers noisy, unruly maniacs who demand from their owner adequate translation. The wormy mahogany of "Stings" divulges a self-anointed queen. Finally, from the black hole of the cellar, the speaker utters a desperate prayer. The optimistic conclusion of "Wintering" depends on a predictive analogy between female generativity and nature's cyclical fruitfulness. In the female bees' death trance ("so slow I hardly know them"), their keeper hopes for a displaced enactment of the Demeter/Kore myth. If she can figure their rebirth, her dumb bulb might flower again into speech. Yet Plath's difficulty with the conclusion of "Wintering" suggests her persistent uncertainty about the adequacy of the natural metaphor that bound the female body as intimately to death and decay as to rejuvenation or, in the terms of this poem, to the present corpses as much as to the barely credible spring. The final questions are far from rhetorical in the first handwritten draft:

> Will the hive survive, will the gladiolas
> Succeed in banking their fires

to enter another year?
What will they taste ⟨like⟩ of the Christmas roses?
Snow water? Corpses? ⟨Thin, sweet Spring.⟩ ⟨A sweet
    Spring?⟩ Spring?
⟨Impossible spring?⟩
⟨What sort of spring?⟩
⟨O God, let them taste of spring.⟩.

Later, in the typed draft, the poet appears more certain of "Snow water" and "Corpses" than of "Spring," which is crossed out and replaced by a tentative echo of the queen's ascent, "A glass wing?" Even through the third full draft of the poem, when all her other choices of image and phrase had been conclusively established, Plath had trouble believing in the certainty of spring as the end of her wintering. Her final revision, when it comes, moves in the opposite direction from her changes in "The Bee Meeting." Rather than introducing more questions, she wills herself to assert a compelling prophecy, continuing to hope, as she has throughout the rest of the sequence, that saying it would make it so: "The bees are flying. They taste the spring."

"Fever 103°" and "Ariel": Rearticulating the Body

How much Plath's new poetics of singularity were a self-conscious effort to write beyond the ending of the narrative of rage is revealed in "Fever 103°." The poem moves from victimization through retaliation toward transfiguration, yet the obscurities of its images and the uncertainty of tone mark it as a transitional poem. The poem revisits the scene of sexual torture in "The Jailer" composed three days earlier, although the speaker finally escapes the earlier poem's sadomasochistic dependency. The poem also anticipates the blasphemous parody of "Lady Lazarus," begun three days later. In its self-dramatization, the poem inflates private suffering to mythic proportions and undertakes, in its ironic cultural allusions, the type of critical quotation "against the grain" that de Lauretis describes.

In its first half, "Fever," like the Vesuvian rage poems, is a performance of intimate aggression. Its success depends on the speaker compelling her lover to witness first her suffering and then her purifying renunciation. The speaker's histrionics demonstrate the same ambivalent dialectic with her audience; her rage commands his attention yet threatens to strangle her: "Love, love, the low smokes roll / From me like Isadora's scarves, I'm in a fright / One scarf will catch and anchor in the wheel." In the drafts it is even clearer that the poem was initially structured by the logic of rage. The original third and fourth stanzas of the poem deploy Plath's familiar trope of persecution in which the speaker's sexual agony is equated with a martyr's smoldering immolation:

O auto-da-fe!
The purple men, gold crusted, fat with spleen

Sit with their hooks & crooks & stoke the light
The tinder cries.

The tinder that cries reminds us of the Joan of Arc figure in the flames of "Burning the Letters," just as the splenetic inquisitors' hooks and crooks recall Hughes's hooked handwriting that was the source of her torment in that earlier bonfire. The speaker of "Lady Lazarus" will also "turn and burn" in a fire tended by an intimate tyrant. This portrait of the speaker as anguished but inextinguishable heretic remains a part of "Fever" through three typed drafts before it is suppressed.[63] Its presence helps explain the oblique retaliation that concludes the first half of the poem.

The speaker's slow, sullen incineration produces global pollution that at first seems indiscriminately lethal, "Choking the aged and the meek, the weak / Hothouse baby in its crib, the ghastly orchid." The naming of the ghastly orchid prompts a burst of revisions in the first draft. Since "Burning the Letters," when the name of Hughes's lover rose from the ashes as a "sinuous orchis," the image served Plath as a coded shorthand for betrayal. Here, as in the earlier poem, the poet's fury is released in a vengeful digression in the draft:

the ghastly orchid
Hanging its hanging gardens in ⟨thin⟩ the air
⟨Oh that floral⟩ Devilish leopard!
Radiation turned ⟨you⟩ it white
And killed ⟨you⟩ in an hour.

Fever 103°

Pure? What does it mean?
The tongues of hell
Are dull, dull as the triple
Tongues of dull, fat Cerberus
Who wheezes at the gate. Incapable,
Of licking clean

The aguey tendon, the sin, the sin.
O auto-da-fé!
The purple men, gold crusted, fat with spleen
Sin with their hooks + crooked stoke the light.
The tinder cries,
The indelible smell

Of a snuffed candle!
Love, love, the low smokes roll
From me like Badass's scarves, I'm in a fright

One scarf will catch + anchor in the wheel.
Such yellow sullen smokes
their own element. They will not rise,

But trundle round the globe
Choking the aged + the meek, The weak
Hothouse baby in its crib, the ghastly orchid

Ceasing the bodies of adulterers
Like Hiroshima ash, and eating in
the sin! the sin!

Hanging is hanging gardens in the air
In to the air
leaped!
Radiation turned
White
And killed in an hour.

MEMORANDUM
SMITH COLLEGE

"Fever 103°," draft 1, page 1, composed October 20 and revised after October 30, 1962, perhaps as late as January 1963

The entire passage appears as a marginal addition to the first draft; its pronouns suggest that Plath's impulse to punish was personal and not easily satisfied. The pall of her wrath expands to megalomaniacal proportions, "Greasing the bodies of the adulterers / Like Hiroshima ash and eating in." Whether the body is burned as sexual martyr or consumed as fuel for deadly retaliation, its fires are suffocating, not purifying: "they will not rise."

The second half of the poem shows the fluid exchange between what have become Plath's stereotypical postures of victimization and the imagery of her transfiguring new poetics. In the rage poems the enflamed body is a sign of poetic dispossession; here creative primacy is asserted as a pleasurable repossession of the body: "Does not my heat astound you. And my light. / All by myself I am a huge camellia / Glowing and coming and going, flush on flush." The speaker insistently rereads the symptoms of her fever as the expression of her luminous, self-sufficient energy. In the narratives of rage the body is reactively defined; because its ravages serve to inscribe the figure of male tyranny, its forms are determined by this unvarying polarity. "Fever" accomplishes the rupture of the metaphorical equivalence between the sexualized body and emotional deprivation, erotic dependence and artistic extinction. The male presence remains in this transition poem, but his power has been diminished to the derivative status of voyeur. The speaker's dazzling self-display demonstrates to the astounded observer her resilient, seductive power and yet her volatile unpredictability. Her pleasure is derived not only from the autoerotic, orgasmic pulse of her fever but from the trespass of her performance that insists her lover watch what he is no longer necessary to produce.

A hallucinatory exuberance marks the speaker's release from the oppositional rhetoric of rage into the transgressive freedom of the outlaw. She appropriates the conventional scripts of religious purification only to critique them through her carnal reenactment. Just as the fever's rituals are a parodic imitation of Christ ("Three days. Three nights. / Lemon water, chicken / Water, water make me retch"), her self-propelled ascension ("Attended by roses, / By kisses, by cherubim, / By whatever these pink things mean") borrows the grandeur of the iconography of the Virgin and the Madonna but ambiguously undermines its spirituality. Her final assertion of her singular identity is not an impersonation, however, but a reconception of female purity as an "acetylene Virgin." The image suggests not only the violent erasure of cultural inscriptions of the body that the evacuated passivity of "Tulips" failed to achieve, but also an aggressive inviolability that, by defying possession, repels any future inscription. Plath's figure for the virginal body recasts the stereotype of virgin as lack, absence, or unconscious materiality; hers is both a wounding presence and the agent of its own ecstatic excess. The final spectacle of "Fever" is also the signature of Plath's poetics. These speakers all predict their flight but defy us to follow it. In their incandescent mutability they are unapproachable; what we notice is the mark they leave behind, the blinding articulation of the body subjectively possessed.

"Ariel" is the last poem in this sequence and the only one composed on fresh memo paper rather than on the Bell Jar manuscript that had been exhausted a few days earlier. It was composed in Devon on her birthday and on the eve of a trip to London that she hoped would inaugurate her career as a poet in her own right. In London she recorded fifteen poems, fourteen of them written in the previous two weeks, including this one, for a BBC broadcast.[64] She was also interviewed by Peter Orr for a radio series on contemporary poets—the only American of forty-five poets chosen for the program. She spent an afternoon with Al Alvarez, the literary critic of the Observer, reading her latest work. She bragged in a letter to her brother Warren, "He is the opinion-maker in poetry over here . . . and says I'm the first woman poet he's taken seriously since Emily Dickinson!" (LH 476). Perhaps Alvarez promised that same afternoon to publish her two birthday poems, "Ariel" and "Poppies in October."[65]

In "Ariel," Plath is the most reckless in enacting her poetics through the fiery transubstantiation of the female subject. Yet even here creative liberty is expressed through figures that are emphatically corporeal and transgressively sexual. In her drafts Plath progressively obliterates the distance and difference between the speaker and the animal energy of her horse, Ariel, and interpolates a revised legend of Godiva in which the heroic wife performs a rebellious striptease. She also transposes the imagery of burning, first associated with Godiva, to the "red / Eye, the cauldron of morning" in yet another mutation of the poet's volatile form. Each of these changes, I would argue, produces a fusion of poetic identity and the carnal subject, not a rejection of it. The poem originally began by marking more explicitly an initial dichotomy between the raw, unguided material force of the horse and the speaker as controlling, yet desiring subject: "God's lioness also, how one we grow / Crude mover whom I move & burn to love." Compared to the hurtling velocity and unitary drive of the finished poem, the earliest draft reveals a pervasive, unresolved tension between alternative figures for the speaker's transformation in the grip of her muse. In the first of these, her presence is dispersed into the landscape:

> Something else
> Hauls me through air, // ⟨I foam⟩, O ⟨I⟩ flakes from my
>   heels, ⟨I⟩
> Foam ⟨In⟩to white wheat, a glitter of seas.

The ecstatic translation of the flesh into other natural forms seems an accelerated version of Whitman's sunset exit from "Song of Myself": "It coaxes me to the vapor and the dusk. / I depart as air, I shake my white locks at the runaway sun, / I effuse my flesh in eddies, and drift it in lacy jags."

The first of three handwritten drafts is incomplete; it breaks off, significantly, at a point at which the speaker's rising, melting motion is confused and contradicted by her embodiment in "plunging hooves":

> ⟨I rise, I rise, now⟩
> ⟨I am⟩ the arrow ⟨I am⟩ the ⟨rain⟩ dew that flies
> ⟨Into the sun's⟩
> In the cauldron of morning
> One white melt, upflung
> to the lover, the plunging
> Hooves I am, that over & over.

Plath tries and rejects in each of the three drafts phrasing about the female subject's dawn "rise" in favor of more urgent and purposeful motion. It seems even more significant that here the attraction that compels the union of dew and sun is not suicidal but sexual. All of Plath's figures in this draft are alike in stressing energy and mutability, but they lack the bodily integrity of the "acetelyne virgin" of "Fever."

As she revises, Plath refocuses the poem along a single trajectory, Godiva's daredevil ride at breakneck speed in which horse and rider are merged. The most significant changes occur in the third handwritten draft. The kinship that is claimed at the beginning of the poem ("Sister to the brown arc / Of the neck I cannot catch") is reconfirmed at the close of this draft. The final movement opens with an image in which horse and rider appear to coalesce: "O bright // beast, I / Am the arrow." The line breaks encourage the reader to interpret this vocative as an appositive, a fluid exchange of identities between radiant carnality and female subjectivity. Plath also reconnects the speaker to flesh in this draft by introducing the figure of Godiva. When, in the sixth stanza, Plath sexualizes the rider by adding "thighs" and "hair," she also considers a much longer treatment of the legend in a digression that covers a full page, or space equal to the draft for the entire poem so far. These stanzas, which are all later discarded, show the intrusion of material addressed in earlier poems. The "old dead men" that had been repeatedly killed in the drafts and finally eliminated from the last version of "Stings" reenter here: "Hands, hearts, dead men / Dead men / Hands, hearts, peel off—." In another stanza, Godiva appears an amalgam of the suffering martyrs of the rage poems and the avenging temptress of "Lady Lazarus":

In a season of burning, I
Am White Godiva
On fire, my hair

My one resort.

In the legend of Godiva, the importance of her naked ride to relieve the town of her husband's unjust tax is that it is an unseen spectacle. Her body is modestly veiled by her hair, and her chastity is protected by the town's willing refusal, except for peeping

Tom, to look. The potency of the icon in the popular imagination, however, is not in its inscription of female purity and its function to validate communal norms of propriety, but precisely in the repressed content of the legend, that is, our fascination with the forbidden image of the unclothed female body as a gesture of female daring and an object of male desire. In her transformation of Godiva, Plath exploits the erotic charge of her self-display and yet refocuses our attention on Godiva as subject rather than spectacle. Plath omits any reference to the male gaze, so prominent in the legend and so essential to "Fever," because she would free her speaker even more unequivocally from this dependence. In the single stanza Plath retains in the final poem, Godiva is defiantly antisocial, her desire an unconstrained liberty of self-definition: "White / Godiva, I unpeel— / Dead hands, dead stringencies." She is unashamed of her guilty pleasure in the exhilarating ride that eludes even maternal obligations and ignores the child's cry that "melts in the wall."

In the close of the poem Plath confronts what I take to be two opposing images for the next incarnation of her speaker and, in them, contrary implications for her poetics. Although the ending forges another blazing signature for the singular poet "at one with the drive" toward morning, the images she would merge have an ambiguous instability. Even more dramatically than in the willed triumph of the close of "Wintering," this poem incompletely suppresses a residual ambivalence between an identification with the flying arrow and the suicidal dew. Both images serve to retell the decade between her twentieth birthday and her thirtieth in a poetic shorthand. The phallic arrow recalls a maternal maxim about gender roles that Plath records in her journals and later revises in The Bell Jar. On the same morning in December 1958 that Plath reports the germ of her novel, she also complains of Hughes's lack of masculine drive: "Dick Norton's mother was not so wrong about a man supplying direction and a woman the warm, emotional power of faith and love. I feel we are as yet directionless" (J 285). Three years later when Plath reworked these journal entries in drafting The Bell Jar, she was the mother of a daughter herself, struggling to prove she was also a writer. When

Buddy Willard (the fictionalized Dick Norton) recites his mother's advice ("What a man is is an arrow into the future and what a woman is is the place the arrow shoots off from"), Esther Greenwood contemptuously dismisses the feminine role that Plath had earlier in her marriage endorsed: "The last thing I wanted was infinite security and to be the place an arrow shoots off from. I wanted change and excitement and to shoot off in all directions myself."[66] In "Ariel," the dichotomy between male ambition and envious female desire is erased in her assertion: "I / Am the arrow."

We have seen how Plath used the figure of suicide in "Daddy" and "Lady Lazarus" to mark psychic deaths and to demonstrate her capacity to manage her own resurrection. The Bell Jar manuscript itself on which she composed "Stings," "Lazarus," and "Fever" was palpable proof of her ability not only to survive her attempted suicide at twenty but to succeed as a writer a decade later. In her October letters, Plath's emotional distress is often apparent. Her urgency about reclaiming her poetic authority is uneasily balanced against her somewhat paranoid fears that everyone around her expects another breakdown. On October 16 she boasts, "I am writing the best poems of my life; they will make my name." Yet in the same letter she fantasizes that Hughes and Assia want her dead: "Ted & his woman (he will have the distinction of being her 4th husband, thank god I think she is barren) have already wistfully started wondering why I didn't commit suicide, since I did before! Ted has said how convenient it would be if I were dead, then he could sell the house and take the children whom he likes."[67] Plath called home on her birthday, and Aurelia later reports that "this second unhappy birthday out of 30" reminded her, as it must have Plath, of her twenty-first birthday spent in McLean's hospital after her attempted suicide.[68] Earlier in her journals Plath associates suicide with her writing blocks and her relationship with Aurelia: "How, by the way, does Mother understand my committing suicide? As a result of my not writing, no doubt. I felt I couldn't write because she would appropriate it" (J 281). In her emotional life, suicide represented one kind of revenge, poetry another. To pretend to court suicide in a poem

Ariel

October 27
1962

Stasis in darkness,
Then the substanceless blue
Pour of tor & distances.

God's lioness!
How one we grow!
Pivot of heels & knees! the furrow

Splits & passes
Sister to the brown arc
Of the neck I cannot catch,

Nigger-eye
Berries cast dark
Hooks, ~~but do not satisfy black~~

Black ~~black~~ sweet blood mouthfuls,
Shadows!
Something else

Hauls me through air—
Thighs, hair;
Flakes from my heels.   white
                                         Godiva, I unpeel—
And now I   Dead hands, dead
Foams to wheat, a glitter of seas.   stringencies!
The child's cry

Melts in the wall.
O bright beast, I
Am the arrow, the dew that flies
Suicidal, at one with the drive
Into the red
Eye, the cauldron of morning.

"Ariel," draft 3, page 1, composed October 17, 1962

~~Hands, hearts, dead men~~
~~Dead men~~
Hands, ~~hearts~~, peel off —
~~Old~~
Dead hands, dead stringencies!
~~I am bare~~
I am white
Godiva

Rising, galloper,
In a season of dying,
A season of burning.

In a season of burning, I
am White Godiva
On fire, my hair
My one resort
Brown furrows, rippling

White ~~Godiva, I~~
Godiva, I unpeel —
Dead hands, dead stringencies!

White
Godiva, I unpeel —
Dead hands, dead stringencies!

"Ariel," draft 3, page 2, composed October 17, 1962

was, I think, a calculated risk; by invoking it she called up her worst demons, but by writing beyond it she could prove both Hughes and Aurelia wrong.

Finally, the compelling evidence of Plath's revisions demonstrates that "Ariel" represents not an urge to disintegration but to articulation. In the third handwritten draft, Plath dramatically accelerates the pace of the poem by cutting the line length in half. She also positions the line breaks to produce a breathless syntactic suspension. The effect of both of these revisions is to focus the reader's attention on isolated words and phrasing while frustrating the desire for resolution. In the original handwritten draft almost the whole poem is composed in complete sentences. By disrupting and fragmenting these in her revision, Plath creates the illusion of pure energy in motion. The shift to intelligible, complete sentences, which comes only with the entrance of "White / Godiva" in the seventh stanza, is especially pronounced. At the same time, in the final third of the poem, Plath relocates the pronoun "I" to the ends of several lines. The poem ends with an intensification of identity rather than with its negation as the speaker's self-assertive "I" is magnified in the "red / Eye" (initially "heart") of the rising sun. Plath literally could not know what lay beyond the "cauldron of morning," yet in the poem she gathers momentum—she fully intended to enter London two days later as a rising star.[69]

Feb. 5
1963

Motherhood

The blood blooms

[...] woman is perf[...]
Her dead

Body wears the smile of accomplishment,
The illusion of a Greek necessity

Flows in the scrolls of her toga,
Her bare

Feet seem to be saying:
We have come so far, it is over,

[...] nothing [...] happen

[...] stiffen in air like beacons
[...] the roads and

Each dead child is coiled, a white serpent

[...] one at each little

Pitcher of milk, now empty.
She has folded

Them back into her body as
            body as
Of a rose close when the garden

Stiffens + odours bleed
From the sweet, deep throats of the night

The moon has nothing to be sad about,
Staring from her hood of bone.

She is used to this sort of thing.
Her blacks crackle + drag.

The Motherknot: "I cower and want, want and cower"

> Then I think of my gross fears at having a baby which I suppose center around that crucial episode at the Boston Lying-In, so many years ago when that anonymous groaning woman, shaved and painted all colors, got cut, blood ran, water broke, and the baby came with bloody veins and urinated in the doctor's face. Every woman does it: so I cower and want, want and cower. I also think of how far I fall short from the ideal of Doris Krook [Plath's tutor at Cambridge]— what a slipshod part-time scholar I am—no nun, no devotee. And how, on the other hand, very far I fall short from writing. . . . I dream and boast I could do it but don't and maybe can't. . . . Oh, the desire to write a novel and a book of poems before a baby. (J 220, April 29, 1958)

What Plath wanted from motherhood and from writing is entangled in knots like this one throughout her journals. She esteemed both as essential forms of self-realization; producing a book of poems or a baby was an accomplishment that would mark her as an adult. Without them she was still a student, an apprentice, a daughter. As intensely as she desired motherhood and writing as products, and as guaranteed sources of approval and recognition, however, she quailed equally before the prospect of self-imposed discipline that writing required and the loss of self-control that maternity seemed to threaten. "Cower and want, want and cower"—desire and dread contended against each other as she contemplated her options and measured her achievements in the years before the birth of Frieda and the acceptance of *Colossus*, her first book of poems, both in the spring of 1960. Not surprisingly, the knot that bound writing and motherhood as twin goals seemed most perplexing in the periods of her life in which she had made a commitment to full-time writing: a summer on Cape Cod, subsidized by her mother, before she returned to Smith College to teach; the year in Boston immediately afterward when she and Hughes tested their ability to survive on an income from writing; and the fall of that year when she accompanied Hughes to Yaddo, just after she became pregnant with Frieda. How thoroughly Plath had internalized the

1950s cultural convention that womanhood is proven by motherhood is evident in her conviction that "every woman does it"; she never questions that motherhood is an inevitable part of the definition of a successful woman in this script, but the legitimacy, even the reality of her writing is always in doubt and often appears a fraudulent dream. She perceived the conflict, the possibility that these might be mutually exclusive choices, but she was determined to prove that both were inherent expressive needs of her female sexual identity.

For Plath, children could be earned. They were anticipated as one of the rewards for honoring her calling as a writer: "All joy for me: love, fame, life work, and, I assume, children, depends on the central need of my nature: to be articulate, to hammer out the great surges of experience jammed, dammed, crammed in me over the last five years" (J 163). They could also be an escape, a justification for not writing: "There is no outer recalcitrant material to blame for snags and failures, only the bristling inner recalcitrance: sloth, fear, vanity, meekness.... I have even longed for that most fearsome first woman's ordeal: having a baby—to elude my demanding demons and have a constant excuse for lack of production in writing" (J 240–41). Motherhood promised to connect her to a world of external reality, of known obligations and recognized purpose when the failure to write seemed "a life of doing nothing," "ridiculously ingrown, sedentary" (J 254). Compared with the impalpable, unrealized identity of a writer who cannot write, motherhood once achieved could not be disproven: "Incompetence sickens me to scorn, disgusts me, and I am a bungler . . . rejected by an adult world, part of nothing—of neither an external career of Ted's— . . . nor a career of my own, nor, vicariously, the life of friends, nor part of motherhood—I long for an external view of myself and my room to confirm its reality. Vague aims—to write—fail, stillborn" (J 252). As here, Plath's failures to produce, to deliver a viable writing self, are often described in images of botched births: "a bloodily breached twenty-year plan of purpose" (J 251). She could also castigate herself as a "purposeless woman with dreams of grandeur" who longs "to fill myself up with some external reality— where people accept phone bills, meal-getting, babies, marriage, as part of the purpose to the universe" (J 261).

While she recognized that some women from the older generation appeared to have sacrificed life for art, or at least heterosexuality for scholarship, she was determined that her youth, her ambition, and her sexual drive could not be compromised: "Are these women, this Miss Burton, this old Miss Welsford (who is coming to the end of her vigor) better for their years reading and writing articles . . . and fearing the bright brilliant young ones like Dr. Krook? I would live a life of conflict, of balancing children, sonnets, love and dirty dishes; and banging banging an affirmation of life out on pianos and ski slopes and in bed in bed in bed" (J 125). Three years later, pregnant at Yaddo, she dreaded that a child might be dangerous to her own self-determination: "Challenge of baby when I am so unformed and unproductive as a writer. A fear for the meaning and purpose of my life. I will hate a child that substitutes itself for my own purpose: so I must make my own" (J 329).

Finally, the knot of motherhood and writing was itself ensnarled with the tangle of mother-daughter relations. Plath's wish to be a mother was connected to her desire to be mothered, to be connected to a matrilineal heritage by reproducing her mother's choices. Yet here, too, her desire for approval, connection, and continuity was contested by her dread of disappointing the other mothers, like her teachers, who recommended nunlike devotion to career: "I cried about other mothers coming to take care of their daughters for a while, with babies. Talked of how I could let Mother have her limited pleasure if I were 'grown up' enough not to feel jeopardized by her manipulating me. I sidestepped this problem ingeniously: talked of M. E. Chase, lesbians. . . . I am also afraid of M. E. C. . . . You think all old women are magical witches. The crux is my desire to be manipulated. . . . How can I find myself & be sure of my identity?" (J 290). Plath recognized that the same gesture that would delight and confirm her mother also meant displacing her; her own maternity was unequivocal proof of her adult sexuality, a sexuality Plath as daughter felt her mother blamed: "Why guilt: as if sex, even legally indulged in, should be 'paid for' by pain? I would probably interpret pain as a judgment: birth-pain, even a deformed child. Magical fear Mother will become a child, my child: an old hag child" (J 287).

The mother's ghost, as self-sacrificing provider and expectant audience, hung over the writing desk as much as the marriage bed, especially during the Cape Cod summer she had funded. Plath's anxiety of authorship, with its cross-gendered metaphors, and the anxiety of a daughter trying to give birth to herself as a writer were so deeply entwined there seems no severing them: "The virginal page, white. The first: broken into and sent packing. All the dreams, the promises: wait till I can write again, and then the painful botched rape of the first page. Nothing said. . . . Slowly with great hurt, like giving birth to some endless and primeval baby" (J 161). What is striking in these entries is that Plath conceives of both writing and maternity as fearful ordeals whose outcome is uncertain; the biological metaphor that links them promises not organic maturation or the relief of delivery but struggle, pain, endless labor, and chthonic fears of monstrous offspring. She depends on writing and motherhood to confirm her identity, yet in the violence of her affirmations she confesses her apprehension that she might instead be extinguished or supplanted in the process.[1]

Domestic Ambitions, Literary Models

There is considerable evidence in both her letters and her journals that Plath was deluded, or at least beguiled, by the prevailing constructions of femininity and female sexuality in ways that exacerbated her self-doubt (in the roles of career woman and mother alike) and that underwrote her deference, sometimes feigned but often genuine, to Hughes in defining her own literary ambitions. Nonetheless, as Plath struggled to forge a link between writing and maternity, I believe she was, more self-consciously than not, aligning herself with approved cultural scripts for women and positioning herself as a writer within two literary traditions, one male and one female.

Plath's domestic ambitions are clearly shaped by the decade's relentless marketing of homemaking and motherhood as full-time vocations, often suitable careers for college-educated women. She and Aurelia heard Adlai Stevenson's commencement address to her Smith graduating class (which also included Stevenson's future daughter-in-law). Ironically, Aurelia, widow and working mother, attended Plath's graduation on a stretcher, debilitated by a bleeding ulcer, one symptom of the stress of mothering Sylvia. Their shared memories of Aurelia's selfless devotion to Otto's career might have made them sympathetic to Stevenson's plea that women "rescue us wretched slaves of specialization and group thinking from further shrinkage and contraction of mind and spirit." Stevenson's address itself, however, suggests he knew his advice ran counter to the expectations of his female audience:

> Once immersed in the very pressing and particular problems of domesticity, many women feel frustrated and far apart from the great issues and stirring debate for which their education has given them understanding and relish. . . . Once they wrote poetry. Now it's the laundry list. Once they discussed art and philosophy until late in the night. Now they are so tired they fall asleep as soon as the dishes are finished. There is, often, a sense of contraction, of closing horizons and lost opportunities. They had hoped to play their part in the crises of the age. But what they do is wash the diapers.

His charge to the class of 1955 counseled not resignation about these contracting horizons but a rededication to the role of moral guide and educator: "The assignment for you, as wives and mothers, has great advantages. In the first place, it is home work—you can do it in the living room with a baby in your lap, or in the kitchen with a can opener in your hands. If you're really clever, maybe you'll even practice your saving arts on the unsuspecting man while he's watching television."[2] Yet the widespread reiteration of these pleas, in popular culture and public ideology, for women to accept their "natural" place in the home no longer masks the cultural strain that was actually under way. Rigid, prescriptive, and no doubt persuasive as the 1950s ideology was for many women, male encomiums to the vocations of housewife and mother were, in part, an anxious reaction to women's actual growing independence from the home.[3] As educated women became rivals in the workplace and competitors for careers, the advice columns (and commencement addresses) more insistently portrayed them as willingly satisfied by the joy of cooking and modern child-rearing or, in popular fiction, punished women as unthinkingly compliant sexual bodies, calculating innocents, or castrating mothers.[4]

Plath was a canny reader of her culture's cues who exploited sources of approval by appearing to conform to cultural norms and yet who revised them to make room for her own exceptional behavior. If she seems unself-conscious in accepting the valorization of motherhood, she also used it as camouflage for her literary ambitions. By twinning these goals she made her desire for public fame appear part of the approved domestic script: "We will publish a bookshelf of books between us before we perish! And a batch of brilliant healthy children" (J 154). She never outgrew her faith that a perfect lemon meringue pie was a triumph worth recording in her journal, but she was capable of mocking her own glorification of domesticity: "I go make an apple pie, or study *The Joy of Cooking*, reading it like a rare novel. Whoa, I said to myself. You will escape into domesticity & stifle yourself by falling head-first into a bowl of cookie batter." Even as she recognized that her absorption in the kitchen was an escape from the study, she claimed a literary model in Virginia Woolf: "She works off her depression over rejections from *Harper's* . . . by cleaning out the kitchen" (J 152).

In privileging the home as both professional working space and spiritualized domestic space, Plath selectively rejected certain assumptions about the nuclear family while ardently embracing others. She often gloated that she and Ted had willingly resisted the American Dream of "a job, a steady career," "a lifelong street address within easy driving distance of an American supermarket" (J 254). At the same time, she insistently interpreted, to herself in her journals no less than to her mother in her letters, the life of full-time writing that anchored her and Hughes to their home as an idyll of togetherness, one that exceeded the most Utopian descriptions of the women's magazines. Nonetheless, she was as often rankled that the dishes, mopping, and bed-making kept her from her desk as she found occasion to rejoice that her husband made the oatmeal. However willing Hughes was as soulmate and exceptional as househusband, Plath was nagged by worries that he lacked direction, that he was too rigid in refusing to work in order to guarantee a household income, and, later, that he was too willing to live off a writing grant she had won. While she aspired to produce the formula fiction of the women's magazines in both America and England, she readily perceived the contradictions between the myth of happy marriages they promoted and the symptoms of female distress such myths produced: "Irony upon irony: *McCall's*, the 'magazine of togetherness,' is running a series of articles on illegitimate babies and abortions, an article called 'Why Men Desert Their Wives'; three stories and articles considered, seriously here, humorously there, suicide from boredom, despair, or embarrassment" (J 212).[5]

Plath's search for appropriate literary models, no less than her selective adoption of cultural values, reveals a need to fuse female sexuality and literary mastery. In the letters to Aurelia in the first flush of her courtship with Hughes, and in the beginning of his role as muse, mentor, critic, and rival, Plath places herself by claiming to have bested the male modernists: "I am . . . drunker than Dylan, harder than Hopkins, younger than Yeats in my saying. Ted reads in his strong voice; is my best critic, as I am his" (LH 243). In a parallel move, she distances herself from female precursors: "Ted says he never read poems by a woman like mine; they are strong and full and rich—not quailing and whining like Teasdale or simple lyrics like Millay; they are working, sweating, heaving poems born out of the way words should be said" (LH 244). Her ambivalent relationship to both the male and the female literary traditions she needed to define herself within and against is clear: Can she claim the male sexual bravado as her own? Can she avoid the taint of "poetess"? Sandra Gilbert and Susan Gubar offer the term "affiliation complex" to describe the twentieth-century woman writer's coexisting, and often competing, allegiances to literary fathers and mothers.[6] An aspiring woman writer wants to adopt female precursors as empowering ancestors but also needs to ward off participating in what she perceives as a trivializing tradition of "lady writers." Plath, like generations of women writers before her, sought to recover examples of female greatness as reassurance that her gender was not an obstacle to literary creativity. Yet in the process of noticing, even isolating, gender as the most salient characteristic of these writers, a would-be poet like Plath with ambitions to be "a woman famous among women"(J 260) simultaneously fears being tainted with all the pejorative associations with which male culture and a male-defined literary tradition have discredited and belittled women's increasing competition in the literary sphere.[7]

Choosing to affiliate with a female literary tradition would mean that, as in any mother-daughter bond, even an elective one, the ambitious writer would find as many points of painful abrasion as models for emulation. Plath constantly rewrote her literary gene-alogy on the mother's side to range herself among the greats and to purge it of any unsuitable characteristics, as in this boast in her journals:

> Arrogant, I think I have written lines which qualify me to be The Poetess of America (as Ted will be The Poet of England and her dominions). Who rivals? Well, in history Sappho, Elizabeth Barrett Browning, Christina Rossetti, Amy Lowell, Emily Dickinson, Edna St. Vincent Millay—all dead. Now: Edith Sitwell and Marianne Moore, the aging giantesses, and poetic godmother Phyllis McGinley is out—light verse: she's sold herself. Rather: May Swenson, Isabella Gardner, and most close, Adrienne Cecile Rich—who will soon be eclipsed by these eight poems. (J 211)

It is significant that she names Rich as her arch-rival; Rich threat-ened Plath on two fronts since, although she was a near contem-porary at Radcliffe, she was already two books ahead and the second was coeval with the birth of her first son. Plath frequently conflated poetic and sexual jealousy. When Anne Sexton's lover George Starbuck won the Yale Younger Poets prize Plath thought she herself deserved, she plotted a short story that killed Sexton's children (to punish her for being a bad mother? for being an adulterer?). She also imagined Starbuck as her lover in revenge for Sexton's vicarious poetic triumph (J 310–11).

Plath mentions more female models in her private writing, especially her journals, and refers to them more frequently than any male writers, often exhorting herself to reread the established women writers of the 1950s, including Katherine Anne Porter, Jean Stafford, and Eudora Welty—women old enough to be her mother. Much as she envied their accomplishments and felt she must learn from them, Plath often faults women writers in sexually stereotyped terms: May Swenson has "mere virtuosity with little root" (J 317); Elizabeth Hardwick creates "characters utterly unlikable in any way" (J 310). For Plath, the stylistic risks of affiliating with women writers were an exaggeration of feminine sensibility ("the facile Isabella Gardner and even the lesbian and fanciful Elizabeth Bishop" [J 189]) or a reaction against it ("an abstractionist man-imitator, or a bitter, sarcastic Dorothy Parker or Teasdale" [LH 277]). She complained of the feminine traits in her own writing, "a bland ladylike archness or slightness" (J 172), a "crystal-brittle and sugar-faceted voice" (J 194). Even in her most admired literary mother, Virginia Woolf, Plath deplored a similar sexual anemia: "Surely this is not Life, not even real life: there is not even the ladies magazine entrance into sustained loves, jealousies, boredoms. The recreation is that of the most superficial observer at a party of dull old women who have never spilt blood" (J 306–7). While it seems altogether plausible that such criticism is a form of self-defense, a way of distancing herself from the powerful female precursor in order not to be overwhelmed by her example, Plath's objections are often focused on Woolf's absence of reproductive sexuality in ways that pointedly recall the dilemma of her own self-definition.[8]

At times Plath represented the necessary focus for her writing as a nunnish devotion and could admire other women writers' solitary productivity, as she did May Swenson's when she was a fellow guest at Yaddo: "Independent, self-possessed M. S. Ageless. . . . My old admiration for the strong, if lesbian, woman. The relief of limitation as a price for surety and balance" (J 329). But more often she fantasized her birth as a writer as a sexualized fusion of her two chosen literary parents, Woolf and Lawrence: "I felt mystically that if I read Woolf, read Lawrence (these two, why? their vision, so different, is so like mine) I can be itched and kindled to a great work: burgeoning, fat with the texture and substance of life: This my call, my work. This gives my being a name, a meaning" (J 196). To repair the damaged or deficient mother, Plath pairs her with Lawrence of "rich physical passion," and after this erotic quickening, she becomes pregnant with her own subject. Plath positions herself as both the issue of this literary fertilization and its bearer, and she marks the moment when the avid daughter-reader renames herself mother-writer.[9]

The Mother Who Writes: Theorizing Motherhood

Does it matter that the woman who writes is also a mother?

Feminist literary critics have amply documented how and why the identities of author and mother have not been personally compatible or culturally conceivable for many writing women in the Anglo-American tradition during the last several centuries. These studies have made visible the ways that both maternity and writing are culturally constructed activities whose shifting meanings are indelibly marked by interpenetrating ideologies of gender and power. For example, Gilbert and Gubar, among others, have detailed a literary history in which the nineteenth-century woman writer anxiously defined her literary vocation against a set of dominant cultural myths that represented woman and writer, motherhood and authorship, babies and books as mutually exclusive categories. If superimposed in the practice of an actual writing woman, these categories had the effect of violently canceling one of the terms rather than of questioning their binary opposition, so that her desire for literary expression could be perceived and experienced as unnatural or unsexing, and her labor over a book could be seen as a monstrously deformed pregnancy whose issue, if brought to light at all, might well be regarded as an abomination by her culture, her family, and the writer herself.[10]

Initially, feminist theorists attempted to disentangle the cultural expectations and the personal experience of motherhood by articulating the discrepancies between them. Reviewing her child-bearing years, Adrienne Rich proposed that she could distinguish motherhood as institution—the social structure of behavior and meanings that claims mother love is selfless and unconditional and that a mother's identity is confirmed and completed by children—from motherhood as experience. The subjective experience of motherhood Rich described is an often conflicted state in which a mother feels both empathy and rage toward her children; the tension between defining herself in terms of her relation to and responsibility for her children and as someone apart from them, who rejects or resents the demands of mothering as an invasion or obliteration of the autonomous selfhood necessary to write, produces paralyzing guilt and silence as often as poetry.[11] Yet in laying bare the idealization of motherhood that made some mothers' stories unwriteable or their authors perverse and unwomanly, Rich was overly optimistic that falsifying ideology and authentic experience were separable strands in the densely woven text of maternity.

Feminist critics who would investigate the subjectivity of mothers have become more self-conscious about the ways that subjectivity itself is always mediated, mapped, or created through discourse, and thus the authentic experience Rich would reclaim is not only unrecoverable but nonexistent. Those who critique the cultural mythology pay increasing attention in their analyses to the ways in which we inevitably internalize and collude in the reproduction of those myths. Feminist theorizing, always in part a reflexive, self-analytical act, now recognizes more fully that any woman who is a mother—or who represents the experience of mothering in art or who theorizes about mothering—was herself the daughter of a mother and so participates doubly in the systems of meaning that structure the mother-daughter exchange. This realization means that even as we search for the mother lost or damaged through her appropriation by the dominant ideology, our search is inscribed by the "Master Mother Discourse," especially in our desire for and fear of maternal omnipotence and our feelings of betrayal at maternal powerlessness.[12]

Still that search continues. In recent literary studies the locus of investigation has shifted from motherhood as ideology and institution toward mothers as psychoanalytic or linguistic subjectivities. A project shared by critics as different as Margaret Homans, Marianne Hirsch, Susan Suleiman, Domna Stanton, and Gilbert and Gubar is a desire to articulate the woman writer's relationship to language and to systems of symbolic representation. Each takes as a necessary task the revision of inherited psychoanalytical scripts for mother-child relations in order to propose an altered understanding of female reproduction and symbolic representation and the links between them. Refuting, revising, or recombining Freud, Lacan, Kristeva, Klein, Winnicott, and Chodorow, these critics seek to formulate or analyze a new myth. They acknowledge that what they hope to produce is not so much a corrected version of female reality as an alternative myth whose explanatory power will prevail in explaining how and why women write. Their theories are alike in the preemptive moves by which they hypothesize female primacy in their narratives of desire and language.[13] Most feminist critics engaged in this revision insistently place mother and daughter (rather than son) at the center of their scripts, and they emphasize the presymbolic communion mother and daughter share during and, most emphasize, beyond a pre-oedipal moment. What they posit are images of mother-daughter connection and continuity that change the register of female development from one of lack, exclusion, and belatedness to one of originary wholeness, pleasure, and precedence. In place of the endless postponement of an insatiable desire that leads to language and symbol, Homans, Hirsch, and Suleiman imagine a continuum of erotic attachment and fulfillment between mother and daughter that survives the daughter's entry into the law of the father and does not require a symbolic substitution of paternal word for maternal flesh.[14]

What feminist literary theorists gain from this reconfiguration of the myths is not only a reconstructed "feminist family romance" that, Hirsch observes, may make available new narratives for adult behavior,[15] but a new myth of origins that rewrites female difference as prehistorical and psychological advantage rather than as cultural damage. As literary critics, their objectives seem to be to locate difference in this mythic, and so unverifiable, realm in order to assign a positive rather than a negative valuation to the distinctiveness they describe in women's literary production and, at the same time, to suggest that this difference is a given rather than something that must be proven. Although a monocausal myth of the origins of difference in women's writing has as a primary motive, I believe, a change in emphasis from reading gender as a liability for a woman writer toward seeing her relationship to language as privileged and polyvocal, these critics acknowledge that such a writer, nonetheless, may be ambivalent about her participation in both the male domain of figurative language and the maternal realm of presymbolic language.

If women enter language differently because of their gender, if they undertake symbolic representation with more ambivalence and with a residual, competing attachment to nonsymbolic or preverbal communication learned as daughters and reproduced as mothers, what would be the signs of such differences in their literary practice? Homans suggests that maternal language may appear as rhythmic nonsense; as an identification with the literal, the natural, or the bodily; as a pleasure in denomination over figuration; or in a variety of symbolic representations she identifies as "bearing the word" that "bring together the thematics of women's experience and some aspect of women's special relation to language."[16] Yet Homans notices that to be in the position of a mother-writer as a "speaking subjectivity within an androcentric literary tradition" is to experience divided loyalties "between her own interest in a literal mother-daughter language and her desire at once to placate and to enter the symbolic realm of literary language."[17] Homans proposes that because the dominant cultural myths suppress the nonsymbolic mother-child language by renaming it silence or nonsense, the mother who writes may feel endangered by maternity, may feel that it threatens her literacy. One of the markers of this phenomenon may be an intense ambivalence, an ambivalence, I would argue, toward both metaphor and motherhood. As a result of this split allegiance, the mother-daughter language may be distrusted or appear to be devalued in the woman writer's own narrative. Finally, although Homans persuasively theorizes the existence of mother-daughter communion, she is less successful in producing unmistakable evidence of its pure presence in literary practice.[18] It seems to me unlikely that such a communion will survive the transition into representation, yet its residue does seem palpable in the tension Homans describes. The markers of maternal discourse evoked by French critics are similarly elusive. The French writers most often appealed to by American feminist literary critics—Kristeva, Irigaray, and Cixous—have variously described its presence as disruption, musicality, plurality, fluidity, sexual pleasure, and emanations from the female body. However attractive these seem as descriptions of an alternative discourse, they remain, as Domna Stanton cogently warns, essentially metaphors for avant-garde literary practice (rather than the signs of specifically female stylistic difference), and these metaphors may themselves underwrite the phallocentric logic they are meant to disrupt or displace.[19]

Rather than attempting to define female difference outside or before the patriarchal order, other feminist literary critics examine how the dominant cultural myths structure the relationship between women's procreativity and their artistic creativity at a particular historical moment. When a woman conceives her brainchild (the novel or poem she would author), does she understand or enact this metaphor—that proposes literary activity is analogous to gestation and birth—in the same way a male writer does? Susan Friedman traces the long literary history of male writers' appropriation of female reproduction as analogy for their mental creativity to demonstrate that the male figuration, rather than dismantling gender distinctions, works to rigidify cultural dichotomies based on gender: men create through mental activity and the agency of language what women more appropriately, and less self-consciously, accomplish through their bodies.[20] Susan Suleiman notes the gender asymmetry that often accompanies an analogy between books and babies: "The male writer, in comparing his books to tenderly loved children (a common metaphor, at least until the recent emphasis on writing as autoerotic activity), could see his metaphorical maternity as something *added* to his male qualities, the childless woman whose books 'replaced' real children too often thought (was made to feel) that she had less, not more."[21] Not only are these gendered distinctions in the metaphor culturally policed to confine women to procreation, they often punish female trespass, as Barbara Johnson notes: "It is as though male writing were by nature procreative, while female writing is somehow by nature infanticidal."[22] For the mother who is also a poet, however, is there a possibility that these two forms of generativity are congruent rather than contradictory? cumulatively powerful and reciprocally self-confirming?

Taken together the range of critical opinion delineates a continuum from, at one end, a conviction that motherhood and authorhood are irreconcilable opposites, both in cultural scripts and in mothers' lived experience, to a belief that a woman's procreative potential could or should make her naturally suited for creative labor. Friedman is the most optimistic that birthing and writing are potentially reconcilable. In tracing women artists' use of the childbirth metaphor, she argues for a historical progression from instances that confirm the patriarchal separation of creativities, to those that suggest a guilty trespass on male prerogatives, to her final prediction of a body-based poetics that privileges motherhood as the model of all creativity.[23] The reversal in the meaning of the metaphor depends not only on shifting attitudes or opportunities of the writer but also on the confirming presence of a female reader who "knows the author has the biological capacity men lack to birth both books and babies" and who will simultaneously appreciate her subversive intention, that "woman's reclamation of the pregnant Word is itself a transcendence of historical prescription."[24] In examining contemporary literary representations of motherhood by mothers, Suleiman finds, by contrast, a persistent and always uneasy tension between a specular self-awareness of the mother who interacts with her child in order to produce art and her self-forgetful involvement that nurtures them. To appease the child (or the mother in herself) the artist may choose not to write the book, or to offer the book to her children. The mother might also court cruelty or madness by distancing herself from the child and its demands in order to feed the artist. Between these two extremes lies the mother-artist's guilty fantasy of her child's total dependence and her own omnipotence that makes her choice for art always an anguished rejection of maternity: "With every word I write, with every metaphor, with every genuine act of creation, I hurt my child."[25] Like Suleiman, Alicia Ostriker contends that writing contradicts mothering. She situates the position of the mother as artist in even more excruciating jeopardy. For Ostriker the birth of the artist requires the rupture of her ties as daughter as well as her bonds as mother: "A woman and her mother, or a woman and her child, already are one flesh whether she wishes it or not. . . . As they commend and blame her, so she does herself. Their power over her seems infinite—until it lapses, frays, wanes, or until she breaks it. The fact is that she can never become a poet—never can become an autonomous being—unless that bond is broken. . . . And then when it is broken, she wants to recover it. Without it, she is not whole."[26] All these feminist literary critics would agree that the distance and difference between maternity and literary creativity are ideologically dependent and historically contingent—that is, at historical moments and in particular cultural contexts in which motherhood is represented as the only, natural, best, or most satisfying identity for women, the chasm between the terms of the metaphor that would join them is experienced by both male and female readers as most profound.

Metaphor and Maternity

For Sylvia Plath the 1950s and early 1960s were such a historical moment. In her journals she inscribed her own twin goals of becoming a famous poet and a perfect mother against cultural myths and family scripts that defined female self-expression as most perfectly realized in the domestic drama of child-rearing. In the poetry she wrote as a mother, I believe Plath needed to revise the central metaphor these feminist critics have identified. Are writing and maternity congruent or contradictory? Is metaphor analogous to mothering or an ambivalent defense against it? Motherhood was not a stable, unified, or transparent category to Plath; rather, what it might mean had to be refigured repeatedly in the Ariel poems.

For Plath, making poems and making babies were persistent metaphors for each other. A pair of poems that illustrate this habit were written at either end of a six-month writing block. "You're" was the first poem she composed in 1960; Plath wrote no more poems until "Stillborn" in July.[27] Roughly midway between these poems, Frieda, Plath's first child, was born on April 1. "You're" is a manic riddle about pregnancy: the developing fetus is anticipated, but never named, through a string of metaphors. The poet's wit and the body's health generate surprising forms ("a sprat in a pickle jug. / A creel of eels"); like a puzzle she works twice in rapid succession, the poem moves through two stanzas of nine lines each with a manner at once exuberantly playful and deliberately offhand.[28] The poet's production of metaphors (mostly similes) confidently outpaces her pregnancy and promises a satisfying solution to nine months of guessing: "Right, like a well-done sum. / A clean slate, with your own face on." By contrast, "Stillborn" represents her failed poems as abortive births. What is particularly revealing here, given Plath's later poems about her children, is the way these stillborn poems fail to acknowledge their creator. Their inert smugness refuses to verify her maternity: "They smile and smile and smile and smile at me. / . . . / But they are dead, and their mother near dead with distraction, / And they stupidly stare, and do not speak of her." What "You're" predicts as a pleasurable otherness about the child ("with your own face on") is lamented here as progeny whose "stupid stare" maddeningly fails to reflect their author. Plath's worst fear about producing babies or words, at least as she represents these activities in her poetry, seems to have been that their inevitable separateness questions rather than confirms her identity as their maker. While the poem written in anticipation of Frieda's birth seems to support Friedman's contention that motherhood and writing are twin creative capacities, the poem written in the aftermath of four months of actual mothering doubts it.

If metaphor represented for Plath her self-conscious poetic authority, blood could sometimes be its opposite figure, the sign of the female body beyond her control. "Cut" is one of a group of poems (including "The Tour," and "Poppies in October") written within a few days of each other in late October 1962 in which her maternal identity is unspoken but, I believe, nevertheless intensely at issue. "Cut" was composed on October 24, the same day Plath wrote two poems to Nicholas, "By Candlelight" and "Nick and the Candlestick." "Cut" is another metaphor-driven poem whose apparent task is to turn a female domestic accident— slicing her thumb badly in the kitchen—into macabre humor. Yet I think what is more centrally at risk are her control and productivity as a poet, both of which are threatened by her vulnerability as a single parent. By the end of October, Plath had been alone in Devon for at least a month; after Hughes moved back to London and his lover in September, Plath had hired a string of nannies, none of whom stayed more than a few days. Her letters to Aurelia indicate that her rancor about money, domestic help, and the neighbors' gossip about her marriage was as virulent as the fevers she suffered. A month later, in a Thanksgiving letter, she is still complaining about the "botched job" her local doctor made treating this injury (LH 481).

Plath drafted this poem, as she did about two-thirds of those she wrote in October, on the back of a typescript of her novel. Yet the day after "Cut" was written, these magical pages ran out. The moment of the accident and the circumstances of composition could have only added to her feelings of desertion, depletion, and exhaustion, in which doctors, nannies, and neighbors all seemed hostile rather than merely unavailable to her. The poem is dedicated to Susan O'Neill Roe, the young nurse who began spending days at the cottage just two days before the accident. The dedication is added later, sometime in late December or January when Plath prepared the typescript for the *Ariel* volume in London. Although Plath's letters reveal how much she enjoyed Susan's companionship and how much she depended on the nurse's help to facilitate her move to London, she was disheartened when Roe left the day after the move for a vacation and to return to work at a children's hospital in January.[29] The dedication of the poem may have ambivalently marked both her remembered gratitude and yet another desertion.

The poem's metaphors tabulate male defections, but they also serve (like the verbal contest in "You're") to prove her poetic fecundity, her imaginative agility. Plath chooses metaphoric mastery as the best defense against the losses incurred in this accident, an accident that reveals, in the end, a particularly sexual wounding. The speaker's tone is unrelievedly bright and flippant, although the images themselves are all of violent conflict:

What a thrill—
My thumb instead of an onion.

> . . . .
> Little pilgrim
> The Indian's axed your scalp
>
> . . . .
> A celebration, this is,
> Out of a gap
> A million soldiers run,
> Redcoats, every one.

The poem challenges the reader to match her metaphoric audacity; we may be put off balance by the disparity in measure (American history reduced to a campy soap opera) and mood, but we are also amused, and for the same reasons. The hurtling rhymes flaunt their comic virtuosity: "turkey wattle" is echoed by "bottle"; patterns of exact monosyllabic end rhymes (run/one, ill/kill, man/klan) and internal assonance and consonance appear and disappear with dexterous unpredictability. It is significant that the wounded woman writer appropriates icons of male history for this mock-heroic skirmish. All but one of her imaginative creations marshaled here are little mannequins (not little women) who betray her by deserting her. The poet's self-parody permits a curious seepage between her astonished pain and a vein of male heroism that is simultaneously pricked. The production of male metaphors speeds up in the second half of the poem to generate "saboteur," "kamikaze man," and "Ku Klux Klan" within four lines. Despite the vengeful exuberance with which the speaker denounces male aggression, the ending reveals distinctively female self-doubts about her creative authority.

Surprisingly, any marker of specifically female gender is nearly absent from the imagery of the published poem. In fact in none of the language of the drafts does any hint of female gender appear until the last three stanzas of the poem, the only ones to undergo substantial revision in the remarkably clean drafts. In the eighth stanza, the darkening gauze bandage is compared to a Ku Klux Klan headdress and then is immediately superimposed, in the next line, over "babushka." The grandmotherly softening of the image, however, seems belated and out of character with an intensifying pattern of male violence and hardly relieves the gore of the stained and bloodied headwrap. Originally the poem closed with a return to male impersonation in which the speaker mocks the injured thumb as a "trepanned veteran / Amputee / thumb stump" and ridicules the heart's pained response to it: "You wince like a girl." Here femaleness is correlated with cowardice or an unheroic self-regard that would acknowledge pain. When Plath first revised the ending (within the first draft), she kept the wince but dropped its negative attribution to a girl. But something much more dramatic happens in her revisions of the final stanza in the second draft. The barrage of name-calling includes a new element:

How you ⟨wince⟩ jump—
Trepanned veteran,
Dirty ⟨Pale amputee, pearly⟩ girl,
Thumb stump.

We jump, especially if we are female readers, at the unexpected "dirty girl." Retrospectively, the darkening bloodstain that tarnishes the gauze wrapping evokes not just a wound but our sexuality. What is strangely disquieting for a female reader is that this final naming is itself a form of self-sabotage; we are pained by the alienation it produces and represents for us, by the evidence that the female speaker has necessarily internalized her culture's revulsion at female blood, sexuality, and domesticity. After all these male masquerades, the ebullient wit and rhyming agility of her performance, the woman writer who is confined to the role of scullery maid rewounds herself by unmasking the misogyny within. In the draft, Plath played with "⟨pale amputee⟩" and "⟨pearly⟩ girl," neither of which delivers the same cultural punch to the solar plexus. Plath pretends in "Cut" to counter a reckless waste of blood by an extravagant display of poetic energy; yet in this final unveiling she recognizes that the sexual bleeding that makes maternity possible also makes assertions of control, mastery, and secure identity more problematic.

In both "Poppies in July" and "Poppies in October" Plath again reads blood as a gendered, in fact, sexualized correspondence between the speaker's expressive health and the scene she witnesses and records. In each, the bloom of blood is the signature of gender—in the first, of female victimization; in the second, of the "astounding" female possibility of generating an unstoppable flow. A poem written almost immediately after her discovery of Hughes's infidelity, "Poppies in July" imagines the poppies marked by domestic violence: "A mouth just bloodied. / Little bloody skirts!" In the first draft for this poem, this passage shows considerable reworking. Earlier attempts include "A mouth just ⟨left by a fist, smashed by bad news⟩" and "O the sudden flush of blood that ⟨means⟩ says: No life." Both alternates testify to the link Plath felt between sexual wounding and poetic silencing. Although the poem also contains images of self-immolation and fever that will emerge as central in "Burning the Letters" in August and "Fever 103°" in October, the primary link between poppies and poet is female blood. If in July the poppies speak to her double wound, in October they offer "a love gift / Utterly unasked for." The poet's glance exposes private female parts in a series of revelations that are unseemly but irrepressibly thrilling: "Even the sun-clouds this morning cannot manage such skirts. / Nor the woman in the ambulance / Whose red heart blooms through her coat so astoundingly." That these correspondences between the poppies, the street scene, and the astonished female witness are gender-linked is underscored by a revision Plath makes in the first draft, when the original "man in the ambulance" becomes "woman." Written on her birthday and marking a trip to London to record her latest poems for the BBC,[30] "Poppies in October" sees the blood rush as an announcement of shared female vitality. Here skirts, blood, and mouths testify not to cultural or marital damage as in "Cut" or "Poppies in July" but to an unexpected and expressive excess that reclaims and implicitly renames her vital poet: "O my God, what am I / That these late mouths should cry open / In a forest of frost, in a dawn of cornflowers."

The Poet at Risk: Mothering the Monster

Many of Plath's poems about maternity visit dark enclosures that feminist critics have explored as specifically female space, whether a mythic underworld or the female body itself. These interiors are often unknowable by rational means; daring to descend within them means risking the loss of vision, speech, mobility, and self-control. In their most benign forms, these caverns are capable of causing mysterious transmutations, including seasonal or personal rebirth. Because they embody the realm of natural processes, they may promise gestation as well as death. But these inner recesses are always ambivalently charged for a woman: they suggest her power to contain new life, and yet what she produces may in turn confine her, as biology overtakes identity and the mother-child dyad swallows the singular poet.[31] Plath exploited the ready female symbolic equivalencies between the womb, a demonic underworld, and domestic interiors. What is distinctive is the way she drew the boundaries around these enclosures. Plath's repeated inscription of these boundaries, I would argue, traces the essential paradox of the poet's relationship to maternity. At times she draws the line to defend herself against the threats to rationality and literacy that maternal language poses. In other poems, the boundary encircles the wordless bodily communion between mother and child that she would protect against disruption or intrusion. The collapse or crossing of these borders always means an extinction of part of the writing or mothering self. The speaker in these poems anxiously has her eye on an edge, a horizon, or a threshold, which, even when it delimits outer from inner dark, is fragile, tenuous, suspect. Whatever its fascination, mystery, or pleasure to the mother, confinement to the body or the nursery is also terrifying. Within these perimeters, the poet finds herself home to "black bat airs," "cold homicides" (in "Nick and the Candlestick"); "unintelligible syllables" (in "The Arrival of the Bee Box"); "asininity, decay, possession" (in "Wintering"); and the "lopped blood-caul of absences" (in "Thalidomide"). Intimacy within these spaces can be chilling, even life-threatening.

In "The Arrival of the Bee Box" the poet investigates the line between poetic control and maternal obligation. Crossing the boundary into the suffocating locked box of her clamoring dependents courts madness; trying to define and defend a barrier between them hints at cultural trespass. Ostriker claims the bizarre imagery of much maternal poetry is born of the awareness that the child is "an uncontrollable other, absorbing and exhausting its mother" and that their interactions are skirmishes in which the mother's craziness is only narrowly averted;[32] Plath's speaker reassures herself "I have simply ordered a box of maniacs. / They can be sent back." When the speaker guesses innocently that the locked bee box might contain a "square baby," she triggers a metaphoric association that unsettles the rest of the poem. While I do not claim that the narrative of beekeeping is only a pretext, and that maternity is the disguised urtext, I would argue that the ways in which keeping bees is not like giving birth allowed Plath to defamiliarize some of the myths about motherhood. Each of the assertions she makes may be literally plausible for bees—not feeding them or sending them back, hoping they will forget her but fearing they will feed on her—but only fantasized about children. As she reenacts pregnancy in the poem, the speaker pretends the mother-child bond can be claimed or severed at will and that dependencies can be controlled. Portraying herself as the half-unwilling listener arrested and implicated in their "furious," "unintelligible" babble, the speaker exhibits what Homans claims is the woman writer's "ambivalent turning toward female linguistic practices" that nonetheless links such a choice to danger and death.[33] Curiously, the best security against the dangers of symbiosis she imagines in this poem appears to be to mimic male hierarchies. The voices confined within are colonized by her metaphors ("swarmy feeling of African hands / Minute and shrunk for export") and objectified as alien others ("a Roman mob," "a box of maniacs") so that her control and even her cruelty become thinkable. In toying with the freedom that male authority might bring to the task of mothering in "Bee Box," the poet's tone teeters between horrified fascination and feigned indifference as she tries these impermissible options; both attitudes are self-indulgent and for opposite reasons pleasurable for the speaker.

"The Tour," composed on October 25, is another Gothic tale in which bad mothering and violent poetic labor serve as metaphors for each other. The trapped housewife vindictively exhibits the horrors within to the censuring gaze of a "maiden aunt."[34] The speaker's feigned feminine solicitude for her guest fails, intentionally, to mask her antagonism toward domesticity. Plath uses malfunctioning domestic machinery to represent both her miserable housekeeping and her creative risks that leave her charred and bare:

I kept the furnace,
Each coal a hot cross-stitch—a *lovely* light!
It simply exploded one night,
It went up in smoke.
And that's why I have no hair, auntie, that's why I choke.

At the hub of the house, the mirror image of the poet's molten center, boils the lethal "Morning Glory Pool" that "ate seven maids and a plumber." Attending the pool is a bald, blind nurse, a "born midwife" who can bring the dead to life for a fee. We recognize in the midwife the poet's bald muse, as well as the sideshow revenant from "Lady Lazarus," which Plath was also composing during the same period. Still, neither the speaker's taunts nor her Gothic interiors succeeds in terrifying. The poem, despite seventeen worksheets, is a botched job. Compared to the witty virtuosity of "The Arrival of the Bee Box," "Tour" sounds genuinely desperate, nearly inarticulate in its repetitive phrasing. It reminds us that Plath's representation of the irrationality that exists within maternity is compelling in the earlier poem precisely because of the poet's unfailing control of language and metaphor.

"Thalidomide," like "The Arrival of the Bee Box" and "Tour," shows the fear of confronting what breeds within the dark interior, but it is unlike them in how Plath tries to manage her dread. Maternal feeling spurs this poem of social conscience; Plath forces herself to conceive what the medical establishment in Britain was denying, the monstrous consequences of a drug administered to pregnant women, "the indelible buds, / Knuckles at shoulder-blades," "the lopped / Blood-caul of absences." The metaphors dare us to forget these casualties; they are intended to be deeply disturbing, wounding, imprinting our consciousness with an "indelible" mark the way a repeated nightmare does. Yet in her response to a public outrage, Plath also questions her capacity for mother love. As in "Bee Box" what is unacknowledged or unowned in this poem are creatures of darkness, whose primary characteristic is their dismemberment: "Your dark, / Amputations crawl and appall." If we compare the metaphors Plath habitually chooses to contain her anxieties about mothering, we notice that the predictive analogies of "You're," while comically subhuman, had an evolutionary certainty about them ("A common-sense / Thumbs-down on the dodo's mode") that, given the rightness of the body's arithmetic, are sure to produce the miraculous sum of a new person. Those she returns to in both these poems written after the birth of her children are of fragmented body parts, hyperbolically reduplicated but never combined to become fully human. The drafts for "Thalidomide," composed on November 4, provide additional evidence for a constellation of images suggestive of infant demands: crawling hands, unreadable countenances, consuming appetite, and unintelligible speech.[35] The speaker initially wards off contact with the "spidery, unsafe" missing limbs with her own gloved "leatheriness." In the first draft, the babies' "two blue eyes & a screech" are coupled with "⟨the teeth that hurt⟩." Although Plath was responding specifically to the Thalidomide deformities, they apparently represented for her an extreme case of a more encompassing maternal fear of finding one's issue unlovable. In a list that follows "the thing I am given" in the first draft, she also includes "⟨the bloodclot⟩ / ⟨the suicide, the idiot⟩."

The poetic labor of this poem, however, in contrast to "The Arrival of the Bee Box," is not to defend against these threats but to "carpenter / A space for the thing I am given." "Thalidomide" takes as its emotional project the fabrication of mother love. As she revises the poem (in four separate drafts over four days), Plath reworks each image for the children to make them less appealing. At the same time, other changes stress that her speaker's central resolve to love them is less a natural or instinctive response than a self-conscious construction. Plath consistently chooses stark, even harsh language to preclude a sentimental response. An early impulse to "make a place in the heart" is soon replaced with "I carpenter a space." Originally the horrific birthing image ("faces / That shove into being, dragging / The lopped / Blood-caul of ⟨guilt⟩ absences") is mitigated by a hint of beauty; "Flower faces" appear as part of the image through two handwritten drafts and two typed revisions. At an even later point in the composition process, Plath makes a series of small adjustments in wording in these four pivotal stanzas in which the monstrous child tests the mother's capacity for owning it as hers. Each underscores the contrast between the product of biology, "the thing I am given," and the willed gesture of maternity. The first explicit reference to "love" occurs as a handwritten addition only in the second typed version: "All night I carpenter / A space for the thing I am given— / A love / Of two blue eyes & a screech." Almost as if to compensate for this addition, the deletion of "flower" comes in the next typed draft, along with the substitution of "wet" for "blue" eyes. Despite her effort to look unflinchingly at these sights, finally the poet cannot see herself as mother in this distorting mirror. The poem ends with what seems a confession of revulsion, the shattering of the image that cannot be accommodated: "The glass cracks across, / The image / Flees and aborts like dropped mercury." The broken mirror reflects the mother's terror even as it hideously proliferates its source.

In these poems the poet's urge for control and for self-preservation exists in excruciating tension with the counterforces of darkness, unintelligibility, monstrosity, and absorption. It would be a mistake to think, however, that these poems demonstrate that Plath was an unnatural mother. What seems more important about them is their timing. It is only after her own biological motherhood is accomplished, with all her idealization of home delivery and natural childbirth, that the poet questions the central terms of maternity in her poetry and finds there may be nothing natural about it. Even more striking than the dismantling of the myth is her reconstruction of the relation between mother and child as a conscious and often conflicted choice.

Reciprocal Definitions: The Mother in the Child's Eye

To choose the image of mirror or reflecting pool, as she did perhaps more frequently than any other, as one of her central figures for the mother-child relationship enabled Plath to meditate on several of her most persistent concerns. She could never look in the mirror of her child's face without simultaneously wondering who she was in this reflection. A pair of poems written to Nicholas two months apart indicate that the reciprocal definition of infant and mother that the mirror metaphor makes possible could be as chilling as it was comforting. "For a Fatherless

• Half-Moon

O half-brain, luminosity!
Negro, masked like a white,

All night your dark
Amputations crawl ~~silty~~ & appal —

Spidery, un safe,
~~As the~~ roots and eater, ~~Past obstruct~~!

~~Past obstruct!~~
~~Hair-legged, big man,~~
~~As the man's hand what~~ glove
What glove
What leatheriness
Has protected

Me from that shadow! —
~~That absence, that turned back!~~
The ~~settle~~ buds,
again, Indelible
Knuckles at shoulder-blades
And the flower faces

~~Shoving~~ that shove into being, chagging
The lopped

Blood-caul of ~~great~~ absences.
~~O carpenter!~~ O   I carpenter,
~~What~~ All night, ~~of my~~ woodwork

I ~~#~~ making a place in the heart
For the thing I am given; ~~the ~~ bleeder

~~The suicide, the idiot~~
two blue eyes & a screech,
The wrong side of the moon & ~~the teeth that hurt~~
~~And~~ the teeth that hurt
The smell of perilous slumber

"Thalidomide" (entitled "Half-Moon" on draft), draft 1, page 1, composed
November 4, 1962

Son," one of only two poems written in September, is a bittersweet game of lost-and-found between mother and infant that is played against the backdrop of the father's "absence," "growing beside you, like a tree, / A death tree." Although the child's inevitable awareness of the missing father is forecast in the opening stanza, the speaker immediately retreats from this loss into the security of Nick's uncomprehending gaze that contains only her:

> But right now you are dumb.
> And I love your stupidity,
> The blind mirror of it. I look in
> And find no face but my own. . . .

The mother-child union seems proof against the disunion of the parents, at least temporarily. The disinheritance announced in the title is postponed or repaid by the mother's discovery of her own sufficiency in her child's eyes: "Till then your smiles are found money."[36]

If the child is a "clean slate" or a "blind mirror," then the mother who is a writer would be tempted to believe that she could inscribe it with images of her own making. In "Child," written at the end of January in London, the mother's metaphors attempt to preserve the infant's unblemished newness: "April snowdrop, Indian pipe, / Little / Stalk without wrinkle." But the mother's language, and its magical powers of imaginative transformation displayed here, are counteracted by her nonverbal communication: "this troublous / Wringing of hands, this dark / Ceiling without a star." The perfect reflecting pool of the child's eye catches both gestures—the poet's prolific promises and the mother's unspoken dread. Rather than gratifying her fantasy, the child's blank mirror makes her failures in her mother role available for scrutiny and self-blame. The scenes in these poems are twice-framed. We see Plath marking a boundary around the mother-infant dyad in which their mutual reflection at first appears to define their whole world. This secure space, however, in which the pair simultaneously constitute each other through word and glance, is shown to be fragile and limited by the second frame, a frame that places these timeless moments in history. The inner circle indulges the mother's feelings of omnipotence, her wish to construct the child's reality through the control of image and language; the second unmasks that construction as an illusion.

In three of her most accomplished poems to her infant children, "Morning Song," "By Candlelight," and "Nick and the Candlestick," Plath deploys a series of reflecting images to represent the mother's link to her child and the poet's objectifying distance from it. Plath's movement back and forth in these mirrors between a maternal subjectivity and a self-ironizing, often comic undercutting of herself as mother, between suspended moments of pre-oedipal bonding and an invocation of historical change, suggests several patterns identified by feminist critics. Ostriker observes that the "most exciting and disturbing mother-child poems tend to group themselves around the periods of infancy and adolescence, when the simultaneous union and division between mother and child generates maximum ambivalence. For the condition of motherhood is then most plainly perceived as both an enlargement and a loss of identity."[37] Homans sees a similar ambivalence but characteristically claims it is generated in the woman writer at the level of language, in the discrepancy between her identification as mother with the natural and the literal and her distrust or devaluing of these identifications as a writer who necessarily chooses representation, figure, and symbol to express herself. Drawing on Chodorow and feminist revisions of Lacan, Homans speculates that "if the baby helps the mother reproduce her presymbolic relation to her own mother without translation into the symbolic terms of the phallus, then her bearing of a child, very much like the daughter's experience of a presymbolic symbiosis, will take place in and model a nonsymbolic discourse." Homans's hypothesis depends on our willingness to entertain the notion that we can "remove the baby from the register of the figurative," that is, agree that it may be a literal reproduction of the mother's own symbiosis and that the resulting "nonsymbolic discourse" has a form that can be discovered in women's writing. Homans is most persuasive in evoking the presence of such a discourse as a tension between the appeal of such mother-child communion and an ambivalent reaction against it: "Not only maternity and mother-daughter language, but also women's identification with nature and the literal, all begin (if we can point anywhere in culture to a distinct beginning) by being distinctly appealing to women. . . . But all are redefined, very confusingly for women, as valueless, precisely for being specific to women."[38]

How does Plath define these moments of presymbolic union, and, more important, how does she represent them in language? All three of these poems employ a similar narrative: the mother rises at night to nurse an infant in whom she does and does not recognize herself. In "Morning Song" the speaker appears to deny, for the first half of the poem, her identity as author of this new being. Awed by the infant's incontrovertible separateness, she reports gestation and birth as if she were rather curiously removed or even absent from these events: "Love set you going like a fat gold watch. / The midwife slapped your footsoles, and your bald cry / Took its place among the elements." Once delivered, it is a "new statue" "in a drafty museum," whose bewildered parents "stand round blankly as walls." In the third stanza the speaker's astonished spectatorship is replaced by an elaborately rational metaphor that effects her erasure even more deliberately: "I'm no more your mother / Than the cloud that distills a mirror to reflect its own slow / Effacement at the wind's hand." Rather than confirm her mother's generativity, the newborn serves to mirror her mortality, or as Beauvoir quotes Hegel, "The birth of children is the death of parents."[39] Yet immediately after this most self-consciously figurative representation of the dissolution of the mother-child bond, the second half of the poem returns to record the preverbal forms of communion that prove it. The mother's wordless acts of instinctive responsiveness seem to contradict the earlier abstraction, or at least to reconstruct another model of the relationship. Nonetheless, the figures Plath chooses to represent this model mock the mother's helpless connection to nature even as the body obeys it: "One cry, and I stumble from bed, cow-heavy and floral / In my Victorian nightgown / Your mouth opens clean as a cat's." Homans would seem to be right that a woman writer's participation in a male-defined literary tradition may lead her to "mythologize the subordination of this language to the demands of the culture that defined women as mothers."[40] Yet Plath also takes an ironic, revisionary stance toward that tradition itself, as she does here. In her maternal aubade, dawn brings a hint of the mother's foreknowledge of language that may spell the rupture of this union; her parting gesture, however, is one of celebration, not regret: "And now you try / Your handful of notes; / The clear vowels rise like balloons." The mother's voice makes way for the daughter to tell her own story.

Another more local appropriation and revision of male language occurs in the echoes that appear in "Morning Song" of two poems that Hughes wrote about Frieda earlier. In "Lines to a Newborn Baby," published in the winter of 1960, Hughes uses a similar mirror image to suggest the randomness and potential violence of the universe she has been born into: "You will find a world tossed into shape / Like a handful of twisted lots. / . . . / Here the hand of the moment—casual / As some cloud touching a pond with reflection / Grips the head of a man as Judith / Gripped." What Hughes portrays as a vision of history that is both casual and murderous, Plath reconceives as a gender-specific metaphor for the ineluctably dynamic process of maternity. Hughes ends another version of the same poem, "To F. R. at Six Months," with the recognition, "You have dispossessed us. / Some star glared through. We lean / Over you like masks hung up unlit / After the performance." While Hughes concludes his poem as a dispossessed onlooker, in Plath's poem this stance exists in tension with the pull toward maternal communion that Hughes's poem entirely lacks.[41]

It is also worth remembering the company this poem keeps in Plath's compositional cycle. As readers we have become used to its placement as the opening poem of Ariel, and we cannot ignore Hughes's report that Plath optimistically arranged the volume to begin with "love" and end with "spring." Yet Plath did not write this poem, as Hughes apparently did his, in the first months after Frieda's birth. Rather, she seems to have composed it as an antidote to the miscarriage of her second child, almost a year later in late February 1961. In a trio of poems written within a few days of each other at the end of February, Plath tries three separate responses to her loss: reconstructing the mother-child dyad of Frieda's infancy, inhabiting the mausoleum of "Barren Woman," or enviously judging the smug, unthinking madonnas of "Heavy Women." What is noticeably lacking in the last two is the concrete-

ness of remembered detail that distinguishes the maternal response of the second half of "Morning Song." Compared with
the ambivalently attached and comically distanced portrait of
motherhood in "Song," Plath's allegories of either barrenness or
pregnancy are abstract and ahistorical. Plath's self-representation
as museum in "Morning Song" is reproduced two days later in
"Barren Woman" (originally titled "Night Thoughts" and then
"Small Hours"), but in these nocturnal meditations she is "Empty,
I echo to the least footfall." The motherhood denied her is mythic,
its issue monumental: she would be "Mother of a white Nike and
several bald-eyed Apollos." She is nursed (or anointed?) instead
by the deathly attentions of her muse figure: "The moon lays a
hand on my forehead, / Blank-faced and mum as a nurse."

The "irrefutable" certainty of "Heavy Women" (initially called
"Waiting Women") seems blamed as much as it is coveted. Unconscious of anything but the body's fruitfulness, which "they meditate / Devoutly as the Dutch bulb / Forming its twenty petals,"
these mothers exist as pure nature. Although idealized as arche-
types by their culture ("beautifully smug / As Venus, pedestaled on
a half-shell"), they will eventually be its pawns: "the axle of winter / Grinds round, bearing down with the straw, / The star, the
wise gray men." Plath suggests in contrasting these myths that the
self-absorption of pregnancy will end with the mother's initiation
into a history of suffering in which she loses the child to purposes
not her own.[42] The draft for "Heavy Women" exists only as a
revised typescript dated February 22 (the day after "Barren
Woman," not February 26, the date supplied by Hughes in the
Collected Poems).[43] In no fewer than twelve attempted revisions of
the opening phrase of the second stanza, "Smiling to themselves,"
Plath's urge to punish their complacent hopefulness seems even
more pronounced; the most frequently repeated term in all the
revisions is "blind." Although the epithet disappears from the
finished poem, it remains in "Barren Woman" signaling the essential narcissism, to Plath, of either condition. In neither of these
alienated, rigidly schematic poems does Plath allow herself to
inhabit the maternal body as she does in "Morning Song" and in
two poems to Nicholas written on October 24, 1962.

The drafts for "By Candlelight" and "Nick and the Candlestick" reveal that Plath initially conceived them as two versions of the same poem and that the same images coexisted in both for a time.[44] The working title for both in the early drafts is "Nick and the Candlestick"; before its final title change, "By Candlelight" was designated "Nick and the Candlestick (I)." In fact, the title makes more sense for this poem, in which the brass candlestick figures prominently in the conclusion, than it does for the second poem, in which seven stanzas about it are entirely deleted from the published version. The marked difference in the way these poems finally end—what they admit and what they hold at bay—reveals the conflict for the poet between the authority of these moments of maternal communion and their vulnerability. The texture of their images and their sound patterns also hint at forms of maternal discourse that move at crosscurrents with the historical knowledge that informs them both.

The mirror of mother-child identity created in "By Candlelight" is repeatedly at risk; the candles that make the vision possible ("The mirror floats us at one candle power") also serve to destabilize it. In their uncertain light, the union can be extinguished or projected as an alarming combat, a disorienting dumb show:

> This is the fluid in which we meet each other,
> This haloey radiance that seems to breathe
> And lets our shadows wither
> Only to blow
> Them huge again, violent shadows on the wall.

As in "Morning Song," the speaker systematically dismantles her own attachment; the infant she watches with held breath is a "balled hedgehog" who "roars" when she sings, and the "yellow knife" of the candle plays against the "bars" of the crib. But if the poet's figures are a mildly mocking self-defense against maternal sentiment, the poet's rhymes seem to surrender to it. The soothing recurrence of the thickly overlapping assonance and internal rhyme domesticates and harmonizes even the bleakest details: "A rough, dumb country stuff / Steeled with the sheen / Of what green stars can make it to our gate." On the first draft a marginal notation indicates Plath planning a nine-line stanza: *abacdedff*. These end-rhymes, mostly exact, connect in ways that contradict the usual sharp divisions between her more common three-line units. In her loving creation of this poetic cave of echoing sound, these lush, dense patterns produce a lingering, elegiac effect, claiming our allegiance to a bond the poem warns us cannot last.

The tenuous perimeter of this candlelit enclosure, the last stanza of the poem reveals, is secured by the "little brassy Atlas." Measured against the inevitable loss of the mother, this diminished figure of male heroism is an inadequate inheritance for her infant son. Using Atlas to foretell Nicholas's future ("Poor heirloom, all you have") Plath predicts a desolate devotion to an impossible task: "No child, no wife, / Five balls! Five bright brass balls! / To juggle with, my love, when the sky falls." The poem ends with an emotional and temporal repositioning of maternity, characteristic of the closure of Plath's poems to her children, that expands outward beyond the locus of mother-child exclusivity and looks forward in time. The "sack of black" that threatens to blot out this scene is more than the winter night; it encompasses the claustrophobia of Devon, the single mother besieged with money worries, who sees no exit from child care or her crumbling house. In her letter home earlier in the month, Plath invented the desperate trope that would reappear in all her complaints: "Stuck down here as into a sack, I fight for air and freedom" (LH 465).

"Nick and the Candlestick (II)," as the second poem remained named through several drafts, begins deep within that sack of black. The speaker announces, "I am a miner," yet where her descent is taking her is not clear, except on the sort of underworld journey that Gilbert and Gubar warn is always dangerous to women, if potentially transformative. The icy Devon nursery is ambiguously indistinguishable from a subterranean cavern in which the slow productions ("stalactites / Drip and thicken, tears / The earthen womb / Exudes from its dead boredom") eerily echo female biology.[45] The mother's body is ruled by entropy; what is nurtured here consumes her. The images and syntax of the first half of the poem are hallucinatory; they mimic the kind of maternal speech that is mad or fears it will become so if imprisoned in the body: "Black bat airs / Wrap me, raggy shawls, / Cold homicides. / They weld to me like plums." The disconnected images seem to spring from the same fears of being devoured in "The Arrival of the Bee Box" or of being engulfed by "the black bunched in there like a bat" of "Wintering." The associative nonsense becomes progressively more unintelligible as the speaker's paranoia intensifies ("And the fish, the fish— / Christ! they are panes of ice"), breeding allusions that seem anxiously reduplicated rather than poetically motivated. In the first draft Plath abandons the poem at this point; the "vice of knives" and "piranha religion" that eventually will reappear in stanza six of the published poem have led, temporarily at least, to a dead end. In the second handwritten draft, the next three stanzas—the vision of Nick on which the final poem pivots—emerge, apparently, without a struggle. What would become the second half of the finished poem appears in this draft with revisions of only a phrase or two.

Unexpectedly, the speaker is released from the terrors of the lower depths by the apparition of her sleeping son:

O love, how did you get here?
O embryo

Remembering, even in sleep,
Your crossed position.
The blood blooms clean

In you, ruby.

After this revelation the movement of the poem is reversed; emerging from the cold, dead underworld of the first seven stanzas, the speaker redefines their shared space: "I have hung our cave with roses, / With soft rugs— / The last of Victoriana." What prompts the speaker's recovery of maternal connection? In the mother's doubled vision the infant reconstitutes her identity as mother, just as the newborn "remembers" the embryo, echoing in sleep his fetal position. As in many other poems to her children, Plath does not claim to have authored the infant ("O love, how did you get here?"), only to have witnessed his existence as bemused outsider. Yet the sudden bloom of her infant's blood seems a miraculous gift ("utterly unasked for" like the vision, three days later, of "Poppies in October"), suddenly apprehended as corresponding to her. The gains of this poem should also be measured against the losses of "Cut," composed on the same day. Here Nicholas, the blood issue of her female sexuality, is not a tarnished stain, dirtied through cultural pollution, but "clean," a translucent jewel. These contradictory representations do not cancel but rather necessarily complicate each other. For Plath maternity was both depletion and enlargement, a threat to her identity and the unexpected confirmation of it.

In marked contrast to "By Candlelight," which closes with the unquestioned certainty of the collapse of the maternal world, this poem holds it off:

> Let the stars
> Plummet to their dark address,
>
> Let the mercuric
> Atoms that cripple drip
> Into the terrible well,
>
> You are the one
> Solid the spaces lean on, envious.
> You are the baby in the barn.

The dangers named recall the falling sky that defeats Atlas, or "the dark fruits [that] revolve and fall" and produce the deformed births of "Thalidomide." Curiously, though, the mother's invocation of the destructive forces of the outer dark does not, for once, erode the pre-oedipal sanctuary. Still, the final enfolding gesture that protects the infant may also figure, perhaps on an unconscious level, a loving, if culturally less speakable, fantasy of reincorporation into the mother's body. The baby in the barn might be the embryo not yet fully relinquished or whom she longs to repossess. The close of the poem jealously hoards the infant; it seeks to preserve the moment prior to the mother's subjectivity splitting in two, when the child's separate identity takes on the alienating otherness that shadows Plath's representations of maternity in nearly all her other poems.

Yet in Plath's original conception, the poem did not end with this gesture. For the first full handwritten draft and through seven typed versions, the poem was over a third longer, twenty-two stanzas rather than fourteen.[46] Seven of the additional eight stanzas were devoted to the candlestick; their focus, however, is the panther pelt Atlas wears rather than his labors. The panther is animated as one of the violent forces that threaten Atlas and, in turn, this scene. The speaker imagines it gnawing Atlas's forehead, performing a "beastly lobotomy," and clawing his genitals, emasculating him. Rather than a juggler, Atlas in this poem's close is a "philosopher," or "Old Athenian, old scholar." Plath's purpose in these abandoned stanzas, even more clearly than in "By Candlelight," is to disparage the masculine legacy of reputed strength or wisdom as hopelessly flawed. The very last stanza of the original poem refocuses attention on what I take to be the central project of these poems, to create through metaphor and sound a model of maternal discourse, a mirror for pre-oedipal intimacy: "The mirror floats us at one candle-power / We smile & stare. / That's you! That's me!"

Uneven Exchanges: "You hand me two children, two roses"

Marjorie Perloff has argued that Hughes's arrangement of the *Ariel* volume "implies that Plath's suicide was inevitable," and indeed, the exclusion of many of Plath's poems about her children from this volume has oversimplified their place and meanings in her poetic narrative.[47] Even within the February poems, however, I suggest there is no linear progression in which maternal connection is severed by the drive of poetry. These poems are, if anything, more deliberately weighed than the poems of rage and betrayal written in October. From day to day, and often on the same day, Plath represented a dialogue between maternity and poetry whose ending was not predictable. Taken together, I believe, the February poems are most appropriately understood as a meaningful but perhaps undecidable juxtaposition of figures for motherhood and authorship, counterpointed by their inscribed reverse sides that sometimes may have played a part in the production of the new poems.

"Balloons" was written a week before Plath's suicide in February 1963 on the reverse of a typed copy of the November poem "Thalidomide." "Balloons" is, at first glance, a whimsical account of living in the London apartment with helium balloons left since Christmas, apparently preserved for the sake of the children. Yet the language and imagery of the February poem might contain some verbal echoes from her much darker poem about constructing mother love on the reverse. The balloons are intrusive aliens ("such queer moons we live with") who "shriek" and "squeak like a cat" and who, the mother complains, are "taking up half the space." In "Thalidomide," which was titled "Half-Moon" through several typed versions including the one Plath reuses in February, the mother's task is "to carpenter a space" for "two wet eyes and a screech." Whatever caused Plath to reuse a typed copy of "Thalidomide" when she drafted "Balloons" in February, the new poem also acknowledges an ambivalent response to her maternal identity.

The speaker of "Balloons," who is belatedly and indirectly revealed in the penultimate stanza to be a mother of two children, takes a childlike delight herself in the balloons. Her imagination animates these "oval soul-animals / . . . / Moving and rubbing on the silk / Invisible air drifts, / Giving a shriek and pop / When attacked, then scooting to rest, barely trembling." As the poem's narrative unfolds, we are given three looks at the balloons; each look revises the one before. The poet-speaker's fantasy at first controls the poem and our view, as every new metaphor invests the balloons with breath, vitality, touchingly human innocence ("guileless and clear"), and vulnerability. It is as if her fascinated attention causes the balloons to levitate, to hang suspended out of reach, while she freights their benign presence with symbolic meanings: "Delighting / The heart like wishes or free / Peacocks blessing / Old ground with a feather / Beaten in starry metals." In the break between what would become the third and fourth stanzas in the published poem, a threat to the poet's richly imagined world appears in the child's unself-conscious, and simpler, desires:

Your small

brother is making
His balloon squeak like a cat.
Seeming to see
A funny pink world he might eat on the other side of it,
He bites,

Then sits
Back, fat jug
Contemplating a world clear as water.
A red
Shred in his little fist.

The second look of the poem, the infant Nicholas's, is governed by unthinking appetite. His pleasures (as they are interpreted and filtered through the observing mother's gaze) lie in teasing balloons as if they were cats and eating whatever comes within reach. The first vision bursts when the poet's metaphoric elaboration collides with the cruder hungers of her child. Interrupting her poetic free-flight, the child tugs the mother's attention back to himself. In analyzing the potential conflicts between maternity and creativity, Susan Suleiman proposes that for a mother to make art from her condition she must step outside an empathetic response and adopt, temporarily, a controlling (Suleiman calls it aggressive) stance toward the child as subject. This objectification of her child makes it available for metaphoric transformation, makes it available for art. A key element in Suleiman's argument is that metaphor is an exercise of power, of holding the imaginative self apart, a potentially unmotherly act.[48] Nick reigns supreme at the end of the poem, a complacent, if startled, Buddha. But while the mother's eye may forgive, or, at least, accept his unintentional destruction, the infant seems judged by her act of metaphorization and by the poet's ear. Like the final stanza in "Cut," the concluding rhymes in this poem are devastating: "He bites, / Then sits / Back, fat jug / . . . / A red / Shred in his little fist." Yet there is also a third look within the poem, the one the speaker shares with a second female presence, the older child who also watches "your small brother." The mother and daughter's communion is mute; Plath deletes Frieda's babytalk "boons, boons" from the second stanza in her draft. The speaker makes an implicit alliance with Frieda as she schools her in what it means to care—that is, to allow the baby to destroy, and to mind when he does. Of course the reader shares in both the imaginative investment that brought the balloons to life and in Frieda's instructed look at the costs—both to the creative self and to the imagined world—of maternal caring.

The unblinkingly honest gaze of this poem should probably be complemented by Plath in a more effusive mood, as in the first letter to her mother after moving to London in December: "Well, here I am! Safely in Yeats' house!... And I can truly say I have never been so happy in my life. I just sit thinking, Whew! I have done it! And beaming. Shall I write a poem, shall I paint a floor, shall I hug a baby? Everything is such fun, such an adventure" (LH 488). Even if the complementarity of roles she professes to feel is emotionally true, it must often have been impossible to answer the simultaneous calls of children and poetry. In a heavily annotated and amended page from her personal appointment book in December, covering the first week after her move, just days after this letter, it is noticeable how many errands do not get accomplished as she paints the whole flat, walls, floors, and furniture. Her circled notes suggest, for example, that three times she means to shop for diapers but does not. For several days in a row she reminds herself to wash her hair, while the whole week is filled with notes to arrange for "baby minders" for Thursday morning, which still seems in doubt when the day arrives. Despite entries that indicate she was seeing Al Alvarez, an important critic and a supportive admirer of the new poems she was writing, as well as Hughes for weekly visits with the children, in January her plans met a series of natural disasters: a crippling blizzard that left her without heat or water, delays in installing a phone that meant every shopping trip had to be with children in tow, and a lack of any predictable or affordable child care. By early February, when "Balloons" was written, both her ebullience as a resourceful homemaker and her hopes for a grand entrance to the London literary scene as a poet to be reckoned with (rather than as Ted's cast-off wife) began to unravel. She was steadily depleting her mother's and Mrs. Prouty's generous Christmas checks; as the bank balance dropped, there was no reassuring income from new poems sold. Then the flu leveled the isolated family, leaving all three feverish and Plath herself sleeping and eating irregularly. By the first of February, the last week in which she wrote any poems, Plath's belief in the optimistic script for her life she constructed in her letters to her mother seems nearly exhausted.

These very late poems not only point to the material conditions of mothering—interruption, loss of energy and focus—but also starkly polarize the options Plath earlier insisted were complementary. Biological and poetic creativity are represented as more and more in conflict—if not mutually exclusive, then mutually eroding. In her struggle to consolidate a persona, to construct and confirm a poetic self, Plath characteristically rejects those parts of earlier constructions she can no longer accommodate by projecting them, in the figures of the poems, onto antagonistic others. In "Kindness" she externalizes the "angel in the house," the sweetly serving voice of motherhood as institution. In the draft, dated February 1, "Dame Kindness" appears initially as "Godmother" (good mother?) Kindness. Whether her saccharine advice is a parody of Aurelia's (and her tutelary spirits, the nicer godmothers of "The Disquieting Muses") or a reaction against the "Sivvy" personality she herself had relentlessly perfected and maintained in her letters about her children, Plath reports it now with mordant politeness: "Sugar can cure everything, so Kindness says. / Sugar is a necessary fluid, / Its crystals a little poultice." Kindness's gestures are recognizably maternal, yet alienating; her soothing, mending, nurturant solicitude seems incommensurable with the speaker's expense of spirit:

And here you come, with a cup of tea
Wreathed in steam.
The blood jet is poetry,
There is no stopping it.
You hand me two children, two roses.

How does Plath now understand the meaning of the paired metaphors, "the bloodjet is poetry" and "You hand me two children, two roses"? The reciprocity between these two gestures, these twin offspring of the poet's generativity, is breaking down, but what exactly is the nature of their opposition? Children could be posed as a critique, a negative judgment of the mother's self-interested priorities, or offered as a bribe, a means of deflecting her energies into healthier channels.[49] Their consolations could be genuine, a poultice to the wound of gender she suffered in "Cut"; children seem to serve, particularly in some of the Nicholas poems, as repayment, recompense for the loss of the unfettered creative self that motherhood implies in "The Arrival of the Bee Box" and "Wintering." Both the claim of poetry and of maternity had considerable weight for Plath. As Suleiman notes, if one way to appease the crying child is not to write the book, another is to "tender her/him the book as a propitiatory offering."[50] It is literally true that exactly coinciding with her move to London to further her career, Plath announced the completion of the *Ariel* volume and her decision to dedicate it to Frieda and Nicholas.[51] Plath's paired images may need to be inserted as well in a lengthier metaphoric exchange between women, roses, and children. In the dominant literary tradition, the equation of roses with budding female beauty assumes that the period of female creativity is brief and is limited to producing biological offspring. The male poets' metaphor operates as a threat as much as a tribute, arguing as it does that a woman's only hope for something like immortality is to breed. In claiming "the blood jet is poetry" Plath refuses the traditional analogy and links her issue instead to metaphor.[52]

While the end of this poem suggests one last attempt at balance, the reverse of this draft reveals the forces arrayed against it. On it Plath has typed two listings for "mother's helps"; perhaps she meant to take the names with her on her next foray out for food and to make phone calls, but the helpers were never hired, perhaps never contacted. In the double-faced testimony of these drafts, the poet's ordinary and ephemeral gestures of mothering are preserved alongside her apparent rejection of the role for her poetry, reminding us that each representation of Plath's experience of motherhood is necessarily a partial one. Her need to construct a persona in an effort to purge herself of ambivalences and her private and poetic habit of self-presentation as a studied performance are also echoed on the reverse of her first typed version of "Kindness." In order to produce just the right breezy tone for a professional contact that she desperately needed for survival, she makes a surprising number of revisions in a two-sentence cover letter to Karl Miller of the *New Statesman* that accompanied a book review she had completed: "After Christmas I should be living at 23 Fitzroy Road, NW 1—Yeats' house no less, plaque and all."

Neither "Balloons" nor "Edge," written on the same day, should be understood as Plath's last word on motherhood. "Edge" is drafted on the reverse of a typescript of "Wintering," yet another poem about mothering that is, I think in an uncanny way, responsible for its original opening. Plath wrote "Wintering" in mid-October as a charm against her thirtieth birthday later that month and as a talisman for living through the winter alone with her children. The struggle in the drafts to produce the willed prophecy of that poem ("The bees are flying. They taste the spring") testifies to the pull in the opposite direction, the drag of maternal depletion and poetic extinction ("Her body a bulb in the cold and too dumb to think"). Plath seems to have been rereading the typescript of "Wintering" as she began "Edge." This page of the typescript ends with the march of the female bees who will carry their dead into the snow:

> —the bees
> So slow I hardly know them,
> Filing like soldiers
> To the syrup tin
>
> To make up for the honey I've taken
> Tate and Lyle keeps them going,
> The refined snow.

"Edge" has a false start. In the first draft its title is "Nuns in Snow": "⟨Nuns in Snow⟩ / ⟨Here they come⟩ / ⟨Down there⟩ the ⟨dead⟩ ⟨terrible⟩ woman is perfected." It is as if the surviving female bees had filed around the edge of the paper to deposit this corpse in the snow.

Compared with the peopled and furnished interior of "Balloons," "Edge" happens in some cold, interplanetary space. The speaker's composure and lucidity in laying out this frozen tableau and her Olympian distance from all its characters make this vision culturally unfamiliar and uncomfortable as a portrait of motherhood. Plath no longer delineates within the poem a perimeter that separates the imperfectly sheltered maternal world from a decaying universe. Instead of the nighttime scenes nursing Nicholas that the speaker both inhabits and observes, this poem's intimacy is resolutely objectified, exposed to the glare of the moon, whose omniscient perspective she seems to share on the events "⟨down there⟩." What is also disturbing is the lack of any maternal split, such as Suleiman describes, any opposing tensions (like those that destabilize "Kindness" or that the speaker accommodates in "Balloons") between the claims of children and the "perfected" woman's "smile of accomplishment." We can uncover no regret, no guilt at the now empty pitchers of her maternal nurturance.

Plath has reinscribed this problematic image of mother love in a lengthy tradition of women who died for love, or who killed because of it. If the woman's pose has "the illusion of Greek necessity" it is because she evokes stories about other women, like Medea or Cleopatra (or Clytemnestra in "Purdah"), whose endings are known and yet who remain figures with culturally contested meanings, mothers whose unnatural acts suggest interpretive indeterminacy.[53] "Edge," even more than "Kindness," represents a series of unreadable gestures that link mother and child yet remain deeply ambivalent and deeply equivocal. The draft suggests even more strongly that Plath realizes she has gone further than the narratives she revises:

We have come so far, it is over,
⟨Now nothing can happen⟩
⟨We stiffen in air like beacons⟩
⟨At the road's end⟩.

The dead mother and "each dead child coiled, a white serpent, / One at each little / Pitcher of milk, now empty" mimic the pose of Cleopatra and her asps, superimposing the poisonous agents of destruction and the fruits of procreation. Rather than staunching the flood of blood as children might be expected to in "Kindness," here the speaker implies they have drawn it.

While the poem suggests that children may be lethal to the mother's selfhood, its central images are, in complex and perhaps unacknowledged ways, reflexive. We have seen enough dead heroines in women's writing to recognize them as signs of self-blame, as an authorial retreat from the cultural trespass the writer has committed in imagining her narrative. The deathly currents flow both ways across this edge, the mother killing the children in

~~Nuns in Snow~~

~~he~~ Edge   Here ~~they come~~

Feb. 5
1963

~~Down~~ ~~the~~ the ~~night~~ woman is perfected.
Her dead

Body wears the smile of accomplishment,
The illusion of a Greek necessity

Flows in the scrolls of her toga,
Her bare

Feet seem to be saying:
We have come so far, it is over,

~~Now nothing can happen~~

We stiffen, in air, like ~~beacons~~
~~At the roads end~~

Each dead child ~~i~~ coiled, a white serpent,
~~She is dying down with the~~
One at each little

Pitcher of milk, now empty.
She has folded
                    body as
them back into her ~~by~~ ~~the way~~ petals
Of a rose close when the garden

Stiffens & odours bleed
From the sweet, deep throats of the night flower.

The moon has nothing to be sad about,
Staring from ~~her~~ hood of bone.

She is used to this sort of thing.
Her blacks crackle & drag.

"Edge," draft 1, composed February 5, 1963

order to perfect the self, the poet killing the mother for daring to think of it. In the draft Plath knew she had created another "terrible" heroine ("⟨Down there⟩ the ⟨dead⟩ ⟨terrible⟩ woman is perfected")—as always in the Ariel poems, an epithet that punishes what it praises. Or there may be yet another motive, hinted at in a line deleted from the draft, not a denial of maternal connection and care but their final expression: "⟨She is taking them with her⟩." This line, in what would become the fifth stanza of the completed poem, introduces an extended metaphor that, like "Kindness," equates children (and now their mother) with roses, and with blood.

> She has folded
> Them back into her body as petals
> Of a rose close when the garden
> Stiffens and odors bleed
> From the sweet, deep throats of the night flower.

The voluptuous garden imagery is borrowed from a poem written three years before, "The Beekeeper's Daughter." In the earlier poem the speaker-daughter expresses an incestuous desire for the authority of the beekeeper-father. The opulent, engulfing sexuality of the female bees far exceeds the aging beekeeper's capacity to match it; still he manages it, by right of his gender. Longing for male authority the daughter dreams of surrogate sex, through identification with the queen bee, as the means to power: "a queenship no mother could contest."

The new poem is a more oblique contest between mothers about the power to manage the blood flood of female sexuality. Now, in February of 1963, barely thirty, Plath found herself a mother alone with two young children, just as Aurelia had been. The family script Plath hoped perhaps most to revise was her mother's self-sacrifice in her devotion to her children. In therapy in Boston, Plath had confronted her guilty dread that her indebtedness to Aurelia's care was so profound it could never be repaid; she had faced the fear it bred that Aurelia would appropriate everything she made, from poems to babies. Yet the gloss from the journals does not lessen the equivocal nature of the image in the poem; its enfolding embrace of the children in the death grip of the mother may resist the engulfing love of Aurelia or it may reenact what Plath most feared and resented in her.[54] The murder of the self represented here, no less than the murder of children, is a gesture whose meanings for Plath were embedded in the nexus of motherhood, as she meditated in her journal in 1958: "When I commit suicide, or try to, it is a 'shame' to her, an accusation: which it was, of course. An accusation that her love was defective" (J 281). If an important subtext for the poem is the rivalry between Plath and Aurelia in representing or reading mother love, there is also an explicit rival for the daughter's filial identification and for her poetic production in the witch-mother moon of the final stanza. In a series of poems during her career ("The Disquieting Muses," "Elm," "The Moon and the Yew Tree") Plath chooses the moon as her muse and as her adoptive mother. The moon is portrayed as aloof and indifferent as her biological mother was overwhelming: "The moon has nothing to be sad about, / Staring from her hood of bone. / She is used to this sort of thing. / Her blacks crackle and drag." As much as these lines seem a reproach to Aurelia's defective love, the speaker's unconcern is insisted upon so firmly that it seems suspect, as if a wish for its opposite underlies the bravado of the poem's final rejection of her need for maternal investment.

"Words" is the fate that "Edge" tries to guard against in its totalizing, hermetic reincorporation of all signs of female generativity back into the self. In "Edge" the poet treats the woman as a made thing, "perfected" through an act of will; authorial control claims to be complete, its creations immutable. "Words" tells a different story, one whose implications I think Plath worries about in all her poems about motherhood. The riddle that "Words" expresses is that authorship, like its twin, maternity, is an act that undoes itself. These parallel gestures of female creativity that she hoped would confirm, extend, and express the self have consequences for their author that are unforeseen and uncontrollable. Whether words or babies, what the poet makes mocks her authority. Oddly enough, Plath signs the first draft of "Words," as if to contest by her autograph what the poem signifies.[55] The centrifugal force generated by the initial metaphor represents the effect of words as infinitely expanding:

Axes
After whose stroke the wood rings,
And the echoes!
Echoes traveling
Off from the center like horses.

This motion seems contradicted (but not contained) by the second extended metaphor, in which words plummet vertically through water and, apparently, disappear:

the rock

That drops and turns,
A white skull,
Eaten by weedy greens.

What is odd about both metaphors is that they reveal consequence but deny or suppress causation; any sign of agency or volition seems absent. In the elusive syntax of the poem, the subject is often withheld, while comparison after comparison reproduces words' aftereffects (echoes travel like horses, sap wells like tears, like water, which, in turn, is a mirror). Yet these chained reactions lead us farther and farther away from their author. Only at the end of the penultimate stanza does the speaker's "I" enter the poem, and then she appears as belated audience for the words rather than as their maker: "Years later I / Encounter them on the road— / Words dry and riderless." This delayed entrance, which problematically situates the poet as only the latest in a string of uncontrollable consequences, is the single most significant revision Plath makes in the draft. Initially she had represented the imperious autonomy of words much earlier, as the poem's second stanza: "Peasants & beggars / Encounter them in the road / Dry & proud, in a lather of sweat."

To relocate this encounter later and to have the horses' ungoverned rush witnessed by the poet, now by implication in the beggar's position, underscores the central paradox of this poem: words once made escape the speaker's control; in fact, the maker is herself mastered by her creation. Once found at the end of the third stanza, the speaker's presence is revealed retroactively in the earlier riddles. Instead of the woodsman or rider that the opening

Words

Axes
After whose stroke the wood rings,
~~The the~~ Echoes/ ~~echoes traveling~~
~~Off from the center like horses~~
Echoes traveling
Off from the center like horses.

~~Peasants & beggars~~
Encounter them on the road
Dry & proud, in a lather of sweat
The sap
Wells like tears, like the ~~water~~
Water striving,
To re-establish its mirror
Over the rock

That drops & turns,
A white skull,
Eaten by weedy greens.
Years later. I
Encounter them on the road —

~~...~~ds proud & riderless,
~~...~~ the spirit
~~Hoof-taps indefatigable.~~
~~...~~ from the past
~~Bottom~~ While the indefatigable hoof-taps.
~~...~~ from the bottom
(Of the pool & fixed ~~stars~~ ~~constellation~~
~~Of pebbles & ferns~~
Governs a life.

"Words," draft 1, composed February 1, 1963

metaphors imply, the poet is displaced in images that suggest the reflexive, destabilizing effect of words on the self:

> The sap
> Wells like tears, like the
> Water striving
> To re-establish its mirror
> Over the rock.

The subjectivity that would be confirmed or consolidated by language finds its integrity injured, its coherence ruptured.[56] The several motions under way in the poem intersect in the speaker; each has the effect of unfixing her autonomy or authority. The centrifugal pulse of the "indefatigable hoof-taps" is met by the plumb line of the dropped rock: "From the bottom of the pool, fixed stars / Govern a life." In the first motion words that originally sped "off from the center" are reencountered "riderless," moving in trajectories that are no longer recognizable as having the speaker as their source. In the second movement, the speaker is the mirror shattered by words, which, when it forms again, reflects only their controlling image. The dissolution of the self by words, and its paradoxical subjection to them, reminds us of similar erasures or subordinations of the mother contemplated in "Cut," "Bee Box," "Wintering," "Morning Song," "Thalidomide," "The Night Dances," and even "Balloons." The broken mirror of "Edge" tells a truth these other poems only glance at—the subjectivities of both the mother and the poet are simultaneously and inevitably disrupted and determined by what they make.

Notes

Introduction

1. The term is used by Nancy Miller, who cautions against such a reductive equation of life and art in *Subject to Change*, p. 111. Margaret Homans rejects the identification of poet and persona as a deadly investment in the literal that defeats the figurative possibilities of poetry in *Women Writers and Poetic Identity*, pp. 218–19.

2. For a review of the pathological early readings of Plath that were later countered by formalist approaches, see Gilbert "In Yeats' House," pp. 147–48, and Linda Wagner-Martin's introduction to the same volume, pp. 8–10. Joanne Feit Diehl and Steven Axelrod, among the most recent and most subtle of Plath's critics, nonetheless subscribe eventually to the conviction that Plath's texts produced her death.

3. De Lauretis, *Technologies of Gender*, p. 3.

4. I have been influenced in this understanding of the cultural construction of the female subject by the work of de Lauretis; Belsey, *Critical Practice*, pp. 65–66; and Alcoff, "Cultural Feminism versus Post-Structuralism," pp. 428–34.

5. Smith, *Discerning the Subject*, pp. xxxiv–xxxv (emphasis in original).

6. Butler, "Sex and Gender in Simone de Beauvoir's *Second Sex*," p. 40.

7. Hughes, "Sylvia Plath and Her Journals," p. 152.

8. Nancy K. Miller, *Subject to Change*, p. 80.

9. Todd, *Feminist Literary History*, p. 86.

10. Miller contends in *Subject to Change* that "the postmodernist decision that the Author is Dead and the subject along with him does not . . . necessarily hold for women, and prematurely forecloses the question of agency for them" (p. 106); see also pp. 69, 74, 107.

11. Alcoff, "Cultural Feminism versus Post-Structuralism," p. 434.

12. Plath reports that she received $280 for about 130 pages of poetry manuscript (November 20, 1961, *LH* 437). These materials, purchased by Ifan Fletcher, form the bulk of the Sylvia Plath Manuscript Collection at Indiana University.

13. In her journal entry for March 3, 1958, Plath identifies the lasting significance she would attach to this paper: "Got a queer and most overpowering urge today to write, or typewrite, my whole novel on the pink, stiff, lovely-textured Smith memorandum pads of 100 sheets each: a fetish: somehow seeing a hunk of that pink paper, different from all the endless reams of white bond, my task seems finite, special, rose-cast" (*J* 201).

14. Kroll, *Chapters in a Mythology*, p. 224 n. 31.

15. This characterization appears in her letter to Aurelia, on February 26, 1961, included in the Indiana University collection (box 9, folder 9b).

16. This sequence of poems includes, in the order of composition, "Purdah" (October 29), "The Couriers" (November 4), "Getting There" (November 6), "The Night Dances" (November 6), "Gulliver" (November 6), "Thalidomide" (November 8), and "Letter in November" (November 11).

1. Rage

1. Coincidentally, Steven Axelrod also perceptively analyzes this scene from the journals. Although we agree that the scene reveals much about the strains in their marriage, we differ significantly in our conclusions. My reading, which emphasizes this scene as a prototype for those she rescripted in the later Ariel poems, was complete before his study was published. See Axelrod, *Sylvia Plath*, pp. 180–84.

2. Her interpretation of the relationship between male teacher and female student as primarily an exercise in sexualized dominance operates as well in her re-vision of Newton Arvin, a known homosexual and a former teacher for whom she now worked as his grader: "see Arvin: dry, compulsively fingering his key ring in class, bright hard eyes red-rimmed turned cruel, lecherous, hypnotic and holding me caught like the gnome" (J 203).

3. For the tensions between old and new paradigms for maturity, personal growth, and familial obligation, see Mintz and Kellogg, *Domestic Revolutions*, pp. 205–7; see also Ehrenreich, *Hearts of Men*, pp. 89–93. Plath's plans for Hughes before their marriage betray a paradoxical wish to help him realize his full potential and to make him over: "You should see how Ted is changing under my love and cooking and daily care! Gone is the tortured, black, cruel look, the ruthless banging gestures. . . . I have saved him to be the best man he can be" (May 26, 1956, Indiana University collection [box 9, folder 6b]). Her journals more frequently record her failures to realize her own goals, either of self-actualization or external measures of success; see J 60, 251, 262, 314, 327.

4. Plath's defensiveness about Ted's inadequacies in each of these areas is a refrain in her journals during their American stay; see J 251, 254, 278–79, 283, 285.

5. Ehrenreich, *Hearts of Men*, pp. 17–24.

6. "Both of us feel we are very late maturers, only beginning our true lives now and need to devote the next two or three years to establishing the depths of our talent and then having children, but not until they can't undermine our work. Our own personalities are still squeaking new and wonderful to us" (April 13, 1957, Indiana University collection [box 9, folder 7]); see also LH 298, 318.

7. J 306. Ehrenreich claims Reisman's analysis of the corporate man as "other-directed" corresponds to traits coded as feminine in Freudian psychology and Talcott Parsons's sociology, and implies that what Reisman fears is a "feminization of American men"; see *Hearts of Men*, pp. 32–34.

8. Mintz and Kellogg, *Domestic Revolutions*, pp. 184, 190; Ehrenreich and English, *For Her Own Good*, pp. 211–17; Ehrenreich, *Hearts of Men*, p. 38.

9. Ehrenreich quotes Hugh Hefner in *Hearts of Men*, p. 44.

10. See also similar vows not to share her writing with Hughes during this period: J 259–60, 278, 288, 304.

11. Dickie, *Sylvia Plath and Ted Hughes*, p. 10.

12. For other comments on Hughes's role as writing tutor, see J 244, 323, and LH 267, 289.

13. As an undergraduate, when Plath heard Auden read at Smith, she claimed, "I found my God in Auden" (LH 108); but when he judged her poems, he called them "facile." Later, Auden was among the judges who rejected her book for the Yale Younger Poets prize in 1957 (LH 315). For Eliot's mentorship of Hughes, see also J 313 and LH 312, 379–81, 395.

14. LH 280 (Cambridge, October 23, 1956) and J 304 (Boston, May 20, 1959).

15. Marcus in *Art & Anger* notes that whining and nagging are "peculiar forms of protest" associated with the powerless (women, slaves, children, servants) that testify to the danger of their anger and its "survival in the form of indirect discourse" (p. 123).

16. For a discussion of Plath's female literary genealogy, see Chapter 3. The most striking difference is that Plath's references to male writers rarely include specific comments about craft, either about what she wants to learn or avoid, while her comments on women almost always do.

17. Steven Axelrod's readings of Plath's debt to Lowell and Roethke, while more extensive than I would grant, is also based on the conviction that Plath's borrowings from her male predecessors, especially Lowell, are violently competitive. See Axelrod, *Sylvia Plath*, pp. 66–68.

18. Ted Hughes, "Sylvia Plath and Her Journals," pp. 157–58. Dickie cites Hughes's "Mayday on Holderness" and "To Paint a Water Lily" as Roethkean experiments that parallel Plath's; see Dickie, *Sylvia Plath and Ted Hughes*, pp. 120, 122–23.

19. Plath, *Johnny Panic*, pp. 110, 114.

20. Ibid., pp. 204–10.

21. Sandra Gilbert recognizes that Yeats was a troubling model for Plath, although for different reasons. Gilbert has difficulty reconciling Plath's veneration for Yeats with his misogyny (shared, she argues, to a virulent degree by all male modernists) that must have "depressed her ambitions." See "In Yeats' House," pp. 211, 216, 219, in Wagner, *Critical Essays on Sylvia Plath*. My point is that whatever specific messages Plath read in Yeats's poetry are less important than that he stood for the unimpeachable greatness she aspired to, that she reinvested that ambition and greatness in Hughes, and that she then symbolically reclaimed her place as Yeats's descendant at the end of her marriage.

22. Woolf, "Professions for Women," p. 286.

23. Ibid.

24. Ibid., pp. 287–88. Jane Marcus, in analyzing the drafts for this essay, in *Art & Anger* offers compelling proof that Woolf's imagination is both gendered and angry: "The imagination comes to the top in a state of fury. Good heavens she cries—how dare you interfere with me" (p. 141).

25. Woolf, *A Room of One's Own*, p. 101.

26. Ibid., pp. 108, 102.

27. Spacks, *The Female Imagination*, p. 10; Showalter, *A Literature of Their Own*, p. 264; Rich, "When We Dead Awaken," p. 92.

28. I refer to the version of Rich's essay reprinted in the Gelpi anthology rather than the 1978 revision published in *On Lies, Secrets, and Silences* because the polarities she proposes and the possibilities for reintegration at the beginning of the decade strongly influenced other feminist readings. Marianne Hirsch comments perceptively on the differences between the original and Rich's revision in *The Mother/Daughter Plot*, pp. 127–29.

29. Rich, "When We Dead Awaken," p. 98.

30. Ibid., p. 91.

31. Ibid., p. 97–98.

32. Marcus, *Art & Anger*, p. 124. Although her book appeared in 1988, Marcus's influential essay "Art and Anger," which is reprinted as chapter 4 of her book, was originally published in 1978 in *Feminist Studies* 4, no. 1, and thus is typical of the readings of rage informed by that decade of the women's movement.

33. Bennett, *My Life, a Loaded Gun*, pp. 242, 258.

34. Ibid., p. 245.

35. Marcus, *Art & Anger*, pp. 153–54.

36. Gilbert and Gubar, *Madwoman*, pp. 77, 85.

37. Gilbert and Gubar adopt this term in *Madwoman* to characterize texts by women "whose surface designs conceal or obscure deeper, less accessible (and less socially acceptable) levels of meaning" (p. 73).

38. Toril Moi's preference is for a feminist criticism grounded in psychoanalytic, British socialist, and postmodernist politics and habits of reading. See *Sexual/Textual Politics*, pp. 58–66.

39. DuPlessis, *Writing beyond the Ending*, pp. 38–39, 41–42.

40. Ostriker, *Stealing the Language*, pp. 141, 137.

41. Feit Diehl, "Murderous Poetics," p. 331.

42. Butler, "Performative Acts and Gender Constitution," pp. 519–20, 525–27; see also her condensation of this essay's argument in Butler, *Gender Trouble*, pp. 137–41.

43. Moers, *Literary Women*, pp. 139, 152–53; DuPlessis, *Writing beyond the Ending*, pp. 42, 44–45.

44. Showalter, *A Literature of Their Own*, p. 264.

45. Gilbert and Gubar, *Madwoman*, p. 79.

46. Ostriker, *Stealing the Language*, pp. 143, 145, 149.

47. Feit Diehl, "Murderous Poetics," p. 331.

48. In the order in which they appear on the reverse of Plath's draft, these are "Toll of Air Raids," "Thought-Fox" (1957), "A Fable," "Cradle Piece" (an unpublished poem to Frieda), "Unknown Soldier," and "Poltergeist."

49. Brackets ⟨ ⟩ within quotations from the manuscripts enclose material deleted by the poet during revisions of the same draft.

50. The same coded reference to adulterers and orchids appears again in "Fever 103°."

51. The London return address on the typescript of "Thought-Fox" indicates Plath retyped this poem along with the group of recently composed poems in the spring of 1960; it appears on the reverse of the second page of Plath's first draft.

52. Originally broadcast on October 6, 1961, Hughes's talk, "Capturing Animals," is collected in *Poetry in the Making*, pp. 20–21.

53. Plath's revisionary strategy is also evident in her borrowing from Hughes's "A Fable," which appears on the reverse of the third page of her first draft. "A Fable" is a hallucinatory account of "a man brought to his knees in the desert" that concludes, "The lost man croaked, like a toad in a baking stone, / Interested only in water, water." In Plath's poem, these lines surface in an early version of stanza one, as a comparison for Hughes's discarded papers in the wastebasket: "Grain by grain they ⟨created a desert⟩ ⟨stretched out⟩ unrolled their sands / In which a dream of water danced." Much later in the revising process, Plath overlays Ted's lines with her own fused image of his deceptive smile and planned defection: "Grain by grain they unrolled / Sands where a dream of clean water / Grinned like a getaway car."

54. Ostriker, *Stealing the Language*, p. 60.

55. Although Hughes did not collect his Crow poems until 1970, Plath would have known this persona and images of marital violence through two verse plays from 1962, "The Wound" and "Difficulties of a Bridegroom." The largest published fragment of the latter is *Eat Crow* (1971). For a discussion of the shared imagery in Hughes's plays and Plath's Ariel poems, especially their violent gender rivalries, see Faas, "Chapters in a Shared Mythology," pp. 114–17. See Dickie, *Sylvia Plath and Ted Hughes*, pp. 200–206, for a discussion of the crow persona in Hughes's poetry and its debts to Plath's vernacular voice in the Ariel poems.

56. Ostriker, *Stealing the Language*, p. 98.

57. Marcus, *Art & Anger*, pp. 216–18. Christine Froula makes a similar argument in "The Daughter's Seduction," pp. 633–36.

58. Plath also reports the title and focus on June 17, 1957, in LH 318.

59. See also, in her October letters, her self-portrait as starving while Hughes squanders their resources: LH 465, 468, 470, 471, 473; see esp. letter of October 16, 1962, Indiana University collection (box 9, folder 10).

60. See Marcus, *Art & Anger*, pp. 64–66, and Axelrod, *Sylvia Plath*, pp. 214–15.

61. See Dickie, *Sylvia Plath and Ted Hughes*, pp. 159–61; Homans, *Women Writers and Poetic Identity*, pp. 219–21; Feit Diehl, *Women Poets and the American Sublime*, pp. 133–35.

62. See Howe, "The Plath Celebration," p. 233; Vendler, "Intractable Metal," pp. 3–4; Dickie, *Sylvia Plath and Ted Hughes*, p. 160.

63. Silver, "The Authority of Anger," pp. 346–47.

64. Gilbert and Gubar, *Madwoman*, pp. 587–94; Cristanne Miller, *Emily Dickinson*, pp. 167–68; Mossberg, *Emily Dickinson*, p. 196.

65. Ostriker, *Stealing the Language*, p. 237.

66. This formulation has been influenced by Barbara Mossberg's insights about the "daughter construct" in *Emily Dickinson*, p. 69.

67. Plath spins out their fantasy in a letter to her mother in August 1960: "There is a fantastic market for plays in London—all youngish authors. All he needs is one really good, successful play, and we would have a good start. Our wish now is to get a car, a beach-wagony affair, tour Cornwall and Devon and buy a spreading country house with some land and settle down to write and raise a family. Once he has a successful play produced, we could do this" (LH 392–93). When Plath began to reuse this manuscript, it was precisely this dream that had been realized and destroyed.

68. The other titles, in probable sequence, were "The Rival," "The Rabbit Catcher," "A Birthday Present," then "Daddy." Plath's typescript for her planned collection, prepared in London in January 1963, is part of the Smith College collection (Ariel Poems—Final typescript). Each of these provisional choices confirms Plath's intention to revise in these poems her relationship with Hughes. Her final selection of "Ariel" refocuses the trajectory of the volume on the avatar of the singular woman poet.

69. For a discussion of the differences between Plath's plan and Hughes's selection, see Perloff, "The Two Ariels." Hughes omits some of the most vindictive October poems in part because he may have judged them artistically inferior and also because he thought he could suppress those that had not been published elsewhere.

70. Ostriker, *Stealing the Language*, pp. 88–89.

71. Cristanne Miller's observations of Dickinson's voice make this important distinction, in *Emily Dickinson*, p. 175.

72. Gilbert and Gubar, *Madwoman*, p. 621.

73. Mossberg, *Emily Dickinson*, p. 193.

74. Feit Diehl, "Murderous Poetics," pp. 336–37.

75. Ostriker is commenting on the poetry of Margaret Atwood, Anne Sexton, and Diane Wakoski; see *Stealing the Language*, pp. 162–63.

2. The Body

1. For a discussion of *Modern Woman*, see Miller and Nowak, *The Fifties*, pp. 153–55, and Friedan, *The Feminine Mystique*, pp. 111–12.

2. Ehrenreich, *For Her Own Good*, pp. 219–20, 245–50. Ehrenreich also discusses the slippery logic through which, in a decade devoted to individual gratification, female sexual pleasure became associated with masochism in the work of Helene Deutsch.

3. See Friedan, *The Feminine Mystique*, pp. 252–56, 315–20, and D'Emilio and Freedman, *Intimate Matters*, pp. 285–87.

4. Plath's associations of these colors with violent eroticism and the imprint of a sexualized body that will reappear in the Ariel poems is also evident in another journal entry: "Put on my red silk stockings with red shoes—they feel amazing, or rather the color feels amazing—almost incandescent fire silk sheathing my legs. I can't stop looking—the stocking goes almost flesh color, but gathers rose and glows at the edges of the leg as it cuts its shape in air, concentrating the crimson on the rounding away, shifting as I shift" (J 222).

5. Banner, *American Beauty*, p. 285.

6. Haskell, *From Reverence to Rape*, pp. 254–57, 261–63; see also Banner, *American Beauty*, pp. 283–85.

7. Beauvoir, *The Second Sex*, p. 249.

8. Ibid., pp. xvi, xxviii.

9. Many later feminists have justifiably found fault with Beauvoir's formulations. Vicky Spelman, who coined the term "somatophobia" for the dark side of dualistic thinking that privileges spirit or mind over body, warns that Beauvoir can imagine no escape for women from the trap of the body except to

emulate the attempted male transcendence of it, thus confirming the mind/ body dualism that makes such escape desirable. See Spelman, "Woman as Body." It is also worth remembering that Beauvoir's longing for male transcendence, mobility, and cultural centrality were Plath's own. Although there is no proof Plath read it, *The Second Sex* was translated by a Smith professor and published in America in 1953, while Plath was an undergraduate.

10. Beauvoir, *The Second Sex*, p. 154.

11. Ibid., p. 138. A similar understanding of the role of the mother's body underlies much of psychoanalytical feminist criticism, whether descended through American object relations theory by way of Nancy Chodorow or through post-structuralism by way of Lacan. For a sampling of the former, see *The (M)other Tongue*, edited by Garner, Kahane, and Sprengnether, and for the latter, see Gallop, *Thinking Through the Body*.

12. Beauvoir, *The Second Sex*, p. 144.

13. Ibid.

14. Ibid., p. 174.

15. Butler, "Sex and Gender in Simone de Beauvoir's *Second Sex*," pp. 40, 45, 48. See also her elaboration of this argument in Butler, *Gender Trouble*, pp. 11–13.

16. Rich, *Of Woman Born*, pp. 220, 237 (emphasis in original), 246–47.

17. Mossberg, *Emily Dickinson*, pp. 45, 64.

18. Hirsch, *The Mother/Daughter Plot*, pp. 10–11.

19. Rich, *Of Woman Born*, pp. 21, 290 (emphasis in original).

20. Marianne Hirsch's *The Mother/Daughter Plot* takes as its point of departure her own disappointment as a mother in the lack of a maternal subject in psychoanalytical or literary discourse. Jane Gallop's *Thinking through the Body*, which takes its title from Rich and its graphic cover art from her birthing of her son, is intentionally and conspicuously self-referential throughout.

21. Ellmann, *Thinking about Women*, pp. 65, 131.

22. Auerbach, *Woman and the Demon*, pp. 63–64.

23. Ibid., pp. 15, 17–18.

24. Ibid., p. 148. For other discussions of the cultural disparagement of the implacability of virgins, see Ellmann, *Thinking about Women*, p. 136, and Gilbert and Gubar, *Madwoman*, pp. 616–17.

25. Moers, *Literary Women*, pp. 163–64 (emphasis in original).

26. Kahane, "The Gothic Mirror," pp. 343, 347–50.

27. Gilbert and Gubar, *Madwoman*, pp. 29–34.

28. Yaeger, *Honey-Mad Women*, pp. 35, 148.

29. Ostriker, *Stealing the Language*, p. 213.

30. De Lauretis, *Alice Doesn't*, p. 109.

31. Ibid., p. 7.

32. DuPlessis, *Writing beyond the Ending*, pp. 106, 108, 110.

33. Ostriker, *Stealing the Language*, p. 235. For similar definitions of women's revisionary relation to myth, see also Friedman, *Psyche Reborn*, p. 212; Lauter, *Women as Mythmakers*, pp. 7–9; and Edwards, *Psyche as Hero*, pp. 4–5, 9–10.

34. Although Hughes dates the piece from 1962 when he publishes it in the posthumous collection of her prose, *Johnny Panic*, Linda Wagner-Martin identifies it as written in London in January 1963, a date Plath's January 22 letter to Olive Higgins Prouty also confirms. See Wagner-Martin, *Sylvia Plath*, p. 236.

Plath's letter to Prouty is in the Indiana University collection (box 6). Page references to "Ocean 1212-W" will be cited in the text.

35. Given the self-conscious gender transformations throughout the narrative, it is significant that Plath appropriated in her retelling several instances of male experience, as Aurelia points out in a letter to Judith Kroll, "It was *her* brother who crept into the waves & a friend's father found the Sacred Baboon on the beach, *not* she" (draft for letter of December 1, 1978, Smith College collection).

36. Mossberg perceptively elaborates the ambivalent connections between Plath's writing and her desire for maternal nurture in "Sylvia Plath's Baby Book."

37. Plath's self-justification, at thirty, of her infantile rebellion against her mother proves the enduring power of Mossberg's daughter construct, a need for a contrary self-definition that rebels against the mother matrix of conventional expectations but that also includes a desire to be mothered and esteemed for her wickedness. See Mossberg's discussion of Dickinson's pose as a naughty child in poems she wrote between the ages of forty and fifty, in *Emily Dickinson*, p. 43. It also seems significant that "Ocean 1212-W" rewrites Plath's undergraduate story "Among the Bumblebees," a story of origins in which her father is equated with the fury of the sea and the power of the pen, and she is his favored but deserted daughter.

38. The drafts for both poems are in the Indiana University collection.

39. See LH 408, 411. In a deleted portion of Plath's letter on February 2, 1961, she reports Dido Merwin's face lift. The unedited letter is part of the Indiana University collection (box 9, folder 9b).

40. "Getting There" (November 6, 1962) discards one body and assumes the next in a similar image: "And I, stepping from this skin / Of old bandages, boredoms, old faces / Step to you from the black car of Lethe, / Pure as a baby" (CP 249).

41. The drafts for "In Plaster" are in the Indiana University collection; a handwritten draft of "Tulips" is in the Houghton Library at Harvard University, Cambridge, Mass. Plath may have considered "In Plaster" a slighter poem; she did not plan to include it in the *Ariel* volume.

42. See LH 408–9. She worries on February 6, "I am as sorry about disappointing you as anything else, for I'm sure you were thinking of the birth as joyously as I was"; on February 9 she promises, "Start saving for another trip another summer, and I'll make sure I can produce a new baby for you then!"

43. Rich, *Of Woman Born*, p. 238.

44. Kahane, "The Gothic Mirror," p. 343.

45. Linda Wagner-Martin reports that Plath and Aurelia shared a bedroom from the time Plath was nine until she was sixteen; see *Sylvia Plath*, p. 34. Such unwelcome intimacy as an adolescent may also underlie this poem's claustrophobia.

46. Plath's appendectomy appears to have been a welcome relief from childrearing, as she reports to Aurelia from the hospital, "I haven't been free of the baby one day for a whole year" (LH 412).

47. October 16, 1962 (LH 468). In the unedited original of this letter in the Indiana University collection (box 9, folder 10) Plath's hyperbole is less a sign

of her poetic self-confidence than a symptom of emotional instability that is also manifested in this letter by extreme paranoid fantasies. Plath's boast to her mother echoes her early courtship letters; in both instances, first her affair and now her divorce, she dares her mother to disapprove of her actions by claiming they spurred her creative gift, dutifully returned to the mother in the promise of literary fame.

48. Both Sylvia and Aurelia recognized that in their letters they attempted to purge their relationship of the ambivalence and competition that accompanied their intense identification and mutual dependence. In her journal, Plath acknowledges that "one reason I could keep up such a satisfactory letter-relationship with her while in England was we could both verbalize our desired image of ourselves in relation to each other: interest and sincere love, and never feel the emotional currents at war with these verbally expressed feelings" (J 282). Aurelia too preferred the idealization of the letters to the emotional abrasion of their "psychic osmosis": "Both Sylvia and I were more at ease in writing words of appreciation, admiration, and love than in expressing them verbally, and, thank goodness, write them to each other we did!" (LH 32).

49. For discussions of the "Sivvy" persona of the letters, see Lynda Bundtzen and Barbara Mossberg, who share my conviction that Plath manipulated this persona to secure maternal nurturance and to repay overwhelming emotional debts: Bundtzen, *Plath's Incarnations*, pp. 85–89, and Mossberg, "Sylvia Plath's Baby Book," pp. 188–90. Marjorie Perloff also notes that Plath had to destroy the part of Aurelia that "Sivvy" had internalized after she had herself reproduced the family pattern of single, and potentially self-sacrificing, motherhood; see "Sylvia Plath's 'Sivvy' Poems," pp. 162–63.

50. Rich, *Of Woman Born*, p. 237.

51. Ostriker, *Stealing the Language*, p. 73.

52. Aurelia confirms that the double meaning of her name, as both "jelly-fish" and "golden," was a private joke between her and her daughter and that she recognized that in the poem Sylvia had chosen the less flattering etymology. See letter to Judith Kroll, December 1, 1978, Smith College collection.

53. In a heavily edited journal entry from the period of Plath's 1958 psychotherapy, Plath reveals her anxiety that the success of her marriage must be balanced against Aurelia's suffering: "My mother had sacrificed her life for me. A sacrifice I didn't want. . . . I made her promise she'd never marry. When [I was nine.] Too bad she didn't break it. . . . She is worried about me and the man I married. How awful we are, to make her worry" (J 269). For Aurelia's account of her promise not to remarry, see her memoir, LH 25.

54. Aurelia's summer visit to Devon was meant to free Plath for writing while Aurelia assumed child care, yet during her stay Hughes's affair was accidentally confirmed. Aurelia reports that the mother-blame in "Medusa" may have resulted in part from Plath's expectation that her mother could somehow prevent the affair. See letter to Judith Kroll, December 1, 1978, Smith College collection.

55. My emphasis on Plath's imaginative refiguring of the sexualized body as her trope for poetic authority reverses the arguments of Steven Axelrod and Joanne Feit Diehl. Although Axelrod claims, as I do, that her poetic persona represents an antidote or alternative to her biography, he represents Plath the

artist and woman as curiously passive and ultimately determined by these inherently destructive fictions: "Encountering a double more meaningful than her empirical self, she at first felt comforted and relieved, but then haunted and possessed. . . . She may have undergone her suicide ritual at least partly to recapture her identity from her poems" (*Sylvia Plath*, p. 201). Likewise Feit Diehl gives primary importance to the suicidal impulse that defeats the metaphoric transformation: "The literal desire to escape bodily articulation conflicts with the metaphoric necessity of the corporeal. . . . Purification, which becomes the means of escape, threatens to destroy the body through which it speaks" (*Women Poets and the American Sublime*, p. 136). Lynda Bundtzen reads Plath's reincarnations as powerful rather than doomed, yet she stresses Plath's transcendence of the body and gender in the figure of the "divine androgyne" (*Plath's Incarnations*, p. 256), while I argue for Plath's reinvestment in the corporeal.

56. Twice during the late fall and winter of 1962, Plath reports in her letters that she has finished her new book, once on November 19 (LH 480) and again on December 14 (LH 490). Hughes claims she made her final selection around Christmas (CP 14). The evidence in the Smith College collection of Plath's latest typescript, a revised table of contents (Ariel Poems—Final typescript), and a list of each poem's prior publication (Poems—Lists, 1959–1963) indicates she removed "The Swarm" after January 25, 1963, when the four other poems in the sequence had been accepted by journals.

57. Ted Hughes quotes this observation in his introduction to *Collected Poems*, p. 14.

58. See Poems—Lists, 1959–1963, in the Smith College collection for submission and acceptance of individual poems in the sequence. During the process of composition, Plath reinforced her sense of the integrity of the sequence. Her handwritten additions to the typescript of the earliest poem, "The Bee Meeting," correct the running title several times. She also calculated the total number of lines in the sequence (266) here. The five-line stanza, despite dramatic differences in line length in individual poems, was a unifying feature of the sequence. Her tabulations show that, with the exception of "Bee Box," they are of roughly equal length, between fifty and sixty-five lines each. Her count also verifies that "Stings" included one more stanza than the published version (or thirteen stanzas, for a total of sixty-five lines) for some time.

59. Plath's marginalia in her journals confirm that she finished the novel by August 22, 1961 (J 273), and her correspondence in the Smith College collection with James Michie, her editor at William Heinemann Ltd., publishers, reveals that the novel was accepted within a few months. On November 14, 1961, she asked Heinemann to delay the publication for a year because she had just received the Saxton grant, allegedly to write the novel. See also LH 437 (November 20, 1961) for Plath's admission that the novel was complete before she received the grant.

60. The typescript of Hughes's poem is dated May 1960.

61. Kahane further suggests, in "The Gothic Mirror," that pregnancy reawakens the daughter's ambivalent identification with her mother and may lead her to "fear the fetus as an agent of retaliation, a mirror of her own infantile negativity" (p. 345).

62. This date appears on a carbon of the final typescript of "Stings" (identified as "typed copy 6" in the Smith College collection), a page that was later reused for the first draft of "Winter Trees."

63. The stanza remained in the poem at least until October 30 when Plath recorded "Fever" in London (*Plath Reads Plath*).

64. The recording was made on October 30, 1962, under the auspices of the British Council and the Woodberry Poetry Room, Harvard College Library. The recording begins with "The Rabbit Catcher," a poem from the previous spring, when Plath may have first begun to suspect Hughes's infidelity. Her selection seems to confirm its originary status for this sequence of poems (it also appears as one of the alternate titles on the title page of the Ariel typescript). Four of the October poems ("Medusa," "Fever 103°," "Nick and the Candlestick," and "Lady Lazarus") include one or more stanzas that do not appear in the published poems, indicating that Plath undertook significant revisions when she prepared the Ariel typescript in London in January 1963. The poems, in the order that Plath read them, are "The Rabbit Catcher," "Ariel," "Poppies in October," "The Applicant," "Lady Lazarus," "A Secret," "Cut," "Stopped Dead," "Nick and the Candlestick," "Medusa," "Purdah," "A Birthday Present," "Amnesiac" (including "Lyonesse"), "Daddy," and "Fever 103°" (*Plath Reads Plath*).

65. On her list of submissions and acceptances, Plath indicates these two poems were submitted to the *Observer* on October 29, the date of their meeting; both were accepted (Poems—Lists, 1959–1963, Smith College collection). Alvarez gives his account of this meeting in "Sylvia Plath," pp. 194–95.

66. *The Bell Jar*, pp. 83, 98.

67. The first quote appears in LH 468. The unedited October 16 letter is in the Indiana University collection (box 9, folder 10).

68. Aurelia Plath's letter to Judith Kroll, December 1, 1978, Smith College collection.

69. Plath vowed in her letter of October 23, "Just wait till I hit London. Ted may be a genius, but I'm an intelligence. He's not going to stop that" (Indiana University collection [box 9, folder 10]).

3. Motherhood

1. For similar entries about her anxieties and the analogies Plath created between mothering and writing, see J 171, 189, 195, 242, 255, 271, 280, 297.

2. Adlai Stevenson, "Women, Husbands, and History," pp. 499–500, 498.

3. Miller and Nowak, among several other analysts of the decade, remind us that 22 million women, half of them married, worked outside the home, comprising about a third of the work force. While most of these occupations were jobs rather than careers for women, women's presence in the work force was sizable and directly at odds with the mythologized vision of the full-time "professional" mother. See Miller and Nowak, *The Fifties*, pp. 162–63. For a discussion of women's permanent place as workers after World War II, see also Chafe, *The American Woman*, pp. 174–84. For a discussion of tensions about gender roles in middle-class marriages, see also Chafe, *The Unfinished Journey*, pp. 123–28.

4. For a recent examination of the role of male fiction in underwriting disparaging gender identities for women, see Gilbert and Gubar, *No Man's Land*, 1:46–48.

5. For an analysis of the role of women's magazines in promulgating a hegemonic ideology during the decade, see Friedan, *The Feminine Mystique*, pp. 28–61. For a perceptive and detailed account of Plath's fiction written for women's magazines, see Wagner, "Plath's 'Ladies' Home Journal' Syndrome."

6. Gilbert and Gubar, *No Man's Land*, 1:168–71, 195–200.

7. For a discussion of the misogyny of male modernists as a reaction to female rivals, see Gilbert and Gubar, *No Man's Land*, 1:149, 156.

8. Elaine Showalter claims Woolf's sexlessness made her a problematic foremother to other women writers; see *A Literature of Their Own*, p. 34.

9. See also Plath's effort to combine Lawrence's passion with Woolf's "sexless, neurotic numinousness" (J 199). Sandra Gilbert makes a compelling case for Woolf and Yeats as Plath's literary parents in "In Yeats' House," pp. 209–10, 216–20, in Wagner, *Critical Essays on Sylvia Plath*. I am not arguing for a greater stylistic indebtedness to Lawrence than to Yeats. Rather my point is that Plath's figuration of her literary parentage is emphatically heterosexual and reproductive.

10. Gilbert and Gubar, *Madwoman*, esp. pp. 48–51, 60, 64.

11. Rich, *Of Woman Born*.

12. See Chodorow and Contratto, "The Fantasy of the Perfect Mother." Chodorow and Contratto remind us that as women we have internalized both the culture's idealization and blame of mothers, and they underscore the mutually reinforcing effect of infantile fantasy and cultural ideology in producing a myth of maternal omnipotence that even feminist analyses of motherhood share; see also Suleiman, "On Maternal Splitting," pp. 29–30.

13. Homans, *Bearing the Word*, pp. 1–13, 23–27; Hirsch, *The Mother/Daughter Plot*, pp. 99–100, 131–32; Suleiman, "Writing and Motherhood," pp. 353–59; Stanton, "Difference on Trial," pp. 164–65; and Gilbert and Gubar, *No Man's Land*, 1:183–84, 263–66. Gilbert and Gubar stay much closer to the Freudian and Lacanian scenarios of language, but they share a revisionary impulse toward the myth: "The idea that language is in its essence or nature patriarchal may be a reaction-formation against the linguistic (as well as the biological) primacy of the mother" (1:264).

14. Homans, *Bearing the Word*, pp. 23–27; Hirsch, *The Mother/Daughter Plot*, p. 132; Suleiman, "Writing and Motherhood," p. 367. Gilbert and Gubar, in *No Man's Land* at least, would demur on these points.

15. Hirsch analyzes in *The Mother/Daughter Plot* specifically how feminist revisions of psychoanalytic plots propose "the pre-oedipal realm . . . as a powerful mythic space, not irrecoverably lost but continually present because it is recoverable in ideal(ized) female relationships" (p. 133).

16. Homans, *Bearing the Word*, p. 29.

17. Ibid., p. 38; see also her similar qualifications, pp. 13, 19.

18. Hirsch also notes that Homans's search for literal mother-daughter language yields only "brief moments of interruption and silence" (*Mother/Daughter Plot*, p. 45).

19. Stanton, "Difference on Trial," pp. 170–72. Discrediting or disputing the French theorists has become a significant movement. Among the many Anglo-

American and Franco-American feminist critics who have warned against the trap of "biologism" or "essentialism" among the proponents of "writing the body" and who have quarreled with its apparent acceptance of the dualisms of patriarchal thinking, see Poovey, "Feminism and Deconstruction," pp. 54–57, and Felski, *Beyond Feminist Aesthetics*, pp. 33–40.

20. Friedman "Creativity and the Childbirth Metaphor," p. 65; see also Ellmann, *Thinking about Women*, pp. 15–17.

21. Suleiman, "Writing and Motherhood," p. 360 (emphasis in original).

22. Johnson, "Apostrophe, Abortion and Animation," p. 198, in *A World of Difference*. See also her discussion of the woman writer's monstrous creation and her failure at mothering, in "My Monster/My Self," pp. 151–53, ibid.

23. Friedman, "Creativity and the Childbirth Metaphor," p. 76; see also Gubar, "The Birth of the Artist as Heroine," pp. 25–26, 39. Gubar, in specifying the difference between Victorian and modernist practice among women writers, sees a historical shift from contradiction to congruence that closely parallels Friedman's.

24. Friedman, "Creativity and the Childbirth Metaphor," p. 58.

25. Suleiman, "Writing and Motherhood," p. 374. See also Rich, *Of Woman Born*: "For me, poetry was where I lived as no-one's mother, where I existed as myself" (p. 12).

26. Ostriker, *Stealing the Language*, p. 179.

27. Hughes also dates the six-line "Hanging Man" from the very end of June. Plath may have been concentrating on fiction instead, as she tells her mother in the letters throughout the summer and fall, but she seems to have been unable to produce either poetry or fiction, as she finally confesses at the end of November: "I am now working hard on something I never really attacked right—women's magazine stories. Very rusty and awkward on my first" (*LH* 401 [November 28, 1960]).

28. Earlier, in March 1959, when she mistakenly thought she was pregnant, Plath tried some of these same comparisons in the slighter poem "Metaphors." The 1959 poem focused on herself rather than the fetus and used metaphoric mastery as a defense against a feared loss of self control: "I've eaten a bag of green apples, / Boarded the train there's no getting off" (*CP* 116).

29. See *LH* 474, 487–88.

30. The dedication "for Helder & Suzette Macedo," the couple she stayed with on her trips to London, was added in ink to the final typescript of "Poppies in October" when she prepared the *Ariel* volume in London (Ariel Poems—Final typescript, Smith College collection).

31. Ostriker, *Stealing the Language*, pp. 218–21; Gilbert and Gubar, *Madwoman*, pp. 93–95; de Lauretis, *Alice Doesn't*, p. 132. For earlier formulations, see Moers, *Literary Women*, pp. 140–51, and Walker, *Nightengale's Burden*.

32. Ostriker, *Stealing the Language*, pp. 181–82.

33. Homans, *Bearing the Word*, p. 30.

34. The poem's vindictiveness seems motivated by a fear of female censure. Plath's letters during October show a hypersensitivity about what her female relatives and Prouty will think of her impending divorce. Yet she much more frequently asked for, and received, material female support. See *LH* 465, 469, 470, 472, 473, 482.

35. Charles Newman reproduces seven pages of these drafts, although not in the order of composition, in *The Art of Sylvia Plath*, pp. 273–79.

36. The poem's final image provides an interesting counterpoint to Plath's letters to her mother during September in which she worried incessantly about money and referred to Ted, in his departure, as having stolen her "nanny money," a sum she had planned to save from her Saxton grant but that had been used on living expenses instead and now would not be repaid by Hughes's future earnings. See Indiana University collection, box 9, folder 10, esp. letters of September 24, 26, 1962.

37. Ostriker, *Stealing the Language*, p. 180.

38. Homans, *Bearing the Word*, pp. 26, 28.

39. Beauvoir, *The Second Sex*, p. 151.

40. Homans, *Bearing the Word*, p. 28.

41. Hughes's two poems may have initially been conceived as parts of a single poem. Both appear in typescript with the same title, "Lines to a New-born Baby," on the reverse of Plath's drafts for an early, abandoned version of "Stings" that she began on August 2, 1962. Both were composed sometime before "Morning Song" (February 19, 1961) and were published in periodicals: "Lines to a Newborn Baby" appeared in *Texas Quarterly* 3 (Winter 1960): 214; "To F. R. at Six Months" appeared with the title "For Frieda in Her First Months" in *Western Daily Press* on February 22, 1961, just a few days after Plath drafted her poem (but no doubt Hughes's poem was submitted before then). Margaret Dickie perceptively documents how both Hughes and Plath appropriated each other's images and recast them in different moods during this period; see *Sylvia Plath and Ted Hughes*, pp. 134–35.

42. A similar fear of maternal dispossession concludes the November 1962 poem, "Mary's Song": "O golden child the world will kill and eat" (CP 257).

43. The drafts for both "Barren Woman" and "Heavy Women" are in the Indiana University collection. No drafts exist for "Morning Song."

44. Hughes's date for the composition of "Nick and the Candlestick" as October 29 in *Collected Poems* is an error; although the first handwritten draft is undated, several successive handwritten and typed versions are all dated October 24.

45. Margaret Dickie suggests this image may be borrowed from Hughes's poem to Frieda, in which "a stalagmite / Of history under the blood-drip" appears; see *Sylvia Plath and Ted Hughes*, p. 134. What is equally significant, I think, is that Plath erases the boundary between interior, bodily, female history and Hughes's violent external forces. Adrienne Rich's poem, "Living in the Cave" (1972, in *Diving into the Wreck*) echoes Plath's metaphoric equation of the mother-poet's body with confinement in the underworld in which the accretion of infant demands obliterate the mother.

46. Plath read this version of the poem when she recorded fifteen of the Ariel poems in London on October 30 (*Plath Reads Plath*).

47. Marjorie Perloff claims that Plath's order emphasizes struggle and revenge, while Hughes's volume concludes with poems "written from beyond rage, by someone who no longer blames anyone for her condition." See "The Two Ariels," p. 11. While I agree with Perloff in her assessment of Plath's intended selection, I see a continuation of struggle, rage, and betrayal (though

against a more complicated array of forces than the husband betrayer) even in the very last poems.

48. Suleiman, "Writing and Motherhood," pp. 373–74.

49. For example, Lynda Bundtzen sides with those critics who see Kindness as an internalized voice of cultural reproach that "prevents her from writing poetry by reminding her of her children's needs." See *Plath's Incarnations*, p. 224; see also pp. 6–7. Rather than offering an insoluble choice, Kindness, according to Margaret Dickie, is trying to prevent the speaker's self-sacrifice, "the blood-jet is evidence both of the heart's persistent life and of its exhaustion of that life in poetry" (*Sylvia Plath and Ted Hughes*, p. 155). Dickie's analysis of the significance of blood throughout Plath's poetry, while not entirely congruent with my own, helpfully distinguishes that its meaning is not monolithic.

50. Suleiman, "Writing and Motherhood," p. 364.

51. See LH 478, 480, 491.

52. Alvarez, following Butscher's biography, claims a more local male influence as the source for several images in the poem. In Hughes's radio play (perhaps "Difficulties of a Bridegroom," broadcast in January 1963) the husband runs down a rabbit in his car, sells it, and then buys roses for a woman (Alvarez and Butscher differ on whether she is wife or mistress) with the money. See Alvarez, "Sylvia Plath," p. 202, and Butscher, *Sylvia Plath: Method and Madness*, p. 361, 377 n. 6. Both men overemphasize Plath's dependence on Hughes's imaginative lead, yet I suspect the final stanza may contain a more oblique comment on the fruits of their marriage. Since Plath's earlier poem "The Rabbit Catcher" already understood Hughes as capable of violence toward her, his murderous wish in the radio play (and the dream the incident is allegedly based on) would have only confirmed her intuitions. If the husband's violence is masked with the love gift of roses in the play, then babies, like roses, might be benign disguises for his destructive impulses toward her.

53. Margaret Higonnet claims that female suicide, especially of classical heroines, remains unintelligible because we read in the text of the dead woman's body our cultural projections of woman's nature while the motives of the actor herself are always inaccessible. See "Speaking Silences," pp. 68, 73–75, 79. See also Ostriker, *Stealing the Language*, pp. 235–36.

54. Elaine Showalter, reading Woolf's *To the Lighthouse*, claims Mrs. Ramsey's maternal devotion to others is both insatiable and suicidal. Showalter's reading uncovers Woolf's ambivalence and may also identify Plath's oblique allusion to another literary mother, Woolf's portrait of the self-sacrificing mother in Mrs. Ramsey: "She seemed to fold herself together, one petal closed in another . . . while there throbbed through her . . . the rapture of successful creation" (quoted in *A Literature of Their Own*, pp. 296–97).

55. Plath's habit is to type her name along with her address on typescripts of the poems. Only "Edge," along with "Munich Mannequins," composed on January 28, 1963, among the Ariel poems has her signature on the handwritten draft. Some of the very few first drafts of earlier poems included in the Indiana University collection have an autograph (usually "S. Plath") that was probably added when she sold these manuscripts to Ifan Fletcher in late November 1961.

56. Plath's image may echo the epigraph to Anne Sexton's *All My Pretty Ones*, a

book she had owned since August 1962 and which she praised in a BBC broadcast in January 1963, a few weeks before this poem. Sexton quotes a letter from Franz Kafka to Oskar Pollak: "The books we need are the kind that act upon us like a misfortune, that make us suffer like the death of someone we love more than ourselves, that make us feel as though we were on the verge of suicide, or lost in a forest remote from all human habitation—a book should serve as the ax for the frozen sea within us."

Selected Bibliography

Primary Sources

Manuscript Collections

Sylvia Plath Collection
Smith College Library Rare Book Room
Smith College
Northampton, Massachusetts

Sylvia Plath Manuscript Collection
Lilly Library
Indiana University
Bloomington, Indiana

Published Works by Sylvia Plath

The Bell Jar. New York: Harper & Row, 1971.
The Collected Poems. Edited by Ted Hughes. New York: Harper & Row, 1981.
Johnny Panic and the Bible of Dreams. New York: Harper & Row, 1979.
The Journals of Sylvia Plath. Edited by Frances McCullough and Ted Hughes.
    New York: Dial, 1982.
Letters Home: Correspondence, 1950–1963. Edited by Aurelia Schober Plath. New
    York: Harper & Row, 1975.
Plath Reads Plath. Cambridge, Mass.: Credo Records, 1975.

Secondary Sources

Alcoff, Linda. "Cultural Feminism versus Post-Structuralism: The Identity Cri-
    sis in Feminist Theory." *Signs* 13, no. 3 (Spring 1988): 405–36.
Alexander, Paul, ed. *Ariel Ascending: Writings about Sylvia Plath.* New York: Harper
    & Row, 1985.
Alvarez, A. "Sylvia Plath: A Memoir." In Alexander, *Ariel Ascending,* pp. 185–213.
Annas, Pamela J. *A Disturbance in Mirrors: The Poetry of Sylvia Plath.* Westport,
    Conn.: Greenwood, 1988.
Auerbach, Nina. *Woman and the Demon: The Life of a Victorian Myth.* Cambridge,
    Mass.: Harvard University Press, 1982.
Axelrod, Steven Gould. "Plath's Literary Relations: An Essay and an Index to
    the *Journals* and *Letters Home.*" *Resources for American Literary Study* 14, no. 2–3
    (Spring and Autumn 1984): 59–84.

————. *Sylvia Plath: The Wound and the Cure of Words*. Baltimore: Johns Hopkins University Press, 1990.

Banner, Lois W. *American Beauty*. New York: Knopf, 1983.

Bassnett, Susan. *Sylvia Plath*. Totowa, N.J.: Barnes & Noble, 1987.

Beauvoir, Simone de. *The Second Sex*. Translated by H. M. Parshley. New York: Bantam, 1953; reprint, 1970.

Belsey, Catherine. *Critical Practice*. London and New York: Methuen, 1980.

Bennett, Paula. *My Life, a Loaded Gun: Female Creativity and Feminist Poetics*. Boston: Beacon, 1986.

Berg, Temma F. "Suppressing the Language of Wo(Man): The Dream as a Common Language." In *Engendering the Word: Feminist Essays in Psychosexual Poetics*, edited by Temma F. Berg, pp. 3–28. Urbana: University of Illinois Press, 1989.

Bloom, Harold, ed. *Modern Critical Views: Sylvia Plath*. New York and Philadelphia: Chelsea House, 1989.

Boose, Lynda E., and Betty S. Flowers, eds. *Daughters and Fathers*. Baltimore: Johns Hopkins University Press, 1989.

Broe, Mary Lynn. *Protean Poetic: The Poetry of Sylvia Plath*. Columbia: University of Missouri Press, 1980.

————. "A Subtle Psychic Bond: The Mother Figure in Sylvia Plath's Poetry." In *The Lost Tradition: Mothers and Daughters in Literature*, edited by Cathy N. Davidson and E. M. Broner, pp. 217–30. New York: Ungar, 1980.

Bundtzen, Lynda K. *Plath's Incarnations: Woman and the Creative Process*. Ann Arbor: University of Michigan Press, 1983.

Butler, Judith. *Gender Trouble: Feminism and the Subversion of Identity*. New York: Routledge, 1990.

————. "Performative Acts and Gender Constitution: An Essay in Phenomenology and Feminist Theory." *Theatre Journal* 40, no. 4 (December 1988): 519–31.

————. "Sex and Gender in Simone de Beauvoir's *Second Sex*." *Yale French Studies* 72 (1986): 35–49.

Butscher, Edward. *Sylvia Plath: Method and Madness*. New York: Seabury, 1976.

Butscher, Edward, ed. *Sylvia Plath: The Woman and the Work*. New York: Dodd, Mead, 1977.

Chafe, William H. *The American Woman: Her Changing Social, Economic, and Political Roles, 1920–1970*. New York: Oxford, 1972.

————. *The Unfinished Journey: America since World War II*. New York: Oxford, 1986.

Chodorow, Nancy, and Susan Contratto. "The Fantasy of the Perfect Mother." In *Rethinking the Family: Some Feminist Questions*, edited by Barrie Thorne and Marilyn Yalom, pp. 54–75. New York: Longman, 1982.

D'Emilio, John, and Estelle B. Freedman. *Intimate Matters: A History of Sexuality in America*. New York: Harper & Row, 1988.

de Lauretis, Teresa. *Alice Doesn't: Feminism, Semiotics, Cinema*. Bloomington: Indiana University Press, 1984.

de Lauretis, Teresa, ed. *Feminist Studies/Critical Studies*. Bloomington: Indiana University Press, 1986.

————. *Technologies of Gender: Essays on Theory, Film, and Fiction*. Bloomington: Indiana University Press, 1987.

Dickie, Margaret. *Sylvia Plath and Ted Hughes*. Urbana: University of Illinois Press, 1979.

DuPlessis, Rachel Blau. *Writing beyond the Ending: Narrative Strategies of Twentieth-Century Women Writers*. Bloomington: Indiana University Press, 1985.

Edwards, Lee R. *Psyche as Hero: Female Heroism and Fictional Form*. Middletown, Conn.: Wesleyan University Press, 1984.

Ehrenreich, Barbara. *The Hearts of Men: American Dreams and the Flight from Commitment*. New York: Doubleday, 1983.

Ehrenreich, Barbara, and Deirdre English. *For Her Own Good: 150 Years of the Experts' Advice to Women*. New York: Doubleday, 1978.

Eisler, Benita. *Private Lives: Men and Women of the Fifties*. New York: Franklin Watts, 1986.

Ellmann, Mary. *Thinking about Women*. New York: Harcourt, Brace & World, 1968.

Faas, Ekbert. "Chapters of a Shared Mythology: Sylvia Plath and Ted Hughes." In Sagar, *The Achievement of Ted Hughes*, pp. 107–24.

Feit Diehl, Joanne. "Murderous Poetics: Dickinson, the Father, and the Text." In Boose and Flowers, *Daughters and Fathers*, pp. 326–43.

———. *Women Poets and the American Sublime*. Bloomington: Indiana University Press, 1990.

Felski, Rita. *Beyond Feminist Aesthetics: Feminist Literature and Social Change*. Cambridge, Mass.: Harvard University Press, 1989.

Flynn, Elizabeth A., and Patrocinio P. Schweickart, eds. *Gender and Reading: Essays on Readers, Texts, and Contexts*. Baltimore: Johns Hopkins University Press, 1986.

Friedan, Betty. *The Feminine Mystique*. New York: Dell, 1963.

Friedman, Susan Stanford. "Creativity and the Childbirth Metaphor: Gender Difference in Literary Discourse." *Feminist Studies* 13, no. 1 (Spring 1987): 49–82.

———. *Psyche Reborn: The Emergence of H. D.* Bloomington: Indiana University Press, 1981.

———. "Women's Autobiographical Selves: Theory and Practice." In *The Private Self: Theory and Practice of Women's Autobiographical Writings*, edited by Shari Benstock, pp. 34–62. Chapel Hill: University of North Carolina Press, 1988.

Froula, Christine. "The Daughter's Seduction: Sexual Violence and Literary History." *Signs* 11, no. 4 (Summer 1986): 621–44.

Gallop, Jane. *Thinking Through the Body*. New York: Columbia University Press, 1988.

Garner, Shirley Nelson, Claire Kahane, and Madelon Sprengnether, eds. *The (M)other Tongue: Essays in Feminist Psychoanalytic Interpretation*. Ithaca: Cornell University Press, 1985.

Gilbert, Sandra. "In Yeats' House: The Death and Resurrection of Sylvia Plath." In Wagner, *Critical Essays on Sylvia Plath*, pp. 204–22. Reprinted in Middlebrook and Yalom, *Coming to Light*, pp. 145–66.

Gilbert, Sandra M., and Susan Gubar. *The Madwoman in the Attic: The Woman Writer and the Nineteenth-Century Literary Imagination*. New Haven: Yale University Press, 1979.

———. No Man's Land: The Place of the Woman Writer in the Twentieth Century. 2 vols. Vol. 1, The War of the Words. Vol. 2, Sexchanges. New Haven: Yale University Press, 1988, 1989.

Gubar, Susan. "The Birth of the Artist as Heroine: (Re)production, the Künstlerroman Tradition, and the Fiction of Katherine Mansfield." In The Representation of Women in Fiction, edited by Carolyn G. Heilbrun and Margaret R. Higonnet, pp. 19–59. Baltimore: Johns Hopkins University Press, 1983.

Haskell, Molly. From Reverence to Rape: The Treatment of Women in the Movies. New York: Holt, Rinehart & Winston, 1974.

Heilbrun, Carolyn G. Writing a Woman's Life. New York: Norton, 1988.

Higonnet, Margaret. "Speaking Silences: Women's Suicide." In The Female Body in Western Culture: Contemporary Perspectives, edited by Susan Rubin Suleiman, pp. 68–83. Cambridge, Mass.: Harvard University Press, 1986.

Hirsch, Marianne. The Mother/Daughter Plot: Narrative, Psychoanalysis, Feminism. Bloomington: Indiana University Press, 1989.

Homans, Margaret. Bearing the Word: Language and Female Experience in Nineteenth-Century Women's Writing. Chicago: University of Chicago Press, 1986.

———. Women Writers and Poetic Identity: Dorothy Wordsworth, Emily Brontë, and Emily Dickinson. Princeton: Princeton University Press, 1980.

Howe, Irving. "The Plath Celebration: A Partial Dissent." In Butscher, Sylvia Plath: The Woman and the Work, pp. 225–35.

Hughes, Ted. Poetry in the Making. London: Faber & Faber, 1967.

———. "Sylvia Plath and Her Journals." In Alexander, Ariel Ascending, pp. 157–64.

Jacobus, Mary. Reading Woman: Essays in Feminist Criticism. New York: Columbia University Press, 1986.

Jacobus, Mary, ed. Women Writing and Writing about Women. Totowa, N.J.: Barnes & Noble, 1979.

Johnson, Barbara. A World of Difference. Baltimore: Johns Hopkins University Press, 1987.

Jones, Ann R. "Julia Kristeva on Femininity: The Limits of Semiotic Politics." Feminist Review 18 (1984): 56–73.

Kahane, Claire. "The Gothic Mirror." In Garner, Kahane, and Sprengnether, The (M)other Tongue, pp. 334–51.

Kahn, Coppelia. "The Hand that Rocks the Cradle: Recent Gender Theories and Their Implications." In Garner, Kahane, and Sprengnether, The (M)other Tongue, pp. 72–88.

Kennard, Jean E. "Convention Coverage or How to Read Your Own Life." New Literary History 13, no. 1 (Autumn 1981): 69–88.

Kroll, Judith. Chapters in a Mythology: The Poetry of Sylvia Plath. New York: Harper & Row, 1976.

Lane, Gary. Sylvia Plath: New Views on the Poetry. Baltimore: Johns Hopkins University Press, 1979.

Lauter, Estella. Women as Mythmakers: Poetry and Visual Art by Twentieth-Century Women. Bloomington: Indiana University Press, 1984.

Marcus, Jane. Art & Anger: Reading Like a Woman. Columbus: Ohio State University Press, 1988.

Marks, Elaine, ed. Critical Essays on Simone de Beauvoir. Boston: G. K. Hall, 1987.

Matovich, Richard M. *A Concordance to the Collected Poems of Sylvia Plath*. New York: Garland, 1986.

Middlebrook, Diane Wood. *Anne Sexton: A Biography*. Boston: Houghton Mifflin, 1991.

Middlebrook, Diane, and Marilyn Yalom, eds. *Coming to Light: American Women Poets in the Twentieth Century*. Ann Arbor: University of Michigan Press, 1985.

Miller, Douglas T., and Marion Nowak. *The Fifties: The Way We Really Were*. Garden City, N.Y.: Doubleday, 1977.

Miller, Cristanne. *Emily Dickinson: A Poet's Grammar*. Cambridge, Mass.: Harvard University Press, 1987.

Miller, Nancy K. *Subject to Change: Reading Feminist Writing*. New York: Columbia University Press, 1988.

Miller, Nancy K., ed. *The Poetics of Gender*. New York: Columbia University Press, 1986.

Mintz, Steven, and Susan Kellogg. *Domestic Revolutions: A Social History of American Family Life*. New York: Macmillan, 1988.

Moers, Ellen. *Literary Women*. New York: Doubleday, 1977.

Moi, Toril. *Sexual/Textual Politics: Feminist Literary Theory*. London: Methuen, 1985.

Mossberg, Barbara Antonina Clarke. *Emily Dickinson: When a Writer Is a Daughter*. Bloomington: Indiana University Press, 1982.

———. "Sylvia Plath's Baby Book." In Middlebrook and Yalom, *Coming to Light*, pp. 182–94.

Newman, Charles Hamilton, ed. *The Art of Sylvia Plath: A Symposium*. Bloomington: Indiana University Press, 1970.

Ostriker, Alicia Suskin. *Stealing the Language: The Emergence of Women's Poetry in America*. Boston: Beacon, 1986.

Perloff, Marjorie. "Sylvia Plath's 'Sivvy' Poems: A Portrait of the Poet as Daughter." In Lane, *Sylvia Plath*, pp. 155–78.

———. "The Two Ariels: The (Re) making of the Sylvia Plath Canon." *American Poetry Review* 13, no. 6 (November/December, 1984): 10–18.

Poovey, Mary. "Feminism and Deconstruction." *Feminist Studies* 14, no. 1 (Spring 1988): 51–65.

Rich, Adrienne. *Of Woman Born: Motherhood as Experience and Institution*. New York: Bantam, 1977.

———. *On Lies, Secrets, and Silence: Selected Prose 1966–1978*. New York: Norton, 1979.

———. "When We Dead Awaken: Writing as Re-Vision." Reprinted in *Adrienne Rich's Poetry*, edited by Barbara Gelpi and Albert Gelpi, pp. 90–98. New York: Norton, 1975.

Ruddick, Sara. "Maternal Thinking." *Feminist Studies* 6, no. 2 (Summer 1980): 342–67.

Sagar, Keith, ed. *The Achievement of Ted Hughes*. Athens: University of Georgia Press, 1983.

Scigaj, Leonard M. *The Poetry of Ted Hughes: Form and Imagination*. Iowa City: University of Iowa Press, 1986.

Showalter, Elaine. *A Literature of Their Own: British Women Novelists from Brontë to Lessing*. Princeton: Princeton University Press, 1977.

————. "Toward a Feminist Poetics." In *The New Feminist Criticism: Essays on Women, Literature, and Theory*, edited by Elaine Showalter, pp. 125–43. New York: Pantheon, 1985.

Silver, Brenda. "The Authority of Anger: *Three Guineas* as Case Study." *Signs* 16, no. 2 (Winter 1991): 340–70.

Smith, Paul. *Discerning the Subject*. Minneapolis: University of Minnesota Press, 1988.

Snitow, Ann, Christine Stansell, and Sharon Thompson, eds. *Powers of Desire: The Politics of Sexuality*. New York: Monthly Review Press, 1983.

Spacks, Patricia Meyer. *The Female Imagination*. New York: Knopf, 1975.

Spelman, Elizabeth V. "Woman as Body: Ancient and Contemporary Views." *Feminist Studies* 8, no. 1 (Spring 1982): 109–31.

Stanton, Domna C. "Difference on Trial: A Critique of the Maternal Metaphor in Cixous, Irigaray, and Kristeva." In Nancy K. Miller, *The Poetics of Gender*, pp. 157–82.

————. "Language and Revolution: The Franco-American Dis-Connection." In *The Future of Difference*, edited by Hester Eisenstein and Alice Jardine, pp. 73–87. Boston: G. K. Hall, 1980.

Stevenson, Adlai. "Women, Husbands, and History." In *The Papers of Adlai Stevenson*, edited by Walter Johnson, 4:495–502. New York: Little Brown, 1972–79.

Stevenson, Anne. *Bitter Fame: A Life of Sylvia Plath*. Boston: Houghton Mifflin, 1989.

Suleiman, Susan Rubin. "On Maternal Splitting: A Propos of Mary Gordon's *Men and Angels*." *Signs* 14, no. 1 (Autumn 1988): 25–41.

————. "Writing and Motherhood." In Garner, Kahane, and Sprengnether, *The (M)other Tongue*, pp. 352–77.

Todd, Janet M. *Feminist Literary History*. New York: Routledge, 1988.

Trebilcot, Joyce, ed. *Mothering: Essays in Feminist Theory*. Totowa, N.J.: Rowman & Allanheld, 1984.

Ussner, Jane M. *The Psychology of the Female Body*. New York: Routledge, 1989.

Van Dyne, Susan R. "Fueling the Phoenix Fire: The Manuscripts of Sylvia Plath's 'Lady Lazarus.'" *Massachusetts Review* 24 (Summer 1983): 395–410. Reprinted in Bloom, *Modern Critical Views*, pp. 133–48.

————. "More Terrible Than She Ever Was: The Manuscripts of Sylvia Plath's Bee Poems." In *Stings: Original Drafts of the Poem in Facsimile Reproduced from the Sylvia Plath Collection at Smith College*, by Sylvia Plath, pp. 3–12. Northampton, Mass.: Smith College Library Rare Book Room, 1982.

————. "'More Terrible Than She Ever Was': The Manuscripts of Sylvia Plath's Bee Poems." Reprinted in Wagner, *Critical Essays on Sylvia Plath*, pp. 154–70.

————. "Rekindling the Past in Sylvia Plath's 'Burning the Letters.'" *Centennial Review* 32 (Summer 1988): 250–65.

Vendler, Helen Hennessy. "Intractable Metal." In Alexander, *Ariel Ascending*, pp. 1–12.

————. "Sylvia Plath." In *Part of Nature, Part of Us: Modern American Poets*, pp. 271–76. Cambridge, Mass.: Harvard University Press, 1980.

Wagner, Linda W., ed. *Critical Essays on Sylvia Plath*. Boston: G. K. Hall, 1984.

———. "Plath's 'Ladies Home Journal' Syndrome." *Journal of American Culture* 7 (Spring–Summer 1984): 32–38.

Wagner-Martin, Linda. *Sylvia Plath: A Biography.* New York: Simon & Schuster, 1987.

Walker, Cheryl. "Feminist Literary Criticism and the Author." *Critical Inquiry* 16 (Spring 1990): 551–71.

———. *Nightengale's Burden: Women Poets and American Culture Before 1900.* Bloomington: Indiana University Press, 1982.

Waugh, Patricia. *Feminine Fictions: Revisiting the Postmodern.* New York: Routledge, 1989.

Woolf, Virginia. "Professions for Women." In *Collected Essays,* edited by Leonard Woolf, 2:284–89. New York: Harcourt, Brace & World, 1967.

———. *A Room of One's Own.* New York: Harcourt, Brace & World, 1929.

Yaeger, Patricia. *Honey-Mad Women: Emancipatory Strategies in Women's Writing.* New York: Columbia University Press, 1988.

Yalom, Marilyn. "Sylvia Plath, *The Bell Jar,* and Related Poems." In Middlebrook and Yalom, *Coming to Light,* pp. 167–81.

Index

Fisher, Al, 8, 13
Friedman, Susan, 142, 143, 145

Gilbert, Sandra and Susan Gubar:
  Madwoman in the Attic, 29, 31, 57,
  81, 135, 139, 162
Gutman, Assia, 8, 38, 45, 123

Haskell, Molly, 72
Hirsh, Marianne, 77, 139–40
Homans, Margaret, 46, 139–40,
  141, 151, 157, 158, 179 (n. 1)
Howe, Irving, 47
Hughes, Frieda, 3, 9, 93, 103, 129,
  144, 145, 159, 167, 170
Hughes, Nicholas, 3, 10, 105, 145,
  154, 156, 160, 163, 164, 167,
  169, 170, 171
Hughes, Ted: as editor of Ariel volume, 50, 101, 165, 184 (n. 69),
  192 (n. 47); as editor of Collected
  Poems, 22, 160, 188 (n. 57), 191
  (n. 27), 192 (n. 44); as literary executor, 3–4, 8, 102, 185
  (n. 34); as teacher and critic, 4,
  14–15, 18–22, 32–33, 109, 135
—Works: The Calm, 9, 34, 50, 103;
  "A Fable," 183 (n. 53); Hawk in
  the Rain, 38; "Lines to a Newborn
  Baby," 159; "Pike," 23; "The
  Thought-Fox," 9, 23, 34, 38,
  40–41; "To F. R. at Six Months,"
  159

Ideology: of female body, 73–76,
  79–82, 88; of female sexuality,
  67–73, 148; of gender and writing, 77–78, 81, 138–39, 140–44;
  of marriage, 72, 134–35; of
  masculinity, 16–18, 49, 52, 122;
  of maternal body, 75, 77–78,
  80–81, 90, 96, 148, 149–50; of
  motherhood, 75, 76–77, 129–35,
  138–39. See also Body: and literary
  imagination of women writers

Johnson, Barbara, 142

Kahane, Claire, 81, 90, 96, 97, 106

Lawrence, D. H., 136–38
Lowell, Robert: Life Studies, 52
Lundberg, Ferdinand and Marynia
  Farnham: Modern Woman: The Lost
  Sex, 69–70

Marcus, Jane, 28, 44, 46
Maternity: metaphor as defense
  against, 144–46, 148, 152–54,
  156, 166–67, 170; poetics of, 6,
  150, 154, 156–58, 162, 165,
  172; textual signs of, as blood,
  145, 148, 149, 163–64, 174;
  textual signs of, as madness,
  143, 150–52, 162; textual signs
  of, as presymbolic discourse,
  140–41, 151, 157–58, 165. See
  also Plath, Sylvia: expectations of
  motherhood
Miller, Arthur, 72
Miller, Karl, 170
Miller, Nancy, 5, 7, 179 (n. 10)
Moers, Ellen, 31; Literary Women, 80,
  90, 104
Moi, Toril, 30
Monroe, Marilyn, 17, 72, 73
Mossberg, Barbara, 63, 77

Orr, Peter, 119
Ostriker, Alicia, 30, 31, 41, 44, 49,
  56, 63, 82, 96, 143, 150, 157

Performance: and appropriation of
  male privilege, 100–101, 107,
  110, 112–13, 122–23; as child,
  47–49, 52; of gender, 30–31;
  of murder, 31–32, 50, 52, 54,
  62–63; and relation to audience,
  47–48, 52, 55–56, 58, 60, 62,
  116, 118, 121–22; of sadomasochistic scripts, 31–33,
  41–47, 51–52, 63, 115–16, 118;
  as sexual outlaw, 101, 118,
  119–22; as virgin, 118–19
Perloff, Marjorie, 165, 192 (n. 47)
Plath, Otto, 49, 104, 109, 133

Plath, Sylvia: expectations of marriage, 16–18, 32–33, 134–35, 144; expectations of motherhood, 6, 97–98, 129–35, 144, 148, 169, 174–75; expectations of sexuality, 67–73, 135–38; literary genealogy of, female, 19, 135–38; literary genealogy of, male, 19–24, 181 (n. 21); poetic rivalry with Hughes, 4, 19, 21–22, 32, 39, 42, 50; and refiguration of life in writing, 1, 7, 46–47, 110, 113, 170, 174–75; relations with Aurelia, 4–5, 67–69, 71, 84–87, 90, 93–95, 97–98, 123, 126, 131–33, 174–75; and writing blocks, 94–95, 123, 126, 144. *See also* Body: poetics of; Maternity: poetics of; Rage: poetics of

—Works: "Amnesiac," 9–10; "Among the Bumblebees," 104, 186 (n. 37); "The Applicant," 9, 34, 56; "Ariel," 10, 36, 57, 60, 73, 100, 101, 113, 115, 119–26; "The Arrival of the Bee Box," 10, 101, 104, 106–7, 113, 150–51, 152, 153, 163, 170, 178; "Balloons," 165–68, 170, 171, 172, 178; "Barren Woman" ("Night Thoughts" or "Small Hours"), 159, 160; "The Beekeeper's Daughter" (*Colossus*), 101, 104, 107, 174; "The Bee Meeting," 101, 102, 103, 105–6, 108, 115; *The Bell Jar*, 9, 44, 70, 71, 102, 122–23, 188 (n. 59); "A Birthday Present," 9, 56, 62, 87; "Burning the Letters," 9, 23, 33–41, 45, 46, 50, 60, 116, 149; "By Candlelight" ("Nick and the Candlestick" [I]), 44, 145, 157, 160, 161–62, 164, 165, 192 (n. 44); "Child," 156–57; *The Colossus*, 50, 51, 87, 129; "The Courage of Shutting-Up" ("The Courage of Quietness"), 41, 42–43, 46; "Cut," 10, 145–48, 149, 164,

167, 169, 178; "Daddy," 9, 23, 33, 34, 44, 47–55, 56, 57, 93, 109, 123; "Death & Co.," 50; "The Detective," 41, 46; "The Disquieting Muses" (*Colossus*), 169, 175; "Eavesdropper," 9, 60; "Edge" ("Nuns in Snow"), 1, 170, 171–75; "Electra on Azalea Path" (*Colossus*), 104; "Elm," 175; "Face Lift," 87, 88–89, 103; "The Fearful," 10; "Fever 103°," 10, 36, 57, 60, 73, 100, 101, 112, 113, 115–19, 121, 122, 123, 149, 189 (nn. 63, 64); "The Fifty-ninth Bear," 23; "For a Fatherless Son," 154, 156; "Getting There," 186 (n. 40); "Heavy Women" ("Waiting Women"), 159, 160; "In Plaster," 77, 90–91, 93, 96, 106; "The Jailer," 9, 34, 41, 44–46, 50, 52, 59, 115; "Kindness," 169–70, 172, 174; "Lady Lazarus," 10, 33, 36, 41, 47, 55–63, 89, 100, 101, 113, 116, 121, 123, 152, 189 (n. 64); "Lesbos," 9, 60; "Lyonesse," 9–10; "Man in Black" (*Colossus*), 50; "Mary's Song," 192 (n. 42); "Medusa," 9, 60, 73, 77, 93–98, 99, 100, 189 (n. 64); "Mirror" ("Mirror Talk"), 87–88, 89, 103; "The Moon and the Yew Tree," 175; "Morning Song," 93, 157, 158–59, 160, 161, 178; "Nick and the Candlestick," 10, 145, 150, 157, 160, 162–65, 189 (n. 64); "The Night Dances," 178; "Ocean 1212-W," 84–87; "Poem for a Birthday," 22; "Poppies in July," 148–49; "Poppies in October," 10, 57, 119, 145, 148–49, 163; "Purdah," 10, 87, 172; "A Secret," 9; "Stillborn," 144, 145; "Stings," 10, 36, 41, 57, 60, 62, 101, 104, 107–12, 114, 121, 123; "Stings" (August version), 103, 107; "Stopped Dead," 10; "The Swarm," 101,

102, 104; "Thalidomide" ("Half-Moon"), 150, 152–54, 155, 164, 165, 166, 178; "The Tour," 10, 145, 151–52; "Tulips," 87, 89, 90, 91–93, 100, 106, 119; "Wintering," 9, 10, 44, 101, 102, 104, 113–15, 122, 150, 163, 170, 171, 178; "Winter Trees," 10; "The Wishing Box," 23; "Words," 175–78; "Words heard, by accident, over the phone," 52; "You're," 144–45, 146, 152–53

Plath, Warren, 85

Rage: and duplicitous texts, 29–30, 35, 42, 48, 50, 52; and poetic silencing, 13, 33, 35, 42–43, 45, 47, 149; poetics of, 5–6, 33, 63, 118; and revenge plots, 15, 31–37, 40–41, 46–47, 49–52, 54–55, 60, 62–63, 108–9; textual signs of, 15, 24–32, 44, 48–49, 56, 62. See also Performance: of sadomasochistic scripts

Reisman, David: The Lonely Crowd, 17

Reynolds, Debbie, 72

Rich, Adrienne: Plath's rivalry with, 136; "When We Dead Awaken: Writing as Re-Vision," 27–28; Of Woman Born, 76–77, 78, 79, 90, 96, 104, 138–39

Roe, Susan O'Neill, 146

Roethke, Theodore, 22

Sexton, Anne, 21; "All My Pretty Ones," 52, 136, 193 (n. 56)

Showalter, Elaine, 27, 28, 31

Silver, Brenda, 47

Smith, Paul, 3

Spacks, Patricia, 27, 28

Stanton, Domna, 139, 142

Starbuck, George, 21, 136

Subjectivity, gendered, 2–3, 5, 7, 63, 74, 76–78, 80–82, 83, 103–4, 119, 121–23, 126, 139–42, 157, 175–76, 178. See also Body: as carnal subject; Maternity: poetics of

Suleiman, Susan, 139–40, 142, 143, 167, 170, 172

Taylor, Liz, 72

Todd, Janet, 6

Van Voris, Bill, 13–15

Vendler, Helen, 47

Williams, Raymond, 30

Woolf, Virginia: A Room of One's Own and "Professions for Women," 24–26, 27, 28, 134, 137

Yaeger, Patricia: Honey-Mad Women, 81

Permissions